"Ann Perkins and Rita Townsend give women back their voices—and their dignity. In this compassionate work, the authors restore to women a basic right—to speak for themselves. To anyone who wonders still why reproductive freedom is fundamental to all women, this book is essential. If we had more collections like *Bitter Fruit* in wide circulation, perhaps *Roe v. Wade* wouldn't be in such grave jeopardy today."

Susan Faludi
Author of *Backlash: The Undeclared War Against American Women*

"These are the stories of women—and girl children—caught in the shame, isolation, confusion, and fright of what in sanitized parlance is referred to as an unplanned pregnancy. These women's voices describe with authenticity their struggles to find solutions, and then to live with the inevitably difficult consequences of their decisions. Over and over again the women demonstrate that one can grieve the loss without regretting the decision.

"Perkins and Townsend have held true to the voices of the women. The result, *Bitter Fruit,* is a relentless succession of graphic and reflective revelations by women forced to choose between abortion and relinquishment. These painful tales serve as an antidote to those who would romanticize the dilemma facing a woman—or girl child—who finds herself pregnant and without the support of family, society, or the man whose sperm left her pregnant. These are not pretty stories because unwanted pregnancy is not a pretty story. But they are stories which need to be told, and need to be read, by those who seek solace in the stories of others who have faced similar dilemmas, and by those who try to offer support to women, either at the time of crisis or in the aftermath of a decision—even one made twenty years earlier.

Michelle Harrison, M.D.
Author of *A Woman in Residence* and
*Self-Help for PMS*

# Beyond Shame, Beyond Grief, Beyond Silence: Voices of Women Who Have Made Life's Most Painful Choice

"When my mom and dad were talking to this person about the procedure, about the saline, I was just kind of sitting there. There was really no permission for me to have any feelings, so I just sat there and took in the information. When the woman said, 'Let's talk about birth control,' my dad said, 'She's not going to do it anymore.'" *(Celia)*

"On one side, I was wrong because I was pregnant, I was an unwed mother, I was a teenager, I was giving my baby up, so there was guilt and shame. And on the other side was that I had kept my child, I had not opted for an abortion . . . . So you had the shame and you had the glory, both . . . . " *(Erica)*

"As the years have gone by, I have calculated periodically how old she would have been . . . . What would I say to that child now? Is it you I have longed for so often at my breast? Is it emptiness of you that leaves this space inside my chest that nothing can fill?" *(Sena)*

"For us, the abortion was a time that we felt closer to each other. And it opened up certain vulnerabilities in each of us that hadn't been there, particularly for me, because I'm sort of a closed person. He was the one who brought up having kids later, and he was ready. . . . But I would say that the abortion did push me, more than him, in the direction of having kids." *(Monica)*

*Bitter
Fruit*

# Bitter Fruit

*Women's Experiences
of Unplanned Pregnancy,
Abortion, and Adoption*

•

Rita Townsend
&
Ann Perkins

Hunter House Inc., Publishers
2200 Central Avenue, Suite 202
Alameda, CA 94501-4451

*Library of Congress Cataloging-in-Publication Data:*
Bitter fruit : women's experiences of unplanned pregnancy,
abortion, and adoption / [edited] by Rita Townsend and Ann
Perkins. — 1st ed.
p.    cm.
ISBN 0-89793-090-8 : $12.95 (pbk)
ISBN 0-89793-107-6 : $21.95 (hbk)
1. Pregnancy, Unwanted—United States. 2. Abortion—United
States. 3. Adoption—United States. I. Townsend, Rita.
II. Perkins, Ann.
HQ766.5.U5B58    1991
304.6'66'092—dc20                                    91-36208
                                                          CIP

Editors: Jackie Melvin and Gina Renée Gross
Editorial Coordinator: Lisa E. Lee
Cover Design: Theresa Smith
Book Design: Qalagraphia
Production Manager: Paul J. Frindt
Publisher: Kiran S. Rana
Set in Adobe Garamond by 847 Communications, Alameda, CA
Printed and bound by Patterson Printing
Manufactured in the United States of America

9  8  7  6  5  4  3  2  1    First edition

# Table of Contents

# Acknowledgments

Our first and greatest thanks go to those of you who shared your stories with us, who sent us your poems and art. We believe that others will understand as they read the book how incredibly generous you have been. You have broken the silence and shared your lives with extraordinary honesty—often through your tears, often for the first time. It is our hope that this has been, and continues to be, a healing experience.

The stories some of you told us are not included in the book, due to the limits of space. Your experiences are no less important, and we thank you no less for your time and your courage.

We would like to acknowledge every woman who has suffered the pain of having an unwanted pregnancy and making a decision concerning it—and every woman who will do so in the future. We offer you these stories and poems and art to let you know that you are not alone, and that your pain is in many ways the pain that we all share.

We are grateful to our publisher for believing in this book, and to all the staff at Hunter House for working so hard to make it something we can all be proud of.

We thank the humor gods, if such there be, for not abandoning us when things got really tough. We would like to thank our assistant, but we didn't have one, so we thank each other and ourselves for our long labor and behold, with relief and awe, the birth of this child called *Bitter Fruit*.

•

*Rita Townsend:* I would like to thank Stephen Levine for teaching me much of what I understand about death as a part of life, the nature of loss and grief, and (together with my other Vipassana meditation teachers) the possibility and wisdom of continuously coming back to what *is* and keeping an open heart in the midst of it all

I want to thank my mom, Opal Townsend, for her long years of toil to be the very best mother she knew how to be to five children, and for loving me so fiercely. I want to thank my dad, Atlas Townsend, for his example of open-mindedness, faith, and resilience, and for his love.

I am inexpressibly grateful to the rest of my family and my incredible circle of friends for their generosity towards me of all kinds, for constant support and encouragement, for believing in me and my ability to do this work when I found it hard to believe in myself, and for being so patient with unreturned phone calls, unacknowledged events, and a generally pretty self-absorbed family member and friend.

For invaluable help with reading and giving feedback on the manuscript, suggestions of all kinds, allowing me to use their equipment when I didn't have my own, and putting me in touch with their friends or resources who could help, I want to thank the following people: the reference librarians at Santa Cruz County Library, Diane Bloch, Debbie Malkin, Bob Taren, Andre Neu, Carolyn Swift, Carrol Moran, Ellen Bass, Charlotte Raymond, Helen Smith, Julia Chapin, Curtis Kopple, Yona Adams, Nina Sonenberg, and especially Connie Gibble.

To Ann, Sira, N.K.B., the firemakers, grandmother, the kids and Mary: we did it.

•

*Ann Perkins:* My thanks first and foremost go to Rita, who was the backbone of this project from start to finish. Secondly, I would like to thank a stockbroker named Bill Wilson and a doctor named Bob Smith, without whose help Rita and I would not have met and probably would have been wholly incapable of completing a project like this.

I would also like to thank my father for the lessons that have come through him about struggle, perseverance and overcoming. My mother for always remembering how to be silly and wishing—like only a mother can—for my greatest good.

In the last, but not least category are: Jim, my partner, for believing in me and helping out wherever he could; my employer, for forbearance and technical assistance; and my four-legged friends who constantly model what I struggle to emulate—tolerance and an open heart.

•

We also gratefully acknowledge permission to reprint or reproduce from the following: "The Bottom Line: We're in a War" by Elizabeth Fernandez, ©1991 *San Francisco Examiner*, reprinted by permission of the San Francisco Examiner; "Abortion and Christian Principles" by Gerald Winslow, Ph.D., *Ministry*, Vol. 61, May 1988; Beverly W. Harrison, *Our Right to Choose*, Boston, MA: Beacon Press ©1983, used by permission of the publisher; Arthur B. Sorosky, Annette Baran, and Reuben Pannor, *The Adoption Triangle*, New York, NY: Doubleday ©1978, used by permission of the publisher; Suzanne Arms, *Adoption: A Handful of Hope*, Berkeley, CA: Celestial Arts ©1990, p. 8, used by permission of the publisher; Sarah Maxwell, *Untitled* on p.103, previously published by *Red Dirt*, 1630 30th Street #A-357, Boulder, CO 80301; Lisa Woods, "Conspiracy" ©1980/1990 and "Conversations" ©1988/1990, reprinted by permission of *MayDay! Quarterly* c/o Rainbow City Publications, Box 8447, Berkeley CA 94707; Lucille Clifton, "the lost baby poem" ©1987 from *Good Woman: Poems and a Memoir 1969–1980* by Lucille Clifton, reprinted by permission of BOA Editions Ltd., 92 Park Avenue, Brockport NY 14420; Lucille Clifton, "to the unborn and waiting children" ©1980 by The University of Massachusetts Press, reprinted by permission of Curtis Brown Ltd.; Kasandra Fox, "Essay on Guilt" ©1990, reprinted by permission of Perfect Page Publishing.

# *Preface*

The process of putting this book together, or actually of thinking of putting it together, began a long time ago, almost twelve years ago as I write this. The original idea came from the feelings of isolation I had after an abortion in the late seventies, when I was eighteen. In spite of the fact that I had women friends I felt really close to, and that I went away to a very "liberal" university not long after this abortion, the feelings of shame and secrecy clung to me like a bad dream.

These feelings of isolation were not abated by the fact that, though I had plenty of opportunity to discuss abortion as a political issue, I never felt free to discuss my *real* experience with abortion. In my circle, I could talk about my "right" to an abortion and my relief at the availability of abortion, but not about the grief or my questioning of what it meant to destroy a developing life. I felt awkward, as though I must be different from other women, because there was no place for me to freely talk about the whole of my experience.

I remember one friend telling me, "It's just some cells. Go get an abortion, forget about it, and go on with your life. It's no big deal." Even though I did decide to get an abortion, and would do it again in the same circumstances, I kept feeling that there was much more to it. Looking at what appeared to be the other way of approaching the question of abortion—that abortion is unforgivable and unacceptable under *any* circumstances for *any* reason, I could not find a place that fit for me.

I felt a strong desire for community support in making the decision and, just as important, in dealing with the aftermath of the abortion. Unfortunately, at the time I couldn't seem to find a safe place to get that support.

I have in my mind this vivid picture of myself standing at a locker, putting on my clothes after my abortion was over. I was not yet finished with high school. I felt exhilarated, triumphant, empowered. I had taken control of my own destiny, without my parents' help. I remember thinking "I have my life back." About ten minutes later, when my boyfriend came to pick me up, I broke down crying. The reality of the possibility, the life, that I had chosen to terminate engulfed me with a sudden and excruciating sadness. This was the beginning of a long struggle for me to understand my own experience with unwanted pregnancy.

Not long after this, I began to think about a book of women's stories about unwanted pregnancy. I first hoped that such a book had already been written. To my regret, I wasn't able to find a book that allowed women's experiences a full hearing. All of the books I found squeezed the reality of unwanted pregnancy into the narrow confines of the two polarized political positions which existed then and continue to exist in the United States.

Many years went by before I started work in earnest on this project. The idea did not leave me, but I was working full-time, preoccupied with starting a career. I credit my friend and co-author, Rita, with keeping the dream alive and pushing the project ahead. Once the work started, the gathering of interviews, the letters to publishers, the book took on a life of its own. It is now a much more ambitious and complete compilation than I conceived of twelve years ago. This is because so many women have been willing to tell their stories, stories which have the power to teach all of us to expand our vision about the issue of unwanted pregnancy.

We started out collecting interviews from women who had had abortions. One out of every three women becomes pregnant before the age of twenty in the United States. The *majority* of these pregnancies end in abortion. This staggering statistic alone shows how prevalent abortion is in this country. Because abortion is the most common end to unwanted pregnancy in the United States, the largest number of interviews is from that group.

There is another very prevalent outcome to unwanted pregnancy which is much harder to track. Many women raise children when they do not want to, or do not feel prepared to. Although this group is less easily defined (or identifiable) we felt their experience really needed to be represented in *Bitter Fruit*. We were pleasantly surprised by the number of women who were willing to share their story of raising children that were unplanned. Most of these stories are accounts of doing *without:* without a partner, without enough money, enough time, or enough community support.

When we were gathering material for *Bitter Fruit,* many women also spoke to us about adoption and the importance of the birth mother's story. Learning about this side of dealing with unwanted pregnancy was one of the most rewarding parts of doing this book for me. Earlier, I had never known a woman who had given up a baby for adoption. After spending countless hours with various birth-mothers, I was extremely moved by their reality and pain. I feel that their stories are in some ways the most poignant and moving in *Bitter Fruit.*

Before reading the adoption stories, as told by the birth mother, I think I believed the same "happily ever after" myth about adoption that many of us do. I admired the women who had the courage and perseverance to carry and deliver a baby they were going to relinquish, and, though I was pretty sure I could never do it, I thought it an almost perfect, though seldom-used, solution to the problem of unwanted pregnancy. Unbeknownst to me, the grief many birth mothers experience, even *decades* after relinquishing a child, is absolutely overwhelming. I was totally unprepared for the magnitude of feelings coming from these women. I had never really considered what it might be like for a woman to say good-bye to her baby, recently born, whom she expected never to see again. Perhaps I didn't want to.

So, *Bitter Fruit* now contains not only accounts of women's experiences with abortion, but also adoption (primarily from the point of view of the birth mother), and it has contributions from women who had children they did not feel prepared to raise. The format has also been expanded to include poetry and artwork related to these themes.

This book has been a very "word-of-mouth" project. Therein lies its weakness as a scientific study and its strength as a grassroots attempt to provide women with a forum to tell their truth about unwanted pregnancy. We tried to get stories from a wide variety of ethnic, socioeconomic, and age groups, and made special efforts to fill any gaps we saw. We advertised on telephone poles, at colleges, in newspapers, and in magazines. Still, our strongest response by far was from friends, friends of friends, and someone whose friend knew someone who knew someone. It seemed to be very difficult for women to come forward to share their story without some personal connection. Still, all their stories are told firsthand.

Through these connections, the book moved from a book comprised solely of interviews with women who had had abortions, to the book it is today. The poetry and art work were important additions. The experience of unwanted pregnancy is nothing if not elusive, contradictory, and difficult to define. These types of feelings lend themselves particularly well to artistic expression.

In working on this project I have been struck by certain themes which run like repeating chords through the stories, such as the shame and secrecy associated with sexuality, and the fear of judgment from God, parents, or members of the community. I offer my observations on these themes not as an expert but as an interested person who has tried to be open to women in their expressions about unwanted pregnancy. I am also someone who has lived with these stories, collecting and working on them for over three years now. Rita and I did not have any assistants, so we gathered the interviews, transcribed them, and edited them ourselves. Though I complained about this situation more than once, I feel it has allowed me an immersion in the subject that wouldn't otherwise have been possible.

I knew that the issues of sexuality and unwanted pregnancy were closely linked, but I expected deep shame and secrecy about sexuality to be primarily found in the stories of women fifty years old or older. Perhaps naively, I assumed that the "sexual revolution" had freed us to a large extent from the Puritanical stigmas about premarital sex, "illegitimate" children, and the like. The interviews in this book show, however, that women of all ages have had to deal with a lot of shame and secrecy around the issue of sexuality.

Much to my surprise, religion often came up as a strong factor affecting decisions regarding unwanted pregnancy. Again, I had thought that we Americans live in a culture that is becoming more and more secular. But many of the women we interviewed had a strong sense of religion, and even if they did not regularly attend church or practice all the tenets of their faith, they were strongly affected by it. It is interesting to me that these women did not get any of the nurturing possible from being a part of a spiritual or religious community, but they did get the condemnation and the sense of shame. Time and time again I saw the dark side of religious affiliation.

One young woman, Sophia, talks about her mother's reaction to finding out she was pregnant. "She got what she wanted. Confirmation that her daughter was a slut . . . . Immediately she started in on how ashamed of me she was. She told me not to tell anyone about it, then she started naming who I shouldn't tell, I was always to keep it to myself." Carol, who is about ten years older than Sophia, from a different part of the country, and raised Catholic rather than Jewish, has some similar feelings. "I can remember thinking when I first heard about sex that I would become a nun, instead of ever having somebody touch me . . . . I was sexually active first when I was fifteen years old. I felt guilty . . . I knew that I could never let my parents know, or they would kill me . . . . "

Elena also talks about her fear of telling her family about her pregnancy. "I was living at home, my parents were just . . . I believed it would really hurt them if they knew. It was clear I was going to have an abortion . . . if I had to die doing it. I was ready to commit suicide . . . feeling that I had done such an evil, bad thing to get pregnant. If I didn't have the abortion, I would be exposed in my evil badness."

To me, this sense of shame about sexuality, which still appears to be very prevalent in American culture, seems to have a great deal to do with how people, particularly women, approach the use of birth control. Carol says, "If you feel guilty about having sex in the first place, then you aren't going to get birth control, because that is an admission that you are deliberately, pre-meditatively, having sex." Taylor, another woman who shared her thoughts with us but whose story does not appear in the book, also talked about the connection between her sense of shame and her seeming inability to use birth control consistently. "I started to ask myself, 'Why can't I get it together with birth control?' I just lose my power in sexual situations and don't take care of myself. When my sexuality started developing, my dad couldn't handle it so he harassed and shamed me a lot . . . . I feel like, when I have sex, I'm such a bad, evil person that I don't deserve to be responsible to myself. I'm so horrible for doing it in the first place, why should I nurture myself by taking care of myself?"

Surely, unwanted pregnancy remains one of the most complex issues of modern times. It raises fundamental questions about what it means to be a human being, how one makes choices, what role community has (or should have) in one's life, what the concept of family means, and so much more. It is my hope that *Bitter Fruit* will serve as an antidote to the easy answers offered on this issue. To me, women's own expressions about unwanted pregnancy are strong testimony to the complex, mysterious, and usually painful truth of unwanted pregnancy.

They are also a testimony to the fact that black-and-white solutions to this problem are not very helpful or realistic. For instance, many people say the solution to unwanted pregnancy is simple: more education about appropriate birth control practices along with affordable, readily available birth control devices. But, what about the scores of women who, like Carol, feel so ashamed about having sex in the first place that preparing responsibly for sex is just too painful an admission of guilt? Women who do not feel empowered to use birth control are not likely to use it.

Other people point to a return of conservative "family-oriented" religious values. That, on the face of it, could be part of a solution. Unfortunately, I did not talk to one woman who felt nurtured and supported by her religious community when it came to dealing with unwanted pregnancy. I do not mean to imply that this never happens, but it certainly doesn't appear to be the norm.

Susan, who gave up a baby for adoption in a Catholic hospital, talks about how she was treated after her baby was born: "When I came to, a nun came in and literally dumped him on my lap. She said, 'You had him, you have to see him.'"

Finally the deeply polarized political situation in the United States, "pro-choice" versus "pro-life," presupposes that black-and-white answers exist to this exceptionally complex human problem. Elizares says, "I didn't feel like I had anyone I could talk to about my mixed feelings. The way the abortion issue is so charged, you have to choose one side or the other. You can't have turmoil." The reality of unwanted pregnancy, in the overwhelming majority of cases, is turmoil, great turmoil.

I invite you to read this book with an open mind and heart. The contributions of the women who shared their stories with such courage and honesty are an invaluable gift to all of us who care about, and struggle with, this issue.

Ann Perkins
San Jose, California, 1992

# Introduction

Dawn is still more than an hour away, but in the chill
Saturday stillness the two camps muster, Christian
commandos on one side, abortion defenders on the
other.

Enmity hangs as thick as the morning mist.

Operation Rescue, the militant anti-abortion or-
ganization known for its blitzkrieg approach to civil
disobedience, is launching its latest demonstration at
a medical clinic somewhere in the Bay Area . . . . Across
the street, dozens of abortion-rights activists sit in their
cars, engines gunning, headlights cutting the gloom,
waiting for the high-speed game of auto chase to begin.

They are the counterforce, the Bay Area Coalition
Against Operation Rescue . . . .

Here in this quiet working-class neighborhood, the
nation's high-stakes abortion battle is being waged by
front-line warriors—on one side abortion proponents
defending a woman's right to decide when to have a
baby, on the other side abortion foes arguing for the
rights of the unborn.

On the weight of their moral convictions, these
activists have taken the abortion debate from cause to
crusade. With compromise out of the question, the
campaign is being staged throughout the country in
legislative and judicial circles, but most vividly here,
on the streets.[1]

It has now been almost two years since this opening for a front-page story entitled "The Bottom Line: We're in a War" ran in the *San Francisco Examiner*. For a while it looked as if Operation Rescue had been discouraged by wholesale arrests, jailings, fines and confiscation of property for their tactics of trying to blockade abortion clinics. But during the two years that we have been at work on this book, the United States Supreme Court has been whittling away at women's access to abortion, and activists on both sides have returned to the battle with renewed vigor.

In May 1991, the Court handed down the very controversial *Rust v. Sullivan* decision. This decision upheld a law prohibiting health care workers in family planning clinics which accept federal funds from discussing abortion as a family planning option. Workers in these clinics also may not tell women where to get information about an abortion, even if the pregnancy threatens the woman's health. Such clinics are the only source of health care for an estimated 4.1 million American women.

Anti-abortion advocates now have at least two test cases aimed at overthrowing *Roe v. Wade* headed toward the Supreme Court. With this on the agenda, Operation Rescue has rebounded with a new, legally distinct entity, Operation Rescue National, and taken again to the streets. Pro-choice advocates, meanwhile, are preparing to mobilize en masse as they face what some believe is an inevitable Supreme Court ruling striking down the right to abortion.

Within this brutally polarized political and moral climate, thousands of women in this country must, each day, come to a decision about how to deal with an unwanted pregnancy. As voices are raised, clamoring for and against, arguing right and wrong, theirs are mostly silent.

Approximately 1.5 million women have abortions in the United States each year. Another 45,000 women bring their babies to term, then give them up for adoption. An unknown number of women bear and keep children they do not want or cannot care for because they are not prepared, or not allowed, to choose either abortion or adoption.

Yet how often have you heard a woman describe her abortion experience, her feelings surrounding and following it? How many birth mothers (women who have borne children and given them up for adoption) do you know? Prior to interviewing women for this book I had rarely heard women talk in depth about these experiences outside of therapy situations, and then only with much prompting. Why is this? Why is it that those of us who talk with friends about virtually everything in our lives, leave this out? And what is the price we pay, individually and collectively, for leaving it out? When Ann first suggested our doing this book together a few years ago, I thought it was an interesting idea. In the intervening time, as we have talked to dozens of women about their experiences, my interest has become a sense of urgency and a commitment. Now as I think back over the hours we have spent listening to women and transcribing tapes of their interviews, I ask myself, what is this book about? What does it say to us as women, and as members of American society?

In its broadest aspect, the book is a series of vignettes or portraits that provide a candid look into the lives of American women in the latter half of the 20th century: their positions in society, their family relationships, how they relate to their bodies and their sexuality, their hopes, their fears, their realities. The sample portrayed is not, by any means, an exhaustive or representative one, but it is a sample.

Beyond that, it provides a forum for at least a few women to tell about the inner realities and outer circumstances of their lives that dictate their decisions about unwanted pregnancy, and what it means to live with those decisions. And what comes to me most strongly out of this is that it is a book about suffering—about confusion, loss, grief, and guilt.

One of the things I understood as I listened to the stories was that many women had believed, before their turn came, that abortion would provide them with a simple and painless solution to an unwanted pregnancy. For some women, abortion *has* been a clear-cut, relatively painless solution. For others, it *might* have been had it not been for lack of money, improper diagnosis which prolonged the pregnancy, medical complications which prolonged the physical recovery, anti-abortion picket lines, and other unforeseeable factors. But many, many women experienced their abortions as a tremendous loss—as, in fact, a death—and suffered a level of grief for which they were completely unprepared. Even more overwhelming was the shame they felt, and how that shame robbed them of their right to grieve. They believed that because the abortion was something that they had *chosen,* they did not have a right to grieve. Moreover, because they were unprepared (by the silence of other women, often including pregnancy counselors) for the emotional consequences, as well as for the physical pain and other aftereffects, they saw it as their own failure—as something wrong with their bodies and psyches, or with their decision.

There continues to be a widespread belief that the decision to have an abortion is made lightly; that it is simply a form of birth control chosen with no more thought or feeling than inserting a diaphragm or taking a pill. What emerges clearly from the stories in this book is that abortion is a choice women make, sometimes at great personal cost, out of deep concern for the quality of the lives of their children, themselves, their partners, and their planet.

What, then, about women who bear children and give them up for adoption? As pointed out by Erica in "I got pregnant on Good Friday," they walk a thin line between glory and shame. On the one hand, society often sends a strong message that not having an abortion and giving an infertile couple a chance to have a child is a more praiseworthy, indeed more moral course. Yet there is no question that pregnancy out of wedlock, or even pregnancy within a marriage when the child is not planned and not wanted, remains an event that is seen as shameful by much of American society. Also, how many of us have heard it said, or thought to ourselves, What kind of woman, what kind of mother, could give her own child up to strangers? In reading the stories of Jenna and other birth mothers, it becomes clear that some birth mothers have kept silent about their experience because the pain of their grief is so excruciating—even 10, 20, 30 years later—that they can only cope with it by keeping it below a conscious level.

The stories of women who have kept children of unwanted pregnancies make clear what a lonely, unrelenting struggle that can be. As Marge, in "And none of them were planned," says after her four children are grown, "When you have your children and you raise them and you love them, it's hard to say you wish you'd had an abortion. But what I wish I had had was more of a *life* that was my own." The strength and courage of these women, in the face of almost no support and incalculable odds, is incredibly moving.

·

The fact that women continue to become pregnant unintentionally and must either terminate the pregnancy or bear children they are unprepared to raise presents us personally and collectively with a social and moral dilemma which has no simple solution. It is a problem within the community, a problem that all members of the community share. It seems obvious that a valid solution must take into account the experience and the needs of all, but there is profound conflict and confusion surrounding the issue. Basic beliefs about individuality, family, and privacy, about life and death are threatened. The usual response designed to decrease anxiety is to look for someone to blame. People take sides and set about fortifying their positions. The need to be "right" overpowers the need to understand.

Gerald Winslow, who holds a Ph.D. in Christian ethics, addressed this issue in the following article written for *Ministry* magazine:

> Abortion cases often present us with genuine moral dilemmas because they introduce conflicts between

values we hold. The only easy way to resolve these conflicts is to deny, or at least underplay, one or more of our values. But the way of moral maturity would rather allow the conflict of values to deepen our understanding of our own firmly held moral convictions. This way is generally more complex and sometimes more painful, but it leads to a clearer enunciation of those Christian principles that should inform our decisions . . . .

In the extended web of human relationships, that anyone contemplates abortion indicates, to some extent, a failure of community. Social and economic deprivation and the lack of adequate helping institutions speak of social injustices in which we all participate. Those who mouth slogans on both extremes of this issue often overlook this fact.

Many who consider themselves pro-life have neglected to consider what it really means to be *for* life. What sort of educational and health provisions might be necessary? Similarly, many who align themselves with the pro-choice forces leave the impression that the one condition necessary for freedom is the removal of restrictions on the procurement of abortion. But to have real freedom means to have real alternatives, including whatever is necessary to make feasible the option of completing the pregnancy.[2]

Most people seem unable to tolerate uncertainty, not to mention paradox, long enough to explore the history and the real conditions of this predicament. Thus the opportunity to find the meaning inherent in the dilemma or to find lasting solutions that move society toward greater health and wholeness is being missed.

The following brief history and analysis of fertility control, adoption, and the place of the child and family in society is offered as a framework for thinking about this issue. This is not exhaustive or scholarly research; it is a brief look into the matter, and refers only to Western European and American civilization. Nevertheless, it may provide some context for contemplation and discussion.

As Beverly Harrison reminds us in *Our Right to Choose:*

> No woman has ever lived untouched at the deepest level by the interaction of her presumed biological power to bear children and her society and culture's expectations for her life. Even under the most adverse conditions, women as a group have attempted to develop some controls in relation to their fertility—in every culture, without exception, regardless of existing morality or religion . . . . For a number of women, nature's sometimes vicious profligacy often has presented a life-threatening situation.[3]

Fertility, childbirth, and parenting—and cultural expectations about them—have varied widely throughout recorded history, and no doubt in earlier times as well. The impetus for this variation has been more often socioeconomic than moral or ethical. Fertility varies greatly with levels of nutrition and health. The age of onset of puberty in both males and females, has dropped rapidly in modern societies, with the typical age of menarche today being twelve, whereas two centuries ago it was sixteen.[4]

In ancient hunter-gatherer societies, the survival of the entire community depended upon limiting procreation, and infanticide was apparently not uncommon. With the domestication of agriculture, not only were the conditions for survival stabilized, but new community members were also needed to enhance the labor pool. Gradually, moral strictures against fertility control began to appear.

Industrialization and the attendant migration of the families from the countryside to the city, the development of suburban living, and more recently the unprecedented mobility of individuals and families have all contributed to the isolation of women. In stable communities and families, grandmothers, aunts, sisters, and neighbors helped to ease the burden of coping with the incessant demands of infants and children. Without this support system, women must have money to assure adequate prenatal care and to feed and care for children. Thus, the modern, middle-strata homemaker is probably *more* economically vulnerable than her grandmother was.[5]

Today, even in households where there are two adults, two paychecks are usually required to meet the escalating costs of housing, food, child care, education and health care. In many parts of this country even couples without children are not able to purchase their own homes.

For women growing up in the fifties and sixties, and I include myself, the seeds of our changing roles in society were being sown even then, yet absolutely nothing prepared us for the lives we were to lead. Most of our mothers had stayed home and kept house. While a significant number of them had married because they were pregnant, we didn't know that until much later. Hygiene and home economics classes prepared us for menstruation (inadequately, and too late in many cases), taught us to cook and sew, bathe babies, and coordinate our wardrobe. They taught us virtually nothing about our own sexuality or about birth control, nothing about the demands of a relationship, and assuredly nothing about the demands of balancing a job and a home and family. We were in no way prepared to make a decision about unplanned pregnancy. Most of us believed that we would marry forever, have children, and stay home and take care of them like our mothers had. For many young women today that myth still prevails, despite all the evidence to the contrary.

By the late sixties and early seventies not only had this lifestyle begun to disappear as an option, due to socioeconomic realities, but it also came to be seen by many women as a sort of second-class existence. The precarious sociopolitical position in which it placed women became clearer as divorce became more common. A woman needed a career, a life of her own, money of her own, freedom.

By then, some of us already had children. Those of us

who didn't felt that it was our duty and our right to put it off until we had found ourselves as women and as people, and had established ourselves in a career. Families needed to be planned. Yet our bodies, and perhaps even our psyches, failed to cooperate. We found in ourselves an intense sexuality that demanded attention and release. This was a big surprise to some of us, who had been taught, covertly if not overtly, that only men possessed or were possessed by that kind of demanding sexuality and that it was our job to soothe or manage or accommodate it. As many women of my generation point out in this book, the messages we received about sexuality were very mixed. Everything told us that we were to be sexy, attractive, alluring, available. But to actually be sexual—and certainly to be caught at it—was fraught with danger and shame.

Then, suddenly, there seemed a way out. There was the Pill and there was permission, and we took both. But for many women the sense of relief didn't last long. We couldn't help sensing that the Pill could kill us, and besides, we were uneasy with this regulation of our bodies by pharmaceuticals. We turned to the IUD: insert it, leave it, forget it. Free at last. Then the infections began. IUDs disappeared, and showed up embedded in aborted fetuses. The incidence of pelvic inflammatory disease skyrocketed. Again, we couldn't help seeing that the IUD worked by poisoning us, little by little. This lesson cost many women the ability to bear children, ever. It brought others years of pain and illness, and a precarious, unpredictable fertility, perhaps regained only through surgery to remove scar tissue from the tubes and uterus. A high price.

The increase in education about and access to vasectomies for men provided some relief. The number of men willing to undergo the procedure, however, remains small. Thus, birth control remains the province of women. And most women feel that there are no good options, only those that are less cumbersome or less dangerous and more reliable than others.

Amazingly, young women today are little better off than their mothers were in this regard. The National Research Council estimates that as many as 3 million pregnancies each year in the United States are caused by contraceptive failure. This is borne out by the experiences of women in this book, many of whom were using some form of birth control when they became pregnant. The teenage pregnancy rate in the United States is the highest of all developed countries, although teenage sexual activity rates appear to be about the same. According to the Statistical Abstract of the United States, approximately 1.1 million (or 1 in 10) teenage girls became pregnant last year. This represents an increase of more than fifty percent since 1970.

Yet the 1990/1992 edition of *Contraceptive Technology* suggests that the trend of increasing options that moved (albeit slowly) in a positive direction for some years in the United States, now appears to be moving in the opposite direction.[6] Federal spending for contraceptive research has declined. Manufacturers face increasing costs of developing a contraceptive, the prohibitive time and expense of gaining FDA approval, as well as threats of liability and pressure from the pro-Life lobby. All this means that women in this country may be facing restrictions on contraceptive options at a time when abortion may also become less accessible. Even with the options currently available, women face a kind of double-bind. Many of the contraceptives with the highest rates of effectiveness (e.g., the Pill, IUDs) also carry the highest health safety risks. Those that are safest in terms of health have a higher failure rate (e.g. the diaphragm, condoms, foam). When abortion is unavailable, women are forced to use forms of contraception that pose greater risks to their health in order to ensure against a pregnancy which they will not have the option to terminate.

Even under the best circumstances—when women are emotionally mature, physically healthy, educated, and financially secure—we continue to be faced, as we have been throughout history, with a fertility over which we do not have reliable control. And clearly, many, many women in this country live in circumstances that are nowhere near ideal, nor, given our current political economy, is their number likely to decrease.

The women who have been most successful at meeting society's current expectations of their role are the so-called "super-women" or "super-Moms." They balance jobs and children, managing to negotiate the work world *and* show up at every soccer game, home-baked cookies in hand. How does even this woman make the perfect decision when she becomes pregnant with her third or fourth child, even though she has been using her diaphragm? When already there are days when she is stretched so thin she feels she may literally come apart at the seams? When she feels that her face may crack with the effort of keeping her composure, maintaining a mask of control in the face of unceasing pressure to do more? What is the *right* decision for her and for her family?

To many people, the solution for this woman, as well as for unmarried women who are pregnant with a child they feel they cannot raise, seems simple and obvious. There are numerous infertile couples in this country who desperately want babies. Why not match one with the other? Adoption is something that most people have taken for granted for a long time. It has always seemed somehow above reproach, a wise and benevolent institution, unchallengable in its mission of providing a home and family for an "unwanted" child. At the same time, the "real" parents of this child were regarded as some mysterious unknown, about which no one was comfortable even thinking, much less talking.

While adoption is often a very good alternative, and one which should perhaps be considered more often than it currently is, it is far from being a perfect or uncomplicated solution. Birth parents and adoptive parents alike come to it with good intentions and great hope, but it is one of those situations where a binding contract is signed at a certain point in time with absolutely no way for either party to foresee the actual circumstances into which they bind themselves.

In looking at the history of adoption, it is surprising and interesting to learn that the overriding consideration, historically, was for the adopter and his family or tribe, and that the imperative of providing an heir was the major impetus for adoption. In fact, as pointed out in the 1978 book, *The Adoption Triangle*, consideration for the welfare of the child is a thoroughly modern concept in the history of adoption.[7] In relatively recent times, the British practice of apprenticing orphaned children was brought by the Puritans to America, and in the early days of the colonies, orphans were in great demand to provide labor. A record from the year 1627 reads: "There are many ships going to Virginia, with them 1400 or 1500 children which they have gathered up in diverse places." As late as the mid-19th century, children were being shipped off by children's societies to uninvestigated, available homes. Newspapers carried advertisements for children wanted for adoption, and parents either sold or gave them away. The first legal regulations came about because of the need to control the wholesale distribution of children to homes where they were used as cheap labor.

By the end of the 1930s, the intention of American law to protect the welfare of adopted children had developed to the point where an adopted child became "reborn" as the child of the new family, with a new identity and new identification in the form of a birth certificate. Part of the reason for this was to erase the stigma of an "illegitimate" past and to ensure that adopted children had equal status and treatment as nonadopted (legitimate) offspring.

It is clear, however, that giving this new identity to the adopted child also served the ancient interests of kinship and loyalty. Adoption into a new family has always meant complete severance from the original family, and the promise of complete allegiance and loyalty to the new family. To seek one's origins or to question one's true identity is for the most part seen even now, as it was in ancient societies, as dangerous, ungrateful, and disloyal.[8]

Nevertheless, adoptees are now seeking their origins and true identities in unprecedented numbers, and there are new laws in many states to aid them in their search. Research has shown that adopted children often experience strong feelings of rejection by their birth parents, and question whether they are defective in some way. They have feelings of not belonging, in some cases even preceding their knowledge that they are adopted. Adoptive parents also have many motives for adopting a child, some conscious and some unconscious. Studies indicate that adoptive family relationships are subject to strains not found in the typical biological family, and that adoptees are significantly over-represented among populations seeking psychotherapy.

> Many adults carry deep within them a sense of having been abandoned or deeply wounded early in their lives. Many children grow up feeling inadequate and as if nothing they do will make them 'good enough' to be loved. Keeping secrets from children and telling lies to children is destructive to their sense of trust. Each of these issues is often part of adoption, because adoption includes either being relinquished or being orphaned, and either one means abandonment to a child. Therefore, I realized, the potential for pain and loss and even abuse existed within most adoptive families.[9]

While the change of emphasis in this century has shifted consideration from adopter to adoptee, birth parents have continued, for the most part, to be shut out of the process. There has been a tendency not to consider them worthy of concern. In a study conducted by Sorosky, Baran, and Pannor and presented at the American Psychological Association in 1976, birth parents were interviewed 10–33 years after giving up their children. Fifty percent said they still had feelings of loss, pain, and mourning over the child.[10]

Of the five birth mothers we interviewed, only one had, at the time of interview, gone on to have another child. All five described spiraling into prolonged periods of alcohol and drug abuse and depression after relinquishing their child. Even if this group is not representative, it is alarming to see the consistency in their experience. Donna, in "I was officially and formally declared immoral," talks about signing the relinquishment papers, and what came after:

> ... I was in my nightgown and bathrobe and there were two ladies in navy blue suits and my mother.
> ... I will never forget that feeling—so vulnerable and so small. Our house had really high ceilings and when I picture it I see this tiny little person in her nightgown, not dressed, with these fully-clothed, powerful people sitting around her. I was sobbing so hard I could hardly hold the pen to sign the papers.
>
> My mom went back to work, I went back to bed, and the women in the blue suits went back to the welfare office and that was the absolute end as far as they were concerned. Of course, it wasn't the end of it for me by any means; it was the beginning. But I didn't know that at the time. What I do know now is that within about six weeks I started taking drugs, and I didn't stop for ten years .... I had so much pain, and ... the drugs helped it go away. It's been a long process to get out of it—it still hurts. I think the hardest part was [the message]: You will forget, everyone will forget, we will forget this, this didn't happen. So I thought that was right, I thought that was true. I had no idea that you can't just make things go away by willpower. I think that's the element that made it last so long.

With the introduction of "open" adoptions and the new "reproductive technologies," the whole issue of adoption has become incredibly complex. The term "open" refers to an adoptive process where there is an exchange of identifying information and continuing contact between birth parent(s), adoptive parents, and the child. The nature and extent of this contact may vary greatly. According to the National Commission for Adoption, less than 10% of current U.S. adoptions are "open." It remains unclear to what extent this may solve some of the problems of birth parents and adopted children—and what new problems it will create.

Private adoption, whether open or closed, has also brought into the arena the acceptability of the direct exchange of money and/or goods and services between adoptive parents and birth parents for the child. When profitability becomes a motive for procurers or middle-men (lawyers, doctors, "baby-brokers"), or for birth parents, babies can become a product. The interview titled, "There aren't enough white babies in the world," refers to a statement made by a doctor to a young woman he was apparently trying to trick into carrying her child to term by denying for several weeks that she was pregnant. Why would he say such a thing? Because most of the people who can afford private adoptions are at least middle-class, married, and white. For the most part, they prefer white babies. Thus, for the doctor, white babies are a superior, more profitable product.

According to the National Commission for Adoption, the number of children adopted in the United States fell from 89,200 in 1970, of which about 80% were infants, to 51,057 in 1986, of which less than 50% were infants. With babies, particularly infants, becoming less available in this country, brokers and infertile couples have turned to third-world and eastern European countries where there is less availability of birth control or abortion, and fewer resources to feed children, to procure them.

Enter the new reproductive technology: *in vitro* fertilization and its many offshoots, including "embryo transfer," which is the transfer of already fertilized eggs into a woman's womb. This allows for what is being termed "pure" surrogacy, where a woman contributes nothing genetically but "simply carries" the child of another couple to term. In 1990, Southern California saw the case of Anna Johnson, who served as a "pure" surrogate for a couple but announced before the birth of the child her intention to sue for custody. The court awarded custody and all parental rights to the genetic parents. It seems obvious that surrogate brokers will turn next to third-world countries for a cheap and compliant supply of surrogate mothers to carry the genetic offspring of affluent parents. If decreased access to abortion results in increasing numbers of children available for adoption, will those children *be* adopted by couples who could, perhaps more cheaply, have their own genetic child carried by a surrogate and be free of future concerns about the birth mother or their legal rights?

•

When women choose neither abortion nor relinquishment, but keep the children of unwanted pregnancies, what kind of support can they look forward to? Figures from the United States Census Bureau Current Population Reports show that, in 1959, 23% of poor families (those falling below the poverty line) were maintained by women with no husband present. By 1986 that figure had risen to 51%. By contrast, only 12% of non-poor families were headed by women, though even this figure is up from 7% in 1959. Two out of five impoverished Americans are children. Of those families headed by a mother aged 14–25, two-thirds live below the poverty level. Even women who have children within a marriage are economically vulnerable if those marriages don't last, as demonstrated by the stories of Marge ("And none of them were planned") and Carol ("If you would just go away, I could be free"). Neither these women nor their children were protected in the divorce courts. Marge, because her second marriage was financially stable, was able to escape the poverty and powerlessness of single motherhood. Carol's story shows what can happen even when the courts attempt to protect women and dependent children by awarding child support if the man decides that he is not going to pay.

A recent, widely-reported study out of Mt. Sinai Hospital in Toronto, Canada, found that women rearing children from unwanted pregnancies often harbor resentment and anger toward those children. The children of women whose requests for abortion were refused were much more likely to be depressed, drop out of school, suffer serious illnesses, commit crimes, and generally have trouble adjusting to life.[11]

The statistics regarding the incidence of child abuse, both physical and sexual, in the United States are abhorrent. And they do not even take into account children who suffer from more benign forms of abuse—lack of attention; lack of adequate food, clothing, health care; neighborhoods too unsafe to play in; resentment; verbal and emotional abuse. One of the pivotal notions in the abortion controversy has been viability: when is the fetus viable? Perhaps our concept of "viability" needs to be extended to question, not only whether the fetus is capable of *living* outside the uterus, but whether the conditions exist to allow it to live, grow, and *develop* once it is born. Perhaps we need to ask: is it economically viable, given the circumstances of this mother, this family, this community? Is it culturally viable?

There has developed in the past several years, in the areas of ethics and moral development, the concept of a feminine approach to moral questions that differs from the masculine. For women, the absolutes of right and wrong and even the notion of individual rights are often less important than concern with the concrete realities of a given situation—the context. They are also subordinate to concern with relationship, caring and responsibility.[12]

This idea is supported by the women we interviewed. For many, making a decision about how to deal with their pregnancy was the most painful part of the process. An unwanted pregnancy poses a dilemma in which choosing is unavoidable, and the consequences must be borne not only by oneself but by others, including one's unborn child. Many women felt incapable of making such a choice, felt as if they were being asked to decide the undecidable, to choose the unchoosable.

Sometimes they prayed to have it taken out of their hands, but it was not. A decision had to be made, and in the end they knew that only they could make it. And regardless of the decision or the pain she experienced as a result, woman after woman stated clearly that the choice she made felt like the only true option open to *her*—the person that she was, in the circumstances in which she found herself. She had done the only thing *she* could do.

Rita Townsend
Santa Cruz, California, 1992

## Notes

1. Elizabeth Fernandez, "The Bottom Line: We're in a War" *San Francisco Examiner,* San Francisco, CA. (October 15, 1989): A-1.
2. Gerald Winslow, Ph.D., "Abortion and Christian Principles" *Ministry,* Vol. 61 (May 1988).
3. Beverly W. Harrison, *Our Right to Choose* (Boston, MA: Beacon Press, 1983), 155.
4. Ibid., 174.
5. Ibid., 159–164.
6. Stewart Hatcher, et al., *Contraceptive Technology* (New York: Irvington Publishers, 1990): 418.
7. Arthur B. Sorosky, Annette Baran, and Reuben Pannor, *The Adoption Triangle* (New York: Doubleday, 1978), 28.
8. Ibid., 26–38.
9. Suzanne Arms, *Adoption: A Handful of Hope* (Berkeley, CA: Celestial Arts, 1990), 8.
10. Sorosky, et al., 50.
11. Natalie Angier, "Women Denied Abortions Said to Resent Offspring," *The New York Times,* New York, NY (August 19, 1991).
12. Nell Noddings, *Caring: A Feminine Approach to Ethics and Moral Education* (Berkeley, CA: University of California Press, 1984) and Carol Gilligan, *In a Different Voice: Psychological Theory and Women's Development* (Boston, MA: Harvard University Press, 1982).

# Note to the Reader

This book contains edited transcripts of interviews, self-written personal stories, one piece of short fiction, poetry, and art.

The interviews and personal stories are offered anonymously. We have changed names, places, and other details to disguise the identities of the people involved. While not all women who participated were concerned with anonymity, because some were, we felt it best to keep their stories uniform in this regard. Interview transcripts were edited for clarity and to minimize repetition, but we attempted to preserve the natural voice of the woman speaking.

The author of the short story and the poets and artists are named, and a short biography of each appears on page 282.

The stories are arranged in chronological groupings, based on age at the time of the interview. Thus, the story of a 23-year-old woman who experienced an unwanted pregnancy at age 19 would appear toward the front of the book, while that of a 60-year-old woman who experienced an unwanted pregnancy at age 17 would appear near the end.

The poetry and art are interspersed with the stories in a rather subjective way. We attempted to place pieces with feelings and themes related to the concerns of younger women toward the front, and those related to the concerns of more mature women toward the back. All of the pieces are contributed by women who have had personal experience with unwanted pregnancy, with the exception of a few pieces of artwork. These were submitted and chosen because of their clear relevance to the theme of the book.

# "You give up an awful lot"

*Shelley had just turned twenty-one years old at the time of our interview. Shelley works full-time as a nursing assistant for an obstetrician/gynecologist. She brought her fourteen-month-old son with her because her mother, who baby-sits, had gotten sick. When I suggested that she lay him down, she declined, telling me that he always sleeps on her or her mother at nap time. He woke up about half-way through the interview.*

•

I'll start when I got engaged to Jim, who is now my husband. We had just moved in together, and it was a month later that I got pregnant. I was on birth control pills, and the doctor had switched me to a lower dose, but she didn't tell me to use a back-up method.

I went through three months of really a lot of problems, because I didn't want to tell my fiancé. He's thirty-two years old and he wanted me to get pregnant when we first started going out, and I was only eighteen. I knew he would be all for it, and it would be harder for me if I decided not to have the baby. I wanted to know firmly if I wasn't going to keep it, then I could tell him that I'd already made up my mind.

It was a really scary time. I would lay in bed and cry at night, wondering if I could support this baby financially on my own, because I had the fear that maybe this relationship wasn't going to work out between me and my husband. I cried a lot. It was just a heavy weight, it felt like a burden, and I felt like I didn't want to be making the decision myself, yet I knew it was my decision to make. I wanted somebody to make it for me. At first I thought I was in a dream, I felt like I was going to wake up, it was just a really bad dream.

I felt alone, because I didn't want to tell my husband. I told my mom, and she said either way she'd support me, but she was really against abortion. So I felt guilty for even considering that idea. I felt my family would think I'd done something that was horrible and destroying and killing, so I felt like I was . . . . I thought of myself as being dirty for even thinking about it. I felt like I was committing a crime or something in my parents' eyes, having been brought up in a Mormon family.

I met with a counselor who suggested I talk to people who had made the various different decisions. I talked to four women who had abortions. Two of them really regretted it, and seeing that regret made me feel like I would even regret it stronger because of my Mormon background. The other two women were completely fine with the decision they made. They felt like their life was better since they had it, that they had more understanding for life, and that they did it for the right reasons. I knew the reasons they were doing it were right and I didn't have nothing against them. I was happy that they could make that decision and I was kind of wishing that I could, that I could make it and live with it.

I think I was trying to find from them an excuse or a way that I could accept it, a way to say it's okay. But I guess I just didn't get enough, so that's why I have him. I think I would have had more regrets with the abortion—well, I know I would have. In ways I wish I could have waited, I wish I could have made that decision and felt that comfortable. Because it probably would have been easier for me, if I could have lived with myself, than to have him. And it's not that I regret him, it's just that it's really hard. After working an eight-hour day, I come home so tired that I don't have the attention span I should have for him. My tolerance isn't as high as it should be, and I spank him for all the wrong reasons, or I scream at him for all the wrong reasons, when he's just being a baby. And that's all I asked for was a baby. So I have to remember that.

Talking to birth mothers scared me, that scared me more than anything. After talking to them I knew I was going to keep it for myself or I was going to give it away so that no one would ever get it. The fear of me wanting to find that baby and not being able to because I gave up the rights, the fear of him thinking there was something wrong with me or that he was not loved because he was given up, I thought about all that. And the open adoption, where you got to see the baby and know the baby, that would have been harder, seeing your son and not being able to tell him why you gave him up, with a good explanation . . . .

That was a very long, long three months. I could feel my stomach getting bigger, I could see the changes, and I knew I had to make this decision faster and faster. The day I finally really sat down and decided, I cried all day, and I called my mom, who was very happy. And then when I told Jim he didn't believe me at first. He thought I was playing head games on him because he had come out of a seven-year bad relationship. So he didn't want to believe me, and wasn't giving me the support for the decision I thought *he wanted,* because I had no proof. He didn't believe me until the fourth month of my pregnancy when he could really see my stomach and we had the ultrasound and found out that it was a boy. Then it sunk in to him that it was real. That time is a part of my pregnancy that I really wish I could forget.

My dad wouldn't acknowledge I was pregnant; he didn't like my fiancé to begin with, he was against our whole relationship. When I first moved out he wasn't speaking to me, and then when he found out I was pregnant, it was like he didn't even want to recognize me as his daughter. As I started showing and would come into his store, he'd be embarrassed, and try to get me in and out as quick as he could. Like he didn't want nobody to know. It was really hard because I always looked up to my dad, he was my main support. My mom always stayed home and raised us, but if we had any problems we could always count on Dad. So the times that me and my husband fought and stuff, it was really hard because I couldn't turn to my dad for a shoulder, as a male support.

Toward the end he started coming around a little bit more, and started to see that maybe the decision I had made wasn't such a bad one. But he never admitted it, because he won't ever admit that he made a mistake. I think the best thing for us was that he was at the birth of the baby. He was in the delivery room by mistake, because everyone thought I was going to be another four to five hours, so he came by just to see how I was doing. But when he walked in I started pushing. So he was one of the first people to hold him. And ever since then we've been closer than we have all of my life. He's never had a son, so he's using his grandson as a son. He's already got him a fishing pole.

My husband had been into drugs really heavy and had given them up when we started going out, because he knew that wasn't my background. When I told him I was pregnant he was upset because I'd kept it from him for three months. He had a big blow-out and went out and did cocaine and didn't come home. So I had no support. I didn't want to tell my mother that he was doing this. I started thinking, What kind of father is he going to be? Then we sat down and talked, and we went to family counseling, but he only went once and he never wanted to go back. I continued one further time, but I felt it was useless without him going. I knew what the problem was and I wanted to work it out, but he needed to be there too. So we talked and he promised that he wouldn't do drugs again.

He was fine until the baby was about a month old. After we had him home I think the shock or the major change of the baby always having my attention, always breast-feeding, and there being no time for him, got to him. One night he got drunk and came home and passed out on the floor. When I got up in the morning there he was with two bottles of booze by him. I started crying, and I took pictures of him. Later I showed him the pictures and said to him, "Is this what you want your son to see growing up? Your father was like this, and it has to stop somewhere." So he's been really wonderful since I took the pictures. He still has a hard time now and then, but if he has a problem he tries to talk about it first. And if he does drink he drinks within reason. I mean he still gets drunk, but it's not to the point where he passes out. And he keeps the stuff put away, so it's not out in the open. It's still not good, but it's better. He's come a long way from the beginning.

But it's scary for me, because sometimes I wonder what I'm doing in this relationship, I mean, back then when I felt like I couldn't trust him. Still my trust in him is a little iffy. But I want to make it work so the baby has a family, and sometimes I feel like I'm trapped in that situation. I think, Am I doing this just for the baby and not for me? Am I going to go with unhappiness for the next eighteen years just to make my son's life happy? And will he really be happy, or will he see the unhappiness?

[Baby wakes up] It's changed my mom's life too, having him, because she doesn't want him in day-care, so she's watching him. She raised us, and she believes a child should be raised by a family. So my problem has turned into hers. I mean, she does it because she wants to, but because of the way she was brought up and I was brought up, she feels she has to. I feel bad that I've tied my mom down. I don't feel secure with my husband's family watching him, because his sister deals drugs. And his mother didn't raise him, she always left him with his relatives growing up, so I don't feel that she is capable of taking good care of him. I can't afford to have a high school student come, or call somebody; it gets really costly. If you're going to go out with your friends and go to dinner or whatever, by the time you pay for dinner or a show and a baby-sitter, you're broke.

The relationship between my husband and me has never been the same because we never have the time to be sexually active anymore. I thought that would never change, that everything would still be the same. It gets pretty sad sometimes, like we have to make appointments for sexual arrangements or something. And the baby is really jealous when me and my husband kiss. He's not jealous of his father, he's jealous of me. So he'll come over and pull my hair, saying, "My Daddy."

I can't get everything out in the way that I feel, or get my feelings out in words. But I just wish there were words to tell the patients who come in at age nineteen—I just feel really bad to see them tied down, because I'll never be rid of my son, I'll always be caring for him, and I'll be thirty-six years old by the time he's able to take care of himself. And that's scary. I mean, thirty-six is not old, but it's older than I am, and I just wonder, what am I giving up between here and there? I turned twenty-one two weeks ago, and I got really depressed on my birthday, thinking, What am I doing? I was upset that I was married, I was upset that I had him. I was upset because now I was twenty-one and I could do all those things like go out dancing, but I'd already given them up before I had the opportunity to do them.

[Taking something away from the baby, again] This is how he always is, always, until ten o'clock at night. He doesn't go to bed until ten o'clock, because he won't go to bed until his dad gets home. I like to put him to bed sooner, but I feel like his father needs to see him too. We're up and out of the house before his dad leaves usually, so the only time they have to see each other is between ten and ten-thirty at night. Sometimes I wonder if I could keep up with him if I was older. I think, well maybe this is good, maybe I'm doing this at the right time in my life and it was the right path to take and things are going to work out.

[Showing the baby his favorite book] Never again will I buy a book with so many words. That sounds horrible, but when you have to read it three times a night . . . .

I have one girlfriend who has stuck with me all the way, and it's even changed her life. With all my other friends, it's

"Hi, how're you doing?" if I run into them. None of them want to go out anymore. Because most of the time when I go out I bring him with me, I mean he's my responsibility and I'm supposed to be his mother; I can't always give him to someone else, or to my mother basically. And I don't blame them, it's just really hard. Most of my friends now are my husband's age, people I've met through the office where I work who have children, so we take the children out together. My friends all thought I was crazy. At first it was exciting: "Oh, how neat, you're going to have something that's yours." They stayed around while I was pregnant and the first month after he was born. But when they figured out what was involved, the responsibility, and how often babies cry and all, they decided, "Hey man, you made a big mistake, I'll give you a call in a couple of weeks." But they don't.

I think there should be support groups out there for young girls, for them and their babies to come to. Because with him I thought I was the only one. He just had problems. He had respiratory problems when he first came out; he stopped breathing. So he got sick easily as he got older, he had colic, and then he was hospitalized with croup, and I had no support. I thought it was me, it was something I had done, until later I realized it was normal for babies to come out with respiratory problems. They have some mother and kid groups but it's so costly, and if you're a young mother, you can't afford it. It's all older mothers.

I left him for four days for the first time two weeks ago on my twenty-first birthday and went to Reno with my husband, and I wish I would have brought him. He would have been the main highlight of everything, he's part of my life. We gambled and that was fun, and we couldn't have done that with him. But he would probably have lit up my birthday more than anything. Because this is who I share my life with. I mean the main people who are important to me are supposed to share my birthday. He wasn't there. He makes me smile, he makes me laugh, and when I cry he's really good, he'll come and say

"Mama" and rub my cheeks. Then I feel like I've got somebody finally who really understands me, loves me for what I am and who I am, no matter what my future looks like.

[Through the screaming of the baby] One hard part was the body change; I was not *even* ready for that. I mean, I knew it would happen, but I didn't think it would be as bad. That's a real shock for girls who think about having a cute cuddly baby to love and to play with. I was always kind of heavy-set, but I had just lost twenty-five pounds before I got pregnant, back into my smallest, size five. And I felt I had saggy skin, but it wasn't as bad as it is now. I can't wear those tight skirts that I used to wear, one boob's larger than the other from breast feeding. You know, I never . . . those things never dawned on me. I knew stretch marks were part of the game, so that didn't bother me, and I didn't get them that bad. But when he was three months old and I'd lost most of my birth weight, I realized my hips have expanded, so I'll never get into a size five, whatever size that I am again. I might get down to a size seven, but still, that's really hard. I could get my pants on, but I couldn't zip them up. My old bras and shirts didn't fit, because my boobs were too big from breast milk.

I cried hard, and I guess everybody ruled it out to post-partum blues. I don't think they were post-partum blues, I think it was real stress. I was really upset because my body would never look the same, and I feel . . . . I don't feel as sexy toward my husband as I used to, sometimes I feel repulsive looking. And I am . . . I mean my stomach sags and I still haven't got over that, it still bothers me. And you're in relationships, situations sometimes, and you wonder, will I ever be sexy enough for another man to be turned onto me and to like me?

We got married a month after he was born. I met him when I was sixteen, we started going out when I was eighteen, in August, November we got engaged, January he moved in, March I got pregnant. So we got married to each other without being friends, and I think that was one of the biggest mistakes. I think if we would have become friends first, our situation today would be better than what it is. And yet I think if I hadn't married, maybe he would have left in certain circumstances, maybe he wouldn't have hung in there. Now when I think back on it, I think that would have been okay if he left, that would mean it wasn't supposed to be. But it's working, and we're happy at this time. But it's real tough.

I guess I've been saying a lot of negatives, but once a baby's here they're rewarding. He's time consuming and costs a lot, but he's my best friend now. He doesn't always understand, but he knows just when to give me love, just when to give me a kiss or do something cute, look up and smile at me. Especially now, he's getting a sense of humor where he'll look at me and he'll start laughing like I look hilarious. He's a real joy; he's worth it, I guess he's worth my decision. It was just hard dealing with something that I wasn't wanting, that was the hardest part. Because I always figured that I was going to plan my pregnancy and have enough money to do the baby's room up and have all the pink and blue frills and ruffles. He got none of it. We got a used crib and used stuff and we live in a one-bedroom apartment, so his bedroom is the living room. There wasn't much to fix up.

Hopefully in a couple of months we'll have a house. We're trying to buy a house in Arizona. My mother-in-law bought an acre of land and you can put more than one house on it, so we're looking to buy a mobile home to put on it. So we'll have that dream after all, we'll have the white picket fence and everything, so maybe it will work out. I feel really, really scared, but my mother-in-law is a nice woman, and the more I get to know her the more I'm starting to trust her. I know if we went to Arizona that I wouldn't have to work because my husband will be making enough money. It scares me because, once again, all I'll have is my life revolving around him. Sometimes I've felt, when my husband brought it up, that he was taking me there to isolate me.

It's scary, that thought. So I try to think positive about it; I think that I'm going to grow up, I won't depend on my parents, and I can stay home and raise my son. But I won't have my mother who is my best friend and my caretaker of my son, I won't have any of my girlfriends, so the only person I'll be going out with until I meet some people is my husband. I mean I love him and we do a lot of fun things together, but it's scary thinking I'll just have him as my husband and my friend, because sometimes he's not the most understanding person.

The other thing that scares me is that he wants another kid, but I swore my *life* on it that I'm not having another one until he's four, at least. I've guaranteed myself that there won't be anymore, I just couldn't. I know now that I've made this decision to keep him, next time I would have an abortion if I were to get pregnant between now and four or five years from now. It would be the right decision, I know now positively. I guess, too, what helps is that I've seen the procedure done. And it doesn't bother me as bad as I thought it was going to. But now I see that everything is fine, and I don't know what they're like when they get home or a month or two down the line, but at the time they don't have second thoughts, they don't seem to get real upset, and it doesn't bother me. I know next time, knowing everything I do now and seeing the procedure, I'll go through with it; it won't be a problem. I can't deal with two of these. [Dealing with a crying child]

I want to get my nursing assistant degree, so that I have a career and can support him if things don't work out between me and my husband. It's not just me I have to worry about anymore. When I wasn't working during the eight months, my husband brought home paychecks that were barely enough to cover the rent. If I hadn't been breast-feeding him during the early months, how would I have fed him? Now, my first priority is food, whether we have the money or not or whether we pay our rent, which we manage now because I'm working.

It's hard because I was used to going out to dinner maybe four times a week, and we'd see movies twice a week. I haven't seen a movie for four months now, and we don't eat out. All those things you don't think about giving up; you give up your sleep, you don't go to bed when you want to go to bed or get up when you want to get up. I just . . . if I would have known all the changes . . . . But there is no way to explain it and no way to experience it until it's yours. Even if you took care of someone else's baby, you would know it was going to end as of some date. That's the hardest thing, you realize you don't know when it's going to end.

It just changes your life so much you could never be prepared to accept those changes, no matter how much you think you know or how ready you think you are, you're just not ready. I just can't get the words to say how much it changes your life and how hard it is.

# "When I saw it on the ultrasound, I couldn't do it"

*At the time of the interview, Darla has just turned twenty-one years old. She completed her high school diploma after the birth of her daughter. After splitting up with the baby's father she spent several months unemployed and on welfare; she now works full-time in a medical office. Darla is about to transition from state support to self-support for herself and her daughter, now almost three. They live alone together for the first time.*

•

I was about fifteen years old when I started going out with the baby's father. The first year-and-a-half of our relationship I lied every day about seeing him because my mom didn't agree with us seeing each other. When I was seventeen I got pregnant, and just kind of ignored it for about six months. Actually, I think I was only six weeks pregnant when I first realized it. But I had four tests, and every time they were different: you're positive, you're negative, you're positive, you're negative. And actually the last time that I went in there I'd had a period when I was pregnant, and they said that my body had aborted itself, that it was just a miscarriage, and it was okay. They never checked me, they never did anything, they just sat and told me that. I remember Todd's mom was really happy, saying, That's good, that's good, your body's telling you it wasn't the right time. I kind of felt a relief because I didn't do it myself. I don't know how long it was then, until I finally went and got another test.

I think my mom realized it, and she made an appointment over at the clinic finally. But she didn't quite know how far along I was; I said about two months. I didn't want to do it, but it was like I was being dragged. The first thing they did was an ultrasound, and I think I was twenty-four weeks pregnant. So I had a week legally left. I saw her actually on the ultrasound, of course. I was seventeen years old, I wasn't going to say, "Turn the machine around; I don't want to see." And when I saw her, I knew that I wasn't going to do it.

So we spent the whole day over there, crying and arguing with the doctors and stuff like that. When it came down to signing the piece of paper that said I could die during this procedure, I said No, I wouldn't do it. We went all the way up to the director of the clinic. They were saying it was best for me, because I was young. My mom was really pushing for it too, so they stood behind her. Maybe she was trying to get people to convince me. She was really worried about the procedure, whether it was safe. They were trying to convince me that it was safe, that in years nobody had died or whatever, that it was relatively safe.

I went in thinking that I was going to do it, but when I saw it on the ultrasound, I couldn't do it. I think she weighed between three and four pounds then, and I mean she was a . . . a big baby. So what ended up happening was that they wanted me to sit in on a group where they explained stuff. I guess they thought they were going to trick me and take me in and do it. I don't know, I remember a lot of stuff that just doesn't seem right now. So I sat through this group and they said, "Okay it's your turn; the doctor's waiting for you." And I said, "No I'm sorry, I'm just sitting in on this group and I'm not going to go in." And I asked where my mother was. They stalled for a minute and I just got up and walked out and said, "I'm not going to do it."

We went out front and sat, and I just cried. It was a real hard decision. And it was hard on my mom too, because she didn't like my boyfriend and I'm her baby. So we sat outside for about an hour and a half, and three or four nurses came out at different times and said, "The doctor's waiting, you're ready, let's go in, come on," and they would take my hands and try to pull me in. And I said no, that I could not do it. So my mom said, "I'm going to ask you one more time, do you want to do this or not?" And I said, "No, I can't." She said okay, and she went in and talked to them and we left.

When I was over at the clinic I called my boyfriend and told him that I was almost six months pregnant, and that I knew I wasn't going to get the abortion. He said, "If you don't get the abortion, don't come back, don't call me." Of course, that all changed when I got home and called. He played a lot of games, and I knew it wouldn't end like that. But I started crying when he said that, and I was in the waiting room and there were a bunch of people listening and I was embarrassed. My mom was sitting there too, sighing at me because I called him.

I guess the original cost was like three hundred dollars or something, and my mom and step-dad and Todd's parents were splitting the cost between them. But when they finally found out how far along I was they said that would change the price and it would be twelve hundred dollars. My mom said, "That's fine, I'll write a check." And I'll just never forget those words, there are just some things you never forget. It showed that she would do anything to get that abortion, that money didn't even matter, she was that strong on it.

I had been using birth control before with another boyfriend, then I stopped. My attitude about abortion was . . . I didn't really think about it, I never had to think about it. They talked about contraception at school, but I don't remember if they talked about abortion. They probably did, but it probably just didn't mean much. I just thought, not me. And I hadn't been using birth control the whole two years I was with Todd.

When I look back it was just real stupidity, and I just think, How could I do that? I went for almost two years without getting pregnant. I mean, that's luck.

I remember when we went home, my mom went in her bedroom and shut the door; she never shuts her door, never, never, never. And I could hear her laying on her bed crying. I just felt so guilty, and I thought, Why am I doing this to her? It was just a real confusing time in my life. I wrote her a letter, because I felt that I couldn't communicate right then, that if I wrote it on paper it would be a lot easier. And I just explained what I felt and told her that I was really sorry, but that this was my choice. So I think that helped a lot. She wrote me a letter back, which I still have, that she loved me and that she was trying to respect my decision, but it was hard for her. And she also did say (this was in the end of February or the beginning of March, because for my eighteenth birthday I got maternity clothes and pots and pans) that she wanted me to move out. Because she thought that if I was going to be a mother, I should be out on my own and realize how it was. A lot of people looked down on her for that, but today I really have a lot of respect for her because I think that it helped a lot. There are a lot of people that live at home, that don't know how it is, that have kids.

When we moved in together Todd started working again, and he had to do some time in jail, for some tickets. So when I was nine months pregnant he was out at the rehab for a month, and when I went into labor, that's where he was. But they let him out to work. I remember him calling and asking how come I wasn't there, because I always picked him up every day and took him to work and took him back out. I told him because I was sleeping, because I was in labor. And I remember there was just this long silence, dead silence. He said that was the scariest part of the whole thing, because he really thought it would never happen. It was like a dream or something. After a while he asked me if I was okay, and I told him that his mom was on her way out to get him. That's how it started.

There were a lot of problems between Todd and me, him not wanting to be a father and stuff like that. I think it was better in the beginning. About two months after the baby was born it got real bad, and we were still together a year after that, so . . . she put up with a lot when she was a baby. He used to hit me and stuff, and he would see other girls; it was a real bad relationship toward the end. And she actually still remembers it. Like now if my boyfriend tickles me—or the other night he had a piece of pie and he smeared it all over my face—she just freaks out. I was asking my therapist about it, saying, "God, she was so young." He said those are the clearest memories.

She's very possessive when it comes to guys, which is understandable, I guess. She still sees Todd. Every weekend she goes to his mom's, because I work on Sundays. She usually stays over there on Saturday nights, and he lives there, so he sees her. If he didn't live there he wouldn't see her, because he just does not care anymore, which is real weird, because he was there when she was born and was there for a year after. And he was good with her, he was a real caring father. Then the day he walked out, he didn't have a daughter anymore. It's strange that you can just drop something out of your life like that. And she knows that's her daddy, she talks about him a lot.

So, he moved out of the apartment in May before she was a year old in June, and a friend moved in with me for a few weeks. This was a boyfriend that I had gone out with before, who said that he would take care of Melanie, that he would treat her as his own. He had said that when I was about two months pregnant, and I just shrugged him off. He said, "Todd's not good for you and you'll realize that," and I did. So Steve and I got back together after Todd and I split up and he moved in, but it didn't work. I wasn't ready to settle down, and I was fooling myself by thinking that I was. All I wanted to do was go out and stuff like that and he didn't want me to do that, he wanted me to stay home.

On the day of Melanie's first birthday I found out I was pregnant again. I never had a doubt, I knew I needed to get an abortion. It was too soon; I wasn't ready. It was Steve's baby, and he thought that this was great and that we were going to have a baby together and all that. He was real heartbroken about the whole thing. My doctor talked to me and told me what I could do, and I ended up getting an abortion. It's something that I never really thought about. It's something that I guess I just put in the back of my mind as soon as I walked out of that place. I don't think about it. I think it was the best thing to do. It was hard, because it really hurt Steve, but there was no way I could have another baby. So he was real upset because I did that and he said that if I wasn't going to keep the baby and settle down, then he wanted me to move out. So I just moved and moved and moved. I lived with a friend after that for a month or so, then another friend and I got a townhouse, but that only lasted about four or five months. I moved in with my grandmother just temporarily until I could find a place. Because this was all new to me; I mean Todd had supported me, I didn't work.

I had worked in my doctor's office for a month or two, and then I left there because I was going to school from nine o'clock in the morning until two o'clock in the afternoon, then I'd work from two-fifteen until seven o'clock at night, and I never knew where my daughter was. Todd would have her out with . . . I never knew who. And so I couldn't live like that. So that was really the only job I'd ever had. So I moved in with my grandmother and got back on welfare, and then March of last year I finally found a place to live. Melanie and I moved in, and that's the first place I've ever had, just Melanie and myself. I sat on welfare for six months or something and didn't do anything. Then I decided that I needed to start looking for jobs, and it took me about three months of trying, and finally I got a job and my welfare's almost completely gone, by the first of the month it will be gone. So I've come a long way, and it feels really good to support myself and support my daughter without welfare. I started getting child support. I got my first check three days ago, after two-and-a-half years. But it's getting a lot better. When I look back I just can't believe what I went through.

I was still in high school when I got pregnant, and the people there treated me like I had the plague, like they were going to catch it. They would stare, they would walk away from me. So of course I ended up dropping out, in October of my senior year. I went to my graduation, which was on June 15; Melanie was born on June 28. I cried, watching all my friends graduate. It was really hard. The teachers were pretty supportive. I think I just didn't want to go to school in the first place, and that was one way of getting out of it. But it was also that everybody was talking and stuff. I didn't go back until Melanie was nine months old and I went to the Teenage Mothers Program and graduated through there, because I felt that I needed to get a diploma. A diploma meant a lot to my mom, and I did it a lot for her, but I did it for myself too.

In the Teenage Mothers Program you can do your regular classes or you can stay in the Teenage Mothers Program classroom. I stayed in the Program classroom because I didn't know anybody from this high school; all my friends were at another school. My daughter went to the day-care, which is right on campus. The classroom is just a big room with desks, a couch, porta-cribs, swings. The younger babies stay in there for two to four weeks—the newborns—then go down to the day-care. During the day you have one period that you volunteer at the day-care. The number of girls there fluctuated. Always in September there were a lot; by October everybody said forget it. When I left there were maybe twenty girls enrolled, but half of those girls didn't come.

I think that probably if I had known how hard the whole thing would be, I don't think I would have done it. I mean that's sad to say, but I think it's true. You just have to put a lot out for kids. A lot of people don't realize that, they think it's going to be great, dressing them and burping them . . . that's not all it is. And especially if you're single, it's really hard. But even in the hardest times I never had any doubts that I wanted her there, until recently. I mean seriously, because she wasn't a problem before, but now it's the terrible twos, and they *are* terrible. I'm seeing a therapist to help me deal with her. We have a good relationship, but she is . . . a brat sometimes, that's just the bottom line; she's constantly testing.

She's two-and-a-half now, she'll be three in June. I just was twenty-one last week. So, it's been a pretty hard life. I mean you see kids having a hard time, but a kid having a kid takes the cake.

# "There aren't enough white babies in the world"

*Sarah was a twenty-three-year-old graduate student at the time of the interview. Her pregnancy and abortion had occurred approximately eighteen months before. Her story illustrates the current outer limits of fertility control and adoption issues: the world of women as incubators and babies for profit.*

•

I was twenty-one years old and attending city college full-time. I was involved in a relationship where I really wanted to be in love and therefore convinced myself that I was, and couldn't figure out why it still wasn't working out. I had never been pregnant before, and I always thought I'd been really lucky to have gotten through high school, because it seemed like in high school all my friends were having abortions.

In a strange way it came at a really bad time, because I had taken my first women's lit class and I was finally becoming aware of abortion as a political issue. I was always pro-choice, but I thought it was a shame that abortion has been abused as a contraceptive. I thought that a lot of people, particularly in high school, took advantage of it. They were careless and thought, Oh well, I can always go and have an abortion. I never really thought that was the right way to go about it.

I was on the Pill at the time I got pregnant; it was just a fluke. I missed my period, and this was the one time in my life where my period was late and I actually felt like this was it for sure, this was the time that I was pregnant. But I went to have a test and it came out negative. The day that I was notified that my test was negative, I started clotting really heavily, so I immediately went to see this gynecologist who my family saw, and who we had always been told was a really wonderful person. He told me that I had miscarried and that I just needed to rest.

Then for about a month and a half, two months, I didn't get my period again, so I went back to see him because I was really worried. I had all along been feeling a little bit unusual, but I trusted him, so I thought I wasn't pregnant. That, I think, was the most interesting part of the whole pregnancy, trusting him over my own body, when I really was determined that something was wrong. He kept claiming that this was a normal thing after miscarriage, that it was normal that I didn't begin to ovulate again immediately, and that unless I really wanted to begin to have children that it wasn't something I should worry about. And so I trusted him, but I did worry. Two months later I still hadn't received my period, and it really began to be awkward. My body was feeling really strange.

So I went back and I said, "Look, I'm feeling really awkward, I'm not ovulating, and I just want to get back into my routine menstrual cycle, because I felt better that way." Finally after examining me he said, "Well, Sarah, it looks like you are pregnant; you're thirteen weeks pregnant." I said, "But how? How? You said I hadn't been ovulating—how could I be pregnant?" I don't know what he said. His answers were never straightforward and I was always too paranoid to really . . . I was a little bit afraid to question further. I really took his word.

My mother was very supportive and very close throughout this. We both really believe that all along he knew I was pregnant and was kind of pushing me to prolong the pregnancy to a point where it would be too late and I would indeed have to have a child. On the day he told me that I was thirteen weeks pregnant (which was a lie, I was actually twenty weeks pregnant), he said that it was too late to have an abortion. And I knew that thirteen weeks wasn't too late to have an abortion. So I said I didn't understand. He just said, "Why don't you just have it and put the child up for adoption; I know plenty of people who would love to adopt a baby." He kept asking me about the color of my boyfriend; I said, "Well, he's white, why?" Still, it was just so weird that it never clicked, nothing ever clicked with me because I was so afraid. The strangest comment was when he mentioned that there weren't enough white babies in the world, and that there were really a lot of people who wanted to adopt a white baby. He said that my baby appeared healthy, that I should really consider giving it up for adoption, blah, blah, blah.

Of course, I was petrified. I went home and talked to my mother and she said, "Well, let's just schedule an abortion then," because we knew I could have one. So we scheduled an abortion for me, and I went in two days later. They did an ultrasound, and said, "I'm sorry, you're twenty weeks pregnant; we can't perform the abortion here."

I had to leave town, because there wasn't a clinic in the city in which I lived that performed abortions after sixteen weeks or something. I was five months pregnant. It was amazing, though; the day they told me I was five months pregnant was the day everything just came together for me and suddenly I was positive. But I had needed that reassurance, I needed to be told. My breasts had been growing, but it was also a period where I was dieting really heavily and working out a lot. I did gain weight, but I just thought it was a normal bit of stomach. It was nothing like showing really, really drastically, even though I felt awkward all the time. So I wasn't listening to my body, w1hich I'm really ashamed to admit.

I went with my mother for the abortion. It was out of town, so we had to stay in a motel overnight. It was a dilation process, where they insert something twenty-four hours prior to the surgery, and that dilates you as if your body is actually contracting, and it kind of prepares you. Apparently some women actually had contractions and had really strong problems, but I was lucky. I just had that one night, but that twenty-four hours was the most painful twenty-four hours in my life. You couldn't figure out whether you were going to vomit or you needed to go to the bathroom. It was constantly this feeling that you just had to get something out of your body. Then I went in the next morning, and there were protesters as usual. In fact, the police had to come that morning, because there were more than the amount allowed on the premises. My mom told me later that they were taken away right when I got out, so it was something I was glad I didn't have to deal with. The actual abortion of course I didn't feel at all, I was out. I awoke, and that was an emotional period, awaking in this room. There were all these women on these beds that had gone through the same thing.

Afterwards I was sick for a while. I had to have a D&C after that too, because I continued to bleed. And then there were just the emotional aftereffects. I never regretted that I had done it, but . . . I want to have children and the fact that I was five months pregnant when I had the abortion is what made it the hardest. Had it been twelve or thirteen weeks I would have been able to handle it better, but I always thought of it in terms of . . . this is a really stupid way, but more than half a baby. Because I always divided it into time and thought of nine months—well that was a child, in effect, it wasn't just the fetus, a potential life. I always thought of it as indeed a child. That was hard. I was sad, I think, that I had to get rid of a child.

I had to wait about one week before I actually had the abortion, so there was one week that I was completely sure that I was five months pregnant and knew that I could really have this child. And it was amazing how at that time I really noticed a lot of changes in my body. And I really tried to make a point at night to feel the baby, and I thought twice that I did, but I didn't know if it was just the anxiety to feel the child or if I actually did feel the child. So I did have a bond with it, and even afterwards I felt sad. And it's interesting, because every time I have my period I think about it. I'm kind of grateful I know I'm not pregnant again and I don't have to do it, but it is also like this potential life thing once a month that I experience and feel. I still to this day am sensitive when I see little babies. During that summer I sort of withdrew from people, and I thought about it a lot. I guess I just gradually got used to the fact that it was done and over with. My aunt had just had a baby and I spent a lot of time with her and it was wonderful. It was painful, but in a strange way it was healing.

I think about the baby in terms of time as well. I mean I always thought about, had I kept the baby, it would have been born in April, it would have been Gemini/Taurus; I always think about how old it would be now. But I also think about how I probably wouldn't be here now. It's hard not to think of yourself as selfish, especially with all the issues that have developed this past year around abortion. It's just amazing what you hear people say, and it's such a feeling inside of . . . it's like sometimes you know you can't even try to talk to these people about it and try to change their views. That's when it develops into an anger, a frustration. Like when I drive by the family clinic and I see the protesters in front I get really angry, because I know that's the day some people are having abortions and I hate those posters and I just really think it's a cruel thing to do. I can't stand the fact that it's mostly men out there, and that if it's women, they have their children with them. It really does hit you all the time. Sometimes I try to imagine her out there— I had wanted it to be a girl. I imagine the child out there, kind of, in another person's life. I didn't believe in adoption, because I just didn't want to have to face a child in later years, and I know I would have wanted to see my child.

My dad was out of the country at the time. I'm an only child, and we're not that close. He's always pushed me educationally, so there's always been a rebellious streak in me—I've never been good enough for Dad. The whole thing just brought back a lot of family problems and I found out a lot of stuff about my family I didn't know. My mom had had an abortion with my father, and as a result was sick and hospitalized for a long time because it was unsterile. And then my father never really wanted to have children, so he kind of forced my mother into having two abortions after that, when she really wanted to have children. So it was a real weird issue at a really strange time. And my father and I, to this day, have never really talked about it.

The gynecologist I saw is still practicing. My mom sought some legal advice because we really did want to sue him—privately—we didn't want to make it a public issue, have it in the papers or anything, which turned out to be the only way we could do it. Plus, my papers disappeared from his office after that last visit, so I had no written evidence of me ever seeing him. My mother went into the office in the middle of this whole thing, and told them that she wanted to see my file, and that she was going to transfer them to another doctor. And they said, "Well, we don't have any files; we must have misplaced them." So we never got those. And then I remembered that every time I went in for check-ups, they never could find my file and he had to start a new one for me, which never dawned on me to consider of any relevance at all.

There were all kinds of little strange things that were happening all along, like him giving me pre-natal vitamins and just telling me that they were good for me and that I should consider using them. I think it was just really subtly planned out, and I hit myself on the head all the time for being that stupid. And he was a gynecologist; I don't know why all these women would write him these letters about wanting babies. And I don't even know if in the field of medicine it's ethical to show people such letters. Because he would always say, "I have all these letters, I can show them to you; people really need children." Is that ethical to do? And do you just pull out these letters when a woman is pregnant, when you've just found out she is pregnant and she's made it perfectly clear that she doesn't want a child?

What's really ironic is that I had a friend who had become pregnant a year earlier, which I didn't know until we talked about my abortion, and who had the same gynecologist and didn't have any of these problems with him. And she's black, so I started relating all these racial issues with it, with that question that he asked me and his comment about white babies. And what I found really astonishing was that he's not a white man, he's an Asian man. So when I thought about that question about whether my boyfriend was white I just thought, What do you mean there's not enough white babies in the world?— Come on. That's when we were really positive that what he had done was intentional. I don't think my father wants to do anything about it, but I would. I just don't know how to go about it, financially or otherwise.

This is something I always really wanted to talk about, and I was so happy when I saw your ad in the paper. There are so many support groups in this town, so many little therapeutic gatherings for post-this and post-that. I find it amazing that in a town that is so predominantly pro-choice and so concerned with women's issues on the one hand, that there was never a group for women who had experienced abortions. I believed, like a lot of other people, that if you had an abortion and you felt it was a healthy decision, then there weren't many emotional problems attached. Now I know that isn't true. That's another reason that I don't understand how women can just use abortion as a contraceptive, because it's not something that I would ever do again; it's not something that I would choose to do again.

# "I'm going to get over it"

*At the time of her abortion, Monica was twenty-four years old; the father was thirty-four. They spent most nights together, but did not live together officially. She has a master's degree from a prestigious university; he works as a professional. She received the abortion at a women's health clinic in a west-coast town. The initial interview takes place five days after the abortion. Monica is reinterviewed approximately five years later.*

•

When it happened, we both got excited in a fantasy sort of way. We started thinking of this little baby of ours in me and pretending we might have it. I got really caught up in it, excited about being pregnant—the changes in my body and the idea of motherhood. And that was funny, because I had always been very sure as a child and growing up that I wouldn't want children. Kevin and I seemed really close while we were dealing with the pregnancy in that way and not thinking about the abortion. But then a decision had to be made, a realistic decision.

And the situation was that if I had this kid there was a good chance I'd end up being a single mother at some time in the future. I realized that I needed at least the commitment to monogamy, even if it ended six months down the line, like many marriages or relationships do. He couldn't say that he could do that.

He could say yes, he'd try, but in his heart he thought that it would be lying to tell me he could. I'm happy he said it, but it was real, real painful to hear. It made me angry toward him, and I started thinking of him as very self-indulgent and egocentric, wanting children but not wanting a commitment. Also I felt he wanted the kid, but not me; I felt very rejected. He said he thought the right thing for both of us was to have the abortion.

So I just said to myself, I've got to do it. It's going to be gross, I might pass out, I might throw up, I might cry my eyes out, and I might suffer from months of depression, those are all possibilities. I'm so depressed over it now, what's going to happen afterward? And I knew all those risks. But I knew that I really didn't have any choice.

It's weird, but what I wanted from him became all-important. I didn't even think, What do I want to do with my career? What do I want ten years down the line? Do I want to have a ten-year-old around? Do I want to be married to this person, do I want to be getting checks in the mail from this person or what? I really didn't deal with—still haven't dealt with—how I really felt. I guess if he'd said, "Okay, let's get married and have this kid," then I would have started thinking about what I wanted.

It's hard for me to describe how I felt, being pregnant. But I think I felt more like a woman and less just like a person. I've always felt that I wanted to make it doing something, preferably in a non-traditional way. That's probably why I figured I'd never want to be a mother. And I always thought I'd be totally grossed out by the changes in my body, having this fat stomach and having this thing kicking around, and the idea of giving birth and the pain of that. But I remember lying in bed one night and Kevin put his hand on my stomach and it was just really exciting to me for him to feel it. All of a sudden it was some kind of erogenous zone for me. And even though it was getting sort of puffy, and I could actually see it growing, I just thought it was so neat. It felt really good. And the idea of walking around with a giant stomach didn't offend me the way I had expected to be offended. It was actually really exciting. In terms of raising kids, I just always figured I'd be a lousy mother, not being able to tolerate it, being too self-centered or something. But then I started fantasizing about me and this kid and taking it places and watching it grow, buying it clothes, and all these motherly sort of things, and it was really appealing to me in a lot of ways.

Even now after the abortion I'm happy to know that I want children, and I'm happy to know I can have them. For a while I was just really sad, thinking, if I don't have it now maybe I'll just get caught up in some career and before I think again, it might be too late. I felt like I'd blown my chance. But at the same time, I was not prepared to have a child and possibly be on my own and have a career and get my head together. I needed more outside support from Kevin. Maybe that's not right. Maybe you shouldn't do it until you are ready to do it alone these days, because of the way things go with relationships.

Before the abortion, you had to go in for an information meeting and blood test. There were four other women who were all in their late teens, maybe twenty years old at the oldest, which was weird. We didn't talk. The lady just told us the procedure, and was talking about what could go wrong, and I started getting very dizzy, then I ended up passing out. The whole thing just really got to me on some level, the blow-by-blow description of sucking the fetus out and how maybe they'd miss something and have to go in and do it again, all these possibilities of things going wrong. I knew, realistically, these things don't happen that often, but when she was going through them, I was thinking, this is what I'm going to be doing in a couple of days. Also, thinking about how good I felt about the pregnancy, and now it was just all so disgusting and so awful. It really got to me. These little girls were just sitting there taking it all, saying, "Okay, when can we sign up for one?"

I sat in that meeting thinking, Okay, we've got to think of something, come up with some alternative to doing this abortion. I can't do it, I know I can't. If I feel this bad hearing about it, I can't go through with it. And so I thought, Well, I could punch myself in the stomach a whole bunch, drink a whole lot of booze and hope I have a miscarriage, or I could have the baby and raise it by myself if Kevin leaves, or . . . I don't know. I just prayed to have a spontaneous abortion in the next two days or have anything happen so I didn't have to go through with it; but that didn't happen. So I made my appointment for three days later, and I was miserable and scared waiting for it. I was just hoping for someone to tell me the answer, tell me what I should be doing. I couldn't stand having made the decision. I wanted something to happen to take it out of my hands, some complication where things would probably be much worse, but where they would be necessary rather than me having to make the decision to go through with this operation. It didn't sit with me at all—to say, Okay, I'm going in there and I'm going to do this, when I didn't have to.

Kevin thought, Oh, Catholic guilt. Probably it is, partly, having that ingrained in you. But it was also just more of a personal thing. I couldn't really stick it to my religion—or my past religion. I could just feel it inside, deep inside, that I didn't want to make the decision. But nothing happened in the next three days. So I had to go in there and do it.

The morning that I was going to do it, Kevin had taken off work to be with me, and the abortion place called at ten o'clock. My appointment was at ten-thirty, and they said, "Could you please change your appointment to tomorrow at eleven o'clock?" I was outraged. It's not like I was going to a check-up or to the dentist. The night before I'd slept horribly and had all these dreams about babies and abortions and stuff. So I just said, "Absolutely no way." They said, "Okay, but you're going to have to wait when you get here." So we waited for a long time.

I thought they seemed sort of resentful toward me for not having changed. This one woman had been sort of rude the time before when I was sick. She said, "You just don't seem like you're ready for this; I think you should put your decision off for a while," but she said it in sort of a cold way. I wanted to do it that day to get it over with, but I would have felt a whole lot better if she had said, "Hey, what's going on?" Because I really wanted to talk to someone, to let them know about my reservations, because they were going to be doing it. To let them know I might be a basket case when I was doing it. And I would have felt a whole lot better if she had said, "Listen, why don't you talk about it?" But she didn't, and I didn't talk to them about it.

My appointment was at ten-thirty and I guess I didn't go in until about twelve-fifteen or so. Oh God, it was awful; I hated it. I've been through some *really* serious surgeries before, and they just didn't compare to this. Because for one, I was awake. And two, because I had chosen to be there. I had on my high-topped tennis shoes, so the doctor talked to me about basketball. He seemed nice; he was real warm. He had this stupid poster on the ceiling, a really weird, spacey poster that you're supposed to meditate on I guess while you're having the abortion. So I was lying there totally freaking about the thing while they were dilating me and giving me this pain shot in my cervix. I was feeling everything they were doing and wishing I could not think about it.

Then they left me in there for probably fifteen minutes while the pain medication was taking effect. I just fell apart; I started crying and couldn't stop. I had these weird fantasies that I was going to die. It was like I was punishing myself or something. I thought, I'm going to die and I'll never be able to tell Kevin that I love him, and I'm losing this baby. Is it a boy or a girl? I want to keep this baby. I was so sad. In fact, it just, it hurt me spiritually or something, like I was really losing something. I also felt that this was going to kill Kevin and me, which I don't necessarily think is true now. But it's touch and go in my mind, whether this is going to kill us, whether I'm going to be resentful of him forever, whether we're going to start hating each other or something. But then again, if we'd had the kid it could have happened too.

When they came back in to do it I sort of pulled myself

together so that I could deal with the physical aspects of it. The lady (I don't even know her name) was really sweet, and she told me to hold her hands. It hurt, physically. I guess it didn't hurt all that much except that, if it had been a natural thing like giving birth, which I'm sure hurts ten times more than having an abortion, it would have felt better, because that's something you're supposed to do to your body. But this was just so *bad* to do to your body; it's so unnatural to strip your body like that; it seemed so unfair. I got really caught up in how the pain was not good at all, and that made me really dizzy and sick, just that it was not the right kind of pain at all.

Afterwards I started crying again. They left me in there alone; I wasn't supposed to get up. My legs were cramped up and my uterus was cramped. I was lying there moaning and groaning, and I heard the pastor outside say, "Is she all right?" I was really uncomfortable, and the only thing to relieve it was to groan. I was sort of embarrassed because the doors aren't that thick. But I thought, I don't care if these people hear me groan, as long as those nineteen-year-old girls who are doing it with no problem don't hear me. Later I went down to the little recovery room where you lie down on a mattress on the floor and Kevin came in and laid down with me. We just held each other, and we were both really sad.

He was incredibly supportive and comforting during and after it and right now. He apologizes a lot, but it hurts him too. He said that it was the most difficult abortion out of all the ones he's been through, because we came so close to having it. He's thirty-four, and he feels like there's a possibility he won't be able to have a family, although men . . . . My father was fifty-nine or sixty when he had another baby. He's got a two-year-old. So Kevin will always be able to do it. *I* can't always do it, *you* can't always do it. But these guys, they just go for younger and younger women. Kevin is ten years older than me. Next he'll have a twenty-year-old and I'll be an old bag at twenty-five.

The first day afterwards I was really uncomfortable. I slept a lot and Kevin was there taking care of me. The next day

I felt good and I got up and worked. I got a lot done and I went running, which I don't think I should have done. I didn't have much bleeding and I said, thank goodness this is over. Then the next day Kevin and I went running. But that night about eleven-thirty I started bleeding, and I've been bleeding ever since. I get so bummed; I thought this was over, and here it is. I was in an awful mood, stomping around, not wanting to talk. I was just so angry that I had to live with this; big napkins, which I hate, and walking around with this reminder. It wasn't a period, it was just like this left-over shit from losing a baby.

The next day I was getting really spiteful toward myself. I said, I'm going to run even though I have cramps and don't feel well. So I started running and I got in real pain after about two miles. I stopped and walked for a while, then started running even harder. Now I think I have an infection, and I have to go in tomorrow. I kind of sabotaged myself; I should have just rested. I get so angry; it's like I'm angry at my body. Maybe I'm angry at myself for having done it. Because today, even though I felt awful, I took my bike out. I ended up riding up about fifteen miles on hilly roads. I started getting cramps and thought, Why am I doing this? It's stupid. It's like I'm trying to hurt myself or something.

I guess I'm afraid of slipping into a depression and not coming out of it. I just didn't want it to linger. I'm afraid if I do allow myself to treat myself special because of this that I'm going to fall into sadness or self-pity or wishing I would have had it. Today I was thinking I wished I'd had it. But I know, really, that I shouldn't have, that I made the right decision.

But I feel like I lost something real. Even though politically we don't like to think of it like that because we want the right to abortion and we don't think of them as babies like that. But it is the loss of a possible or potential child. I mean actually it's more than the potential, it's there, the genes are all there. I mean, I'm absolutely not against abortions or anything, but it is the loss of something. And when you have a lot of meaning between two people, it hurts, it really does.

It's funny, I was thinking, either you get over it right away or you become immersed in it and go crazy over it—it's like *the* event that makes you go crazy or changes your whole life and you get bitter for the rest of your life. This is how I pictured it. It's like a TV show, a mystery. And the psychiatrist comes to the abortion and says, Oh, this is why this person hates men or this is why this person is suicidal or something. I said, Well, I'm not going to be that way, so I'm going to get over it.

I don't think many people have a respect for what you go through. I feel embarrassed that I can't just say, Okay it's over, good-bye. You think most people do. And when you read people's accounts and how horrible it is and stuff, I used to say, Well, I don't think I would be that way. I think I'd just go through with it and that would be it. I mean, I couldn't attach emotion to that. But I did. And I fight it.

## Re-interview with Monica

*Five years later, Monica reads a transcript of our prior interview before we begin. As we talk, she nurses an infant son, her second child. She and Kevin were married a year after our initial interview and their first child, a daughter now four years old, was born nine months later.*

I didn't realize I was so angry. Actually, what happened when I went back to the doctor was that they found they hadn't gotten everything out, and they had to give me some medication to make the rest of it come out. It was really awful. So I was more at risk for infection, because there was some of the fetal matter still there.

It's interesting that in retrospect I don't remember feeling that strongly about it. I do remember pretending we were going to have the child; but it was pure fantasy. I never expected for it to be such a difficult decision. I mean it almost wasn't a decision; it was a decided thing that I was going to have the abortion, it was a given. But then actually having to bring myself to do it was one of the most difficult things I've ever been through.

But I don't think I was prepared to have a child, and our relationship wasn't at a point where it would have been good for us. We did end up staying together, but I don't think if we'd had that child we necessarily would have. There were too many things that weren't right between us.

It's not an easy thing to go through. I think it tests you in a way. You really think about what your goals are, what you believe in. Because before I was pregnant, I always thought it would never be a problem; it would be just like an extension of birth control. But when it happened it brought up so many issues. It made me look at my relationship; it made me look at myself. And it did totally change my perspective on having kids; it was the first time I could imagine having a child. It never occurred to me what it would be like having children; it wasn't something that I fantasized about until that time. But now I have two great kids, and I don't think about that abortion as being a third child, wondering what that one would have been like. Because I'm happy, I'm fulfilled, I have really enjoyed being a mother. I don't regret doing that abortion, but I don't look at it as just a light little thing in my life.

I think I've mellowed a lot since then—I don't think I would fight my body so much now. It sounds like I was trying to conquer myself or something. I *felt* the pregnancy. Even though I'd never been pregnant before, I knew. There were real changes in my body, all the hormonal changes. My body, every time I've been pregnant, just springs into action. And when it's over, your body does have to heal. And it seems like I didn't want to let it do that; I just wanted to fight back and pretend like it didn't happen.

It made me sad to read that, the description of going through it. I can be tough, but that one . . . . I couldn't even stand sitting in that room and facing up to it, hearing the physical description of it. And in these times . . . I mean things have changed even since *this*, people's attitudes have changed. It's not something you'd want to talk about with most people, having gone through an abortion. I think people hold it against you. Times have changed, people are much more conservative, and obviously, people are trying to change the laws. It's really scary; I would never want to see that happen.

Because I think there'd be a lot more kids in the world that had troubles. I can't say that my kid would have had trouble, but I don't think it would have been necessarily a good life. I can't say that I was emotionally prepared to be a good mother, which is the most important thing. And I also know, having had children, that even if I thought I didn't want the child and I was going to go through the pregnancy and give the baby up for adoption, it's probably one of the most difficult things you could do, much more difficult than having an abortion. If they didn't allow abortions, I think there'd be a lot more women who held onto their babies, even though they knew they weren't capable or prepared. Like in my case where I was with somebody, I don't think *he* would have been able to say, okay let's go through this birth and give it up. We would have had the kid. And whether it would have turned out, I can't say.

We definitely decided to have our daughter, that's why we got married. For us, the abortion was a time that we felt closer to each other. And it opened up certain vulnerabilities in each of us that hadn't been there, particularly for me, because I'm sort of a closed person. He was the one who brought up having kids later, and he was ready. When we decided to, our relationship was a lot better than it had been before. But I don't think our relationship was really tight until we had the kids. It's an amazing thing that it does, because it's even more emotional vulnerability and more bonding. It's one of the most amazing experiences that you can ever go through. I mean it puts marriage to shame. Getting married is nothing compared to having a child, in terms of bonding and just the miracle of it. But I would say that the abortion did push me, more than him, in the direction of having kids.

# Growing Up with Marie

## by Melissa Tinker

when I was in fifth grade, Marie and I
would climb into the fragile plumeria
tree in my backyard, our hands and knees
itching with sticky white sap, our nostrils
full of sweet scent and our feet
dirty red-brown
Marie would tell dirty stories about
people covered with grime,
crackling nests of hair, crust
Marie knew more than I did,
she was a small girl, but the pictures
her voice drew in my mind planted
a warm and sick seed in the pit
of my stomach, and her laugh
could open so wide I was afraid
it would swallow me

we grew up fast, those days rushing by
like a thick door clamping shut
so heavily I could smell the must
Marie never left the house without heels
she said they make your legs look thinner
and her breasts bulged beneath

neon-pink mini dresses, she said men
like that, men, they were everywhere even
hanging from her walls
like paper prisoners, tormentors
exuding sweat or mahogany

a man with hard muscles and maybe
a pimply back, groaning his hot
breath on her face, teeth
clenched gritted straining,
grunting over her, his penis
chafing her insides, rubbing them down
like sandpaper, deposited sperm
spit in an ashtray, plumeria sap
running down her thigh

then another man, then another
until one day, one of them
stayed, latched onto her ballooning
above her cervix
they had to scrape it out of her
scrape out her insides, scrape the
sex out of her, scrape out the
grimy bodies and all that sperm

in the sterilized waiting room
she pulls her pumps over her
calloused feet

no sex for three weeks
the doctor says

©1991 Melissa Tinker

64

# First Response

## by Alison Mazer

Phone ringing 9:00 A.M. Saturday
your far-away voice crying, "It's PINK"
"What?" I ask
"Oh God, Al, It's Pink"
"O.K. now Seline calm down, just calm down"
my heart pounding under wet terry towel
water running down the back of my legs onto cracked
    wood floor
"Is John with you?" I ask
"Yeah" you say, "stuck in the kitchen reading the
    instructions over and over
he's convinced I did it wrong"

Having to leave for my 10:48 to Brewster
I leave you, alone with John

As my thighs stick to the blue vinyl seats
I stare out the gray train window
seeing myself there with you
the doctor's office
cold and white
nurses smile as you try to swallow
the puke that wants to shower their
beautiful beige carpet

listening to this professional
give you your
options
I wonder, will the Supreme Court ruling affect his advice?
Will he be permitted to mention abortion?

Your 250 pound Mother
hands on her huge flower-covered hips
towers over you and your clutched stomach
"Selina, I would rather you not have an abortion!"
black and white James Dean photos shake with each syllable
paint chips flurry down onto your un-made-twin-size-bed
and your father cannot know
your swollen breasts
puffy face
pink and splotchy from crying

This pregnancy is a huge
pink water balloon
crashing down on your tiny skull as you
skip down 181st street
blue print sun-dress
bouncy blond hair soaked
from the
crashing liquid

You lay on the
bumpy gray concrete
spanish-speaking voices
gather echoing concern for
legs sprawled
ankles twisted
your tiny hands try to

wipe wet hair
out from bloodshot eyes

Small sharp stones
press into my bare knees as
I shade your
pink face
from the
bright sun

Your turquoise eyes
stare through me
past Washington Heights
flying over the bright green football field
where you graduate college
the stained-glass
temple where you and John
are married
to the blue and white
Mamaroneck house
where you live
with your four noisy-blond kids
running around the kitchen table
chasing bandits with yellow
and blue water guns

You are a Mother with sweaty bangs and
        cranberry-stained tank-top
nursing one baby as you snip
ends off green beans talking to
clients on cordless phones

You do it all
have it all      but your

eyes slowly shut
tiny hands slide down
to the hot gray pavement
your mouth opens as if
to tell me
how much
easier it is
to sleep
for a while
and dream

# It's Salty on Your Olive Skin

## by Alison Mazer

AT TIMES
WHEN I'M WITH YOU
I LOSE CONTROL
SURRENDER

FORGETTING ALL
SAFESEX
I
RUN AND HIDE
FOR A WHILE
AS YOU
USE MY NAKED
BEAUTY
FILL ME
WITH YOUR LIVENESS

THE MISTAKE IS I
DON'T KNOW YOU
LIKE YOU
ALL THAT MUCH

GENERAL OR LOCAL
ANESTHESIA
DOESN'T REALLY MATTER
THE BUCKS MATTER
NO
THE HURT

MATTERS
PAIN

LONG DREAMT ABOUT
CURLY BABIES
AT
WRONG TIMES
NERVOUS TIMES

UNPLANNED PARENTHOOD AND
TWOHUNDREDTHIRTYFIVEDOLLAR
ABORTIONS
FORCING THE WORDS OUT OF MY MOUTH
KISSING YOUR BODY
FELT DIZZYGOOD TASTING
SO SWEET
BUT BITTER NOW

WITH COLD YELLOW TAPE MEASURE
WRAPPED ROUND MY NAKED WAIST
SWOLLEN WITH
EARLY SIGNS OF
BABIES BABIES BABIES

I
FEAR THE DAY
BUT MOSTLY
I WISH I
LOVED YOU
KNEW YOUR FAVORITE COLOR

*©1991 Alison Mazer*

# *Water Torture*

## by Ann Perkins


You . . . forbidden one
stay far from me
with your strange glue

My quiet whisperings
(desperate urgings)
Make no difference
to your tiny persistence

As if you were
the logical consequence
of some earthly action

A curious question mark
bears down on me
Too heavy for my basket
I don't want to answer


*©1990 Ann Perkins*

# 17th Spring

## by Cosette Dudley

Love with a stomach, Love without heart—
I am cold all spring.
Heat is in a hand closed tight inside me,
Life makes a fist against me.

My belly swells dark,
Under a coat fooling no one.

# "I don't ever have to do this again"

*Sophia is a twenty-five-year-old professional woman currently working on postgraduate education. She was born in Israel and now lives in the United States on the West Coast.*

•

My first abortion happened in April of my eighteenth year. At the time I was really going through a lot of pain. I was actively taking a lot of drugs, primarily speed, and drinking. I was also going to school, but ditching classes all of the time. I was very overweight. I had no self-esteem. My parents had recently divorced. It was just me, my mother and my younger sister at home. I had been sexually active for about a year.

It was high school and I was always going to parties. I went to this particular party with some friends. There was this guy who was having the party, his name was Steve and he was really good-looking. He was known to be, you know, he slept around with a lot of women.

Oh, one thing I need to say is, as the result of all the drinking and drug-taking, I experienced a lot of black-outs. That happened that night. I had been drinking quite a bit and was very ashamed of myself. Very, very much so.

I lived in a fairly middle-class to upper-middle-class area, where all the teenagers I hung around with were rich. They had all the clothes, the cars, the drugs, etc. It was a real Southern California atmosphere, and I was very poor. I had no money, and for me it was a real issue. I was always comparing myself to everybody else. It was a very typical Southern California thing where everybody was tall, beautiful, blonde, [laughs] and I was about 5 feet 4 inches, 160 pounds.

While I was at this party, I remember Steve coming on to me. I remember thinking, Wow, he's so cute. It was a real big thing, I felt honored in a way, flattered. I remember going to his bedroom after a lot of people had left and he put on a rubber. He couldn't penetrate me because I was dry. We tried Vaseline, everything, it just wouldn't work. At that point I was out, that was the last thing I remember.

I recall waking up the next morning and I was very sore, so I knew something had happened. We had never talked about it, as a matter of fact when I got up the next morning, he was gone. He didn't even wait. I remember going home and feeling really hung-over and weird. A horrible feeling. I was so full of guilt and shame, but not dealing with it at all, trying to do everything I could not to think about it. I watched a lot of TV trying to escape.

The next month, my period didn't come and I started getting really worried. At the same time another woman I knew had missed her period and had an abortion. All of a sudden it became real for me. Could this really happen? It was strange because I didn't even have any verbal confirmation that Steve had had sex with me while I was asleep.

I went to the clinic and had a urine test, it came out negative. I was so relieved and expected my period to come. It did not come, so I went in for another test. It was negative again. I was really worried by that time and I asked them if there was anything else they could do. They offered a blood test and it was positive. Without blinking an eye, I picked up the phone. My mother was on welfare, so we had state-sponsored medical care. So I called up the county clinic, and made an appointment.

A woman named Maria took me to the clinic. There was a broad cross-section of women there, but they all had a flat and lifeless affect in common. My own agenda was to get in, get out, get it over with. I got in there, and I filled out all of the forms. I declined counseling, seeing the movie, and all that.

When they finally got to me, they had spelled my last name incorrectly on their sign-in sheet and when they called my name they pronounced it "Dyke." I remember cracking this joke, saying "Gee, if I were that I wouldn't be here." [Laughs] Everybody looked at me, still with that flat affect. I was really laughing to myself. It was really dark humor. That is what really stands out to me. Me, making this stupid joke.

I put on this little outfit, including a little pair of shoes, and went into a room. It all happened quick, quick, in a flash. I got on the table, the doctor came in saying "Hi, I'm so and so," putting the IV in my arm.

All of a sudden I woke up hyperventilating and crying at the same time. They gave me juice and cookies. I got dressed and was bleeding very badly. A friend of mine took me home.

No one knew about my abortion, including my family. Afterwards, I remember being in my bed, listening to my mother, telling her I got out of school early. I wrote in my diary, "Today I killed my baby, and this will be a day I'll never forget." I wrote down all the details of my abortion, and included the joke.

The next page I went into an incredible inventory of how terrible I was. "I'm fat, I drink, I smoke, etc., etc." I wrote down every horrible thing about me and it was actually about four pages long, it was a litany of terrible things about myself. I signed it. I didn't write in my diary after that for a really long time. It was very painful.

I blamed myself for getting in that situation. I never looked at Steve as the person in the wrong, never. I was the one who totally fucked this up. It was all my fault because part of me knew better. But, a small part of me also knew that I couldn't help myself. There was also relief.

My second abortion was two years later, about the same time. I was living at home, it was my birthday. I was turning twenty. A friend of mine was having a party for me. I had been going with this fellow named Randy. Randy and I had a big fight right before my party and he came to the party anyway. I continued fighting with him right through the party. I got lots of gifts which were bindles of coke, pills, champagne, and I just partied galore that night. I went crazy and then blacked out.

With Randy I had always used protection, always. I remember waking up the next morning feeling hung-over and sore. Randy was next to me. I remember asking, "What did you do last night, did you have sex with me?" He was real coy about it, kind of wouldn't answer me, made a joke of it, giggling. Eventually he said, "I did." I said, "Well did you use anything?" He said, "No, but I pulled out." "Oh, great." I remember thinking, Oh, fuck. Right then and there I knew. I was sure I was pregnant.

Sure enough, next month came along and I didn't get my period. I had a urine test, it was negative. I had another urine test, it was negative. I had the blood test, it was positive. [Laughs] Same situation all over again. Abortion revisited. At that time, it was my first year of college, and I was doing a lot better. Although I was still doing drugs, I was not bulimic anymore, I had lost some weight, and I was doing really well in school.

I was madly in love with Randy, just nuts about this guy. I remember calling him and saying, "Well, guess what? I'm pregnant." He felt pretty bad. That weekend we went out with some friends to the Comedy Club. There was this comedian, and he got up and did a schtick on abortion jokes. That's what he went into for a good half hour. Everybody was laughing. I was stone-faced. It was surreal. All this laughter about abortions.

Randy and I went back to his house afterwards, and he kept wanting to have sex and I had no desire for it. I went ahead and did it. I really numbed out, kind of went away. Emotionally I was gone. We had sex and that was the last time I saw him. I tried to call him and he was "never home." I got the message.

That was it, I never saw him again. He was to have taken me to have the abortion.

Another painful part of my memories of this is my mother's reaction. I had always gotten messages from her that I was the black sheep of the family. My sisters were very virginal, definitely not sexually active. I started out real brazen, I made my way in the world, I wasn't afraid. My mother was always really uptight about it. Any time I brought a guy home, she would start asking, "When are you going to get married?"

She had this long-standing habit (it was weird) of looking through the trash to see if I had had my period. Lo and behold, she wasn't finding anything and she knew the exact date I was supposed to get my period. Needless to say, she badgered me day after day. It wasn't just in the morning, she followed me around all day. "When are you going to get your period? Did you get your period? What's going on?" Sex was something I never discussed with her, because I realized it was not a good idea. She and I were in different places altogether.

After a month-and-a-half of this had gone by, I finally said something. I just blew up, she was driving me crazy. She got what she wanted. Confirmation that her daughter was a slut. She asked me what I was going to do. I told her I had scheduled an abortion. She was very upset. Immediately she started in on how ashamed of me she was. She told me not to tell anyone about it, then she started naming who I shouldn't tell. I was always to keep it to myself.

The day of the abortion I felt totally ashamed and alone. I didn't have anybody to talk to about it. Randy wasn't there. My mom definitely wasn't there, so I drove myself. I wanted to be alone with my secret. I got in, went through the whole thing by myself. This time I was flat and lifeless. I was "one of them."

I remember talking to this woman who was afraid because it was her first time. She was married and already had two kids and couldn't afford another child. I remember feeling worse after hearing that because she had a reason. She had a valid reason.

All I could say was "I fucked up." Again, I was blaming myself for every ounce of what had happened. Randy did not do anything wrong, it was me. Obviously it wasn't his fault because he left me.

After I had the abortion, I woke up hyperventilating and crying again. As I walked out of the clinic there were all these people picketing. I was drugged out and the sight of these people just walking up and down picketing was so strange. I felt horrible, so horrible. Part of me wanted to be where they were, holding up a sign, because I felt so ashamed, so horrible about it. Here it was right in front of my face, they made the shame so real.

This very nice woman and her husband saw me standing there. I was really out of it, just standing there staring at the picketers. They asked me if I had anybody to drive me home. She had just had an abortion too. They took me over to Denny's.

We had some breakfast. I was just flat. I had nothing coming out of me at all. It was not even numbness. It was a sense of depletion.

I got in my car and drove away. I went home and there was my mom waiting for me. She asked if I was okay. I went into my room and closed the door. She came in and started her routine. "I hope you've learned your lesson." She ended it with "Make sure you don't tell anybody, I don't want anybody to know about this." The following night my sister and brother-in-law came over. I got into a long conversation with my brother-in-law about politics. As soon as he left, she barged into the room demanding, "Did you tell him?" That was her big thing, that I had told and humiliated *her*.

I went to work the next night. My supervisor was a good friend of mine, and she noticed there was something wrong with me. She asked if we could talk. It all came out, I found myself telling her the whole story. It was such a relief. I was out until three o'clock in the morning talking with her.

When I got home my mom was standing there, looking at me, awake and pacing. She said, "Well who were you with tonight?" The implication being, whom had I had sex with that night? Then she started asking me why I hadn't learned my lesson. I totally ignored her and went to bed. The following day I woke up and there she was, waiting at the foot of my bed. "Who did you have sex with last night?" The first moment I opened my eyes. I remember looking at her and just screaming. I mean screaming my head off. She drove me fucking nuts. I let it out. We did not get along after that. I totally ignored her. I think I moved out two months later.

Now, the third abortion. You know it's weird, but that word abortion still kicks for me, I don't want to accept that. There was part of me that was tempted to lie to you and say, "Oh, I only had one." It's part of myself I really don't own very consistently. Even with that, I think I have gotten to some good realizations. I know now that both guys contributed to the problem and that they both had a lot of things wrong with them for having seized the time and taken advantage of me. I think many would call that rape. I try to call it rape as well. I think I verbally put that out, but don't feel it inside. A large part of me still accepts fault. It's nothing I remember too easily or too well. My heart goes out to anybody who's been through this. There's a sigh of relief in me because of this interview. There is someone here who can understand.

The third abortion happened when I was starting the relationship I'm presently in. I think this one was really a matter of inappropriate birth control. This one was very different from the others, very different. Most importantly, I was with someone I really cared about and who I knew cared about me.

We had been using the sponge, I had only used it a couple of times before. I feel like I had that thing inserted properly. I'm really not sure how it happened, because, I can tell you right now, after the first two abortions, I became very rigid in my use of birth control. No matter what, I used it. I got to a point where I really did not do too much drinking anymore, because that was a real instigator for what had happened.

When I found out I was pregnant this time, I didn't

numb out. I really felt the pain through and through. I went into a deep depression, I went to work and could barely function. I was bursting into tears all the time. My boyfriend was supportive and willing to listen to me. We went away for the weekend after we found out. I could not have sex, and I honored that for the first time.

I remember walking around Golden Gate Park and starting to cry. I was heaving and sobbing and I just couldn't stop. I think I was grieving all three abortions. I don't believe I grieved the first two when they happened. I had absolutely no control over my crying, it was just coming out in spite of me.

My boyfriend took me to have the abortion. I scheduled it first thing in the morning again. It was very fast, we were in and out in half an hour. I had the choice of being awake or put under. No way did I want to be awake, so they put me under.

Afterwards, my boyfriend was not there. He was pretty anxious about the whole thing and was out driving around. So I had some time waiting for him on the stairs outside the clinic. There were no picketers this time. I thought to myself, I don't ever have to do this again. Not ever. I could feel it inside me. It was a relief. No matter what. I really heard myself. Whatever I had been doing, or acting out, it was over now. I could have gone into a big psychological explanation, but I didn't feel like it. I think a large part of me grew up right then and there. I was saying to myself, I'm going to take care of you, you don't have to do these things to yourself anymore.

This time was also different in that I did not do a lot of blaming, either of myself or my boyfriend. I still knew that I was nowhere near ready to have a child. I was still in a lot of pain, emotionally crazy a lot of the time. I was definitely not mature enough to have a child. To me, having a child is an amazing thing which requires the utmost commitment and maturity. There is no way in hell I had enough of that. I was having a hard enough time dealing with myself, let alone a baby.

My boyfriend came to pick me up, and I slept in the car the whole way home. I remember feeling very calm, even peaceful. I had a real sense of relief. I knew that I had done the right thing. I wasn't angry this time. I felt like the grieving in the park really did a lot for me.

The following week I broke up with my boyfriend, in fact, it was the next time I saw him. I told him it was over between us. About a month later, I changed my mind. I realized that I was ready to associate him forever with this horrible situation. Part of me then realized that he is a wonderful man and I didn't need to take the pain of that situation out on him. I'm glad I did not lose out on the wonderful relationship we have had, and have now.

This last abortion, I was really present in my body. The first two, I was really cut off. I don't remember ever looking at my belly or my vagina, it was like they did not even exist. This last time, I remember touching my stomach and looking at it. I felt like there was something incredible going on. I was really amazed by it all.

I don't regret any of the abortions. I was doing the best I could at the time. They are probably the worst situations I've been in. They are marked, I'll never forget any of them. The first two I look upon as the worst situations in my life, when I bottomed out emotionally. I think I'm getting to a place of not blaming myself so much anymore. I know this conflicts somewhat with what I said earlier, but I think those are the normal conflicts we all feel. Part of me doesn't feel that angry at myself anymore and really can appreciate the work I've done to get through it.

# "If I couldn't have an abortion, could I handle having a child?"

*The first interview with Mira takes place in her home. Initially her ten-month-old daughter is sleeping, but she wakes and plays and nurses during the course of the interview. Mira has been married for about a year. She is twenty-six years old and has a master's degree in social work. She is reinterviewed about fifteen months following the first interview.*

•

It feels strange to talk about the abortions now that I have Elinor, so I think I'll just start with her. Elinor is ten months old, and when I got pregnant with her it wasn't planned, but I had just married my husband. A part of deciding to stay pregnant was that I had gone through the other two abortions. They not only were the loss to me of raising a child, but they also really damaged my relationships; they contributed to why things didn't work out. So I was finally with the right person, one I wanted to have a child with, and it didn't make sense to have another abortion.

I had the first abortion when I was seventeen. My boyfriend was older; he was in college in Michigan. I lived in Chicago and visited him on the weekends. I think what we had was pretty good for a high school relationship. There was a lot of communication. When we decided to have intercourse, I had said that I would handle the birth control and had gone to a local clinic or the county facility. I was very uncomfortable as a seventeen-year-old doing that—it was terrible, walking in there, not knowing what to say or what to do. I decided that I was going to use a diaphragm because I thought taking the Pill was really bad—altering your body that way. The interesting thing about the diaphragm is that I don't think I was ever properly instructed by male gynecologists about how to use it. It wasn't until I went to a women's health center here when I was twenty-one or so did anyone ever show me that I had a cervix that was way far back and that I could actually insert the diaphragm, feel that it was in place and that my cervix would be behind it. No one had ever showed me that. The second time I got pregnant, I know the diaphragm was in and I presume that I just didn't have it in right.

So what I remember about the first time I got pregnant is that he was never responsible—he never said, "Do you have your diaphragm in?" And he was just as uncomfortable with my putting it in as I was, because neither of us had ever dealt with people's bodies. So it was always that I would go into the bathroom and put it in and come out and we would have intercourse. And I didn't, a lot of times I just didn't. When I got pregnant, I had driven him up to school in Michigan for his second year, then I was leaving for Chicago for my first year. We were in this awful dorm room, and I knew that I got pregnant from the minute it happened. We had intercourse and I knew that I didn't have it in, but I didn't say anything to him at that time. I remember crying for the whole five hours on the way home in the car with my friend, but I didn't even tell her at that point.

I left for college a couple of weeks later, didn't get my period, and found out I was pregnant. Luckily, I had made a friend in college right away who seemed very open to me. She was kind of a loose woman who didn't wear a bra, kind of like a hippie. I was relieved that there was someone like that who wasn't totally shut down about her body. I had this crazy dorm mate who would get up at five o'clock in the morning and spend two hours blowdrying her hair and putting on makeup. So right away I told this friend I thought I was pregnant, and she went with me for the test. She went with me every time that I dealt with the gynecologist. He was the worst of any of the people that I encountered at any point in having my abortions. He would go on and on every time I was in there about how people my age shouldn't be using diaphragms, we should be taking the Pill, we weren't responsible—never that we didn't know how to put it in right, but just that we weren't responsible.

I talked to my boyfriend a lot on the phone. I never considered having the child. I don't know if he did—I don't think so. Actually, at that point in my life I didn't think I was going to have kids. I was very adamant about the political situation in the world and that there were too many children and you should adopt. But in spite of that, it was still incredibly painful. I don't think I realized until many years later that we, together, had created this being, and understood the pain that that had caused.

I was really scared about the procedure. He did the kind of abortion where you put something in the day before to help you dilate. So when I went in for that, I was really freaked out and really in pain when he put it in—really screamed. He said, "Looks like we're not going to be able to do it on you," which was just . . . oh God. I remember my friend saying, "Mira *has* to have an abortion." She talked to him; she was really good. There was no choice: I was seventeen years old, my parents didn't know, I was in my first year of college. He was saying, "You just can't handle it." I don't know what he thought. If I couldn't handle an abortion, could I handle raising a child? But he ended up doing it.

I went to Michigan after the abortion and stayed for four days there with my boyfriend—and just cried for four days. We would lie in bed, and I would just cry. They had told me not to be physically active for a while. About two days after the abortion, I got up and went jogging in the late afternoon, came back and went to bed. The next morning when I woke up, my sheets and everything were covered with blood. I really freaked out and was dizzy and nauseous and passing out. I called the doctor and he said that nothing was wrong, I just needed to rest. I never saw him again; he never saw me to confirm that there wasn't something going on.

The partner that I was with for the second abortion I met in school in Chicago right after the first abortion. We were together for a couple of years, then he moved back out here to continue school and I went to Costa Rica for a year. We met in Mexico when I was on my way back and at that point decided that I would move out here and we would live together. That fall, the same time of year as before, I got pregnant. It's been the same time of year every single time, and in the two years between the first and second pregnancy, at the time of year that I had the abortion, I did not have a period. I totally missed a period, which I don't do. So when I got pregnant the second time, I thought, Okay, this is this issue that comes up for me every year, that I haven't resolved about the abortion. It's my body's way of remembering, and that's why I'm not getting my period.

But then, I didn't get it the next month either. I didn't know exactly when I got pregnant that time, because we were having sex regularly, and I always used the diaphragm. I was always trying to teach him that he needed to put it in, and he never did, but I always did put it in. So this was a real big surprise. The first time I almost felt like I was playing with fire and knew it was going to happen—and it almost needed to happen so I would realize what the whole thing was about and take it more seriously. But with this one, by the time I found out I was pregnant and set up the abortion—or decided, because that was a longer process—I was at the end of my first trimester, so I was already experiencing morning sickness. That really made me feel it was in there. I had started gaining weight, and I felt a real connection with it.

For him, there was no way we weren't going to have an abortion. We were both still in college and pretty committed to each other, but not real sure about it. I was really torn, I felt, Yeah, I want to finish college, have my B. A., I know this would not be a good time to raise kids, I'm not going to have enough money to make it, I'm not going to be able to get work, etc. etc. But, like I said, I felt connected with this baby and wanted to have a baby and raise a baby.

I don't know why, but they don't allow partners in the procedure. That was difficult for both of us. But the counseling before and after was really effective. What happened after this one was the exact opposite of before. I didn't bleed, and they ended up giving me medication that made me do the rest of the bleeding that would make my uterus contract. It was the most painful thing that I have ever in my life experienced. It was more painful than childbirth—and different. I mean there wasn't a reason behind it necessarily, a good reason anyway. We went up to the mountains afterward and spent a week at his parents' cabin. So with both of them I had a sort of retreat afterwards.

Bob and I stayed together for a couple of years, but he really didn't want to have kids for a long time—that just became clearer and clearer with him, that he was not going to settle down for a while. By the end of that time with him, I realized I needed something more settled in my life.

I find it hard to imagine myself with two more kids—a ten-year-old, a seven-year-old, and Elinor. I remember having a hard time with both of them, getting the money together to do it, and realizing: God, if you're having trouble getting the money together to have an abortion, can you imagine getting the money together to have a child?

With Elinor, we got married in September and I got pregnant in October. I had finished my master's degree in May, and Elinor was born in July. It was difficult, but in some ways it was sort of perfect timing. We would have waited a *lot* longer, but I think our relationship was ready to have a child in it. I was going to wait until I had done two or three years of full-time work. What having her has really changed for me is my sense of what I want to do, where I'm headed.

We knew when I was only about two weeks pregnant. At that point we were using the cervical cap and condoms. When I got pregnant we might just have been using one or the other, but a lot of times we used both. We went together to do the pregnancy test. It was a real process for both of us. We wrote down the things affecting our decision, both for and against having her. My husband's biggest thing against it was financial. We just kept looking at that, saying, well, you make finances work. It probably never will be easy to have a kid financially, so in that way it was sort of a moot point. And I didn't really have many considerations against having her. The biggest one for me was that I have a lot of friends, and none of my friends were having children. But then, that just seemed ridiculous.

I never thought seriously about adoption, because I always knew that that would be incredibly painful to have the child and go through the pregnancy. And having now been through a pregnancy, I know that that would be really hard. The last month of pregnancy is the most incredible thing—you can just talk to this being, it's right there. You feel its head, its feet, its butt, its arms. And then birth itself is so difficult.

It's been a big change in our lives, it's been up and down. One thing that's really clear to me is the line that I walk between being really excited about her changes and being sad that the different stages go so quickly. And it's been hard on our relationship. We've recently gotten a baby-sitter, and we try to spend some time together every weekend by ourselves. I notice there's always this underlying tension about whether things are going to work out for her—it's just this incredibly new focus. And we're tired all the time, because babies wake all the time during the night, and we've struggled with all these decisions about her. It's like you have to make ten times as many decisions as you do when it's just the two of you.

In the past six months I started working two nights a week. That made a big difference for me, and for her, in terms of my getting some space away from her and doing some stuff I felt good about. That increased my self-esteem, instead of just hanging out with her all the time. It really helped. When I started thinking about going back to work, I just couldn't see how I could do it, because I'm just so tired and disoriented all the time. I guess it's different if you plan a child. There have been so many times when I've just thought, Oh, God, wouldn't it have been easier if we hadn't had her? I guess if you plan it, you probably say that, too.

My mom is a therapist and was the administrator of a Montessori school for years, and she also worked with teenaged mothers. She gave me lots of mixed messages about abortion. She feels that it's really important that it be available, but that it's a very traumatic thing for someone to go through, and they should receive extensive counseling to deal with it. That's the message she always gave me growing up. We would fight about it; I would say, "Look, not everyone is going to get extensive counseling, and I'm sure for everyone it's not that big a deal." Well, now I know, she's right. But the unfortunate part of that message for me from her was that it wouldn't be okay for me to have an abortion unless I was going to have extensive counseling, so that's why I didn't ever tell her.

There have been many occasions in the past five years when I've wanted to tell her and have gone back and forth. Once again I'm dealing with it; she's coming out to spend a week with me while my husband is gone. I'm trying to figure out what would be the point in telling her, what would I want to get out of it? I mean, who knows how she's going to react? We have a close relationship. I even wanted to call and tell them when we were deciding what to do when I was pregnant with Elinor. My husband really discouraged me from doing that. When I called to tell them I was pregnant, I told them it had been a hard decision, so they were aware we had considered having an abortion—after the fact, of course, which is good. I mean, they didn't have any business giving input into our decision, which they would have.

## Re-interview with Mira

*Elinor is now about two and naps in the other room as we talk.*
*Mira works half-time. Just about a year ago, two or three months*
*after our first interview, she became pregnant a fourth time, and*
*ended up having another abortion.*

I realized I was pregnant at about this time last year; Elinor was
about one. I was once again using a cervical cap—without sper-
micide, however. This one, like pretty much all my pregnancies,
I started feeling even before my period was late, getting anxious
and nervous and on edge. We went away for a weekend. We
decided that we needed to know, so we took a pregnancy test
with us. It was an amazing time because we really considered
keeping the baby after we found out, especially being away and
being totally relaxed. It was strange—there was a whole fantasy
level of it that we allowed ourselves. We considered once again
Nick staying home from work and me working, because it's
obvious that his salary couldn't support all of us, and with me
working full-time, I might be able to. Elinor was in a place
where she was really fairly easy to take care of. She wasn't walking yet, but she was crawling and was really independent and
happy.

But then we moved. While I was pregnant, we were dealing with the move and not making the decision and kept putting it off. Nick's grandmother died and he had to fly to the
Midwest the same day that we moved. So I was here in the new
house with Elinor, by myself, pregnant. And that weekend I
just got so clear that there was no way that my body could
physically stand it. It didn't make sense to me that I could even
get pregnant when I knew how exhausted I would be if I went
through another pregnancy. She was still nursing, so that was
an issue too, because I didn't want to wean her because I was
pregnant. So it ended up being a lot harder for Nick than it
was for me . . . because he wasn't part of my body and it was
clear that it was about my body, to a certain extent.

But the thing that was amazing was that when I had been pregnant with Elinor I had seen a psychic and we had gone through this thing about the spirits of the other babies that I had been pregnant with before Elinor. . . that it was possible for you to have an abortion and still have those spirits stay in your life and learn the same lessons that you needed to learn. And a friend of mine in Oregon also said something that really freed me up about it. She said that there are a lot of spirits out there that don't really want to be full human beings—they know how miserable it is. But they do have this idea that they want to experience what it is to be in the physical form. She believed that they came to people that weren't going to have the baby, because they didn't want to be in that form; they just wanted to experience it briefly.

We had a whole ceremony around this one, which I had never had with any of my abortions before. We went down to the beach and we found a rock that we felt resembled the spirit. We said good-bye to it and we sang songs—Nick and Elinor and I. We still have the rock to this day and I still think about it. And I went through an amazing thing right before the abortion. I had this period of writing letters to all these people in my life that I had unfinished business with. Having just moved, it was amazing that I found the space to do that. But that was what the message was about for me . . . that was something that I needed to learn in my life. And there was something about this particular spirit that was urgent. Everything was happening quickly and there were things that needed to be dealt with because if they didn't get dealt with it would just be forgotten.

The abortion itself was actually healing, because Nick was there with me and so I was finally having one with someone who I'm going to maintain the relationship with—or at least I'm committed to. We dropped Elinor off at her godparents' house, and we were making them a card, so we had pictures of her with us. We were cutting up pictures and making a collage of her the whole time we were waiting. So I was feeling, here is this life that we do have, and this is the important thing to cherish.

Because I was nursing, I didn't take pain medication, which was also a real difference. My memory of the others—and of course I was much younger, but in talking to other women I have found this to be the case—is that with the pain medication, afterwards you feel totally wiped out. I remember just sleeping, needing to sleep for days. And that didn't happen. I was awake the rest of the day. With the other two, I remember this haze—I came home, I slept—what happened? Did I cry? Whereas with this, we went out to lunch, we came home, I rested, Nick played with Elinor, and I was awake the whole time, processing it. It was very different and really good to have seen that some of the haze around the other ones wasn't necessarily me, but was maybe the result of having taken the medication.

And I really don't think it was more painful, because it's such a short procedure, really. I mean, I think the pain is emotional—it was emotionally painful while it was happening. Just the lying there on the table and having someone do this thing to you. I knew I was doing the right thing, and yet it's such an awful way to have to do the right thing. And as much as I can divorce the body and the spirit and say the spirit is around, just thinking of this thing being sucked out of me and put in this vacuum box . . . . I really wanted to have something to take with me to bury or something. We talked about doing it the herbal kind of route, going through labor, but I decided I just couldn't deal with it. With having a one-year-old child and nursing, it was just too much.

But I think the physical pain is like the pain of some menstrual cramps. And it certainly wasn't painful afterwards. I didn't have any of the complications that I'd had before of either too much bleeding or not enough bleeding.

For Nick, I think it wasn't so much that he wanted to have the baby as that it wasn't as clear for him . . . the separation between the body and the spirit. So it was more a sense of killing a child that was ours, that we had made. Even now he doesn't want to have another child, so it wasn't an issue of him wanting it, really. He was just trying to understand why it had happened to us and feeling like maybe we weren't living up to what we could do. We had had Elinor in a tight situation, and we didn't think that was going to be possible. Maybe it actually was possible to have this one, even though it didn't seem like it. He seems real fine about it now.

I think I told you before that I had never told my mom about either of the abortions I had had. I went back to Chicago in October, about four months after this last abortion. The man that I had had my first abortion with had married and had just had a baby two weeks before I got there. His mom is friends with my mom, and she was in town, so we all went over and saw the baby together. And this guy is someone who is not available to talk about this kind of stuff with, plus he's married and he's got his own family. I had to step back and see that this wasn't appropriate to bring to his life either, to talk about all this.

So I was there by myself basically—Nick was at home and none of my friends are there. I ended up feeling really, really emotional about it and was able to tell my mom in that space, and say to her, "Here is something that I need to tell you is going on because it's just overloading me right now." I ended up telling her about all of them and getting a lot of support both from her and my dad, particularly about the last one. They were glad that we had decided not to have another baby.

I had some good discussions with my mom about the mixed messages she had given me as a teenager about sexuality and why I didn't tell her about the abortions then. And she was aware that it would have been too much for her to deal with at that time. She apologized for that and said that she was sorry and that she was glad that I hadn't told her. So that was kind of good, that there wasn't any guilt trip of: "I wish you would have told me; I would have been able to help you." There was just the acknowledgment that she wouldn't have been and she was sorry for that. It was wonderful.

It's so curious to me that I'm not really in touch with either of these men I had the first abortions with, and yet it feels like there's this link with them that's in the unconscious.

But there hasn't been a way for me to talk about it with them. I've just had to let it go. The man that I was with before Nick, that I had the second abortion with, I have a lot of dreams about. The relationship with Nick came right after the relationship with him, there were times when I was seeing both of them. But I often have dreams about him, as if Nick is this guy—they're just totally mixed up. And I feel like that wouldn't happen with just anybody, that has to do with the fact that we had to go through this intense experience together that's somehow different from other experiences.

# "Okay, solve the problem"

*Lisa is a twenty-six year old African-American woman living on the West Coast. She had an abortion at age sixteen. At age twenty, while in college, she became pregnant by a man she had been living with for two years, and bore a son. They stayed together for two more years, then separated. Then after several years of struggling with the issue, she came out as a lesbian. She now lives with a lesbian partner, and they are co-parenting her six-year-old son.*

•

I had somewhat of a . . . I don't want to say troubled childhood, because I wasn't a troubled child. I was molested by a great-uncle, and that was the beginning of a cycle of sexual abuse from relatives, neighborhood kids . . . it became almost a vicious cycle. This was in Tacoma. Then I moved to Seattle. My mother talked about it as starting her life over. My mother didn't have that choice of abortion when she was nineteen; I was born out of wedlock, and the things that happened in her life followed from that. She went to one year of college, but she couldn't continue because she had to work, and she couldn't afford childcare.

So she was going to start her new life by coming here and looking for a job. She was just going to leave all those bad memories back in Tacoma and start afresh and try to go to school and better herself. I also termed it as my starting anew, because no one knew of my past, of the sexual abuse. For some reason I thought that I would leave that mark behind me, that people wouldn't be able to sense it. I guess I thought it had to do with the city, the location.

The first year I was in school in Seattle there were no incidents, no nothing. I didn't know anybody, I didn't have any relatives or friends, I was kind of on my own. I didn't really make any friends until the very end of eighth grade, when I met this girl and we hit it off. She invited me over to her house, which amazed me because when I was in Tacoma, nobody ever invited me over to their house. I didn't have any girlfriends. Most of my friends were the boys in the neighborhood, that's just the way things were.

So we became friends, and in fact I still have her as a good friend. Then we entered high school, and I started hanging out over at her house a lot, and from that point I just became very promiscuous. I used to have this piece of cardboard that had names on it; one side was the names of all my boyfriends, on the other side was the names of normal friends.

I can remember that my thinking was that I would have sex with these guys, but they would end up getting no satisfaction out of it because I would really make them feel bad. In other words, I was not the type of person that they would sleep with and then go tell their friends about it, because this was nothing you wanted to tell your friends about—simply because I was more experienced, I knew more. I felt it was a pay-back in one respect. I did this for my freshman and part of my sophomore year. I tried to count how many boyfriends I had, and basically I had a new boyfriend every two weeks.

Then, I don't know, I was outside one day playing Chinese jump rope with my sister, and it hit me that all this time I had been playing this game, and how was it making me feel? I didn't have any real boyfriends, someone who really cared about me, someone who would call me just to see how I was doing, who would take me to the movies or would show any affection towards me as saying I was his girlfriend. I didn't have any guy who would walk down the street and hold my hand;

I was missing that part of, you know, a relationship. That just made me so sad, and I felt like I had wasted so much time . . . and that what I was doing . . . I was losing out more than I was gaining. So at that minute I told myself that I wasn't going to do it anymore, and I didn't. All the events that happened after I made that decision just screwed me up even more. I thought it was something that was really great, but the timing —I guess it was just the right place, wrong time.

Because that day I met this boy that was walking down the street, very friendly. I used to be mean to some guys. If they tried to make friendly conversation I'd just give them these mean looks; it was my game with them. Either we are friends sexually or we are just basic friends—I'll go play basketball with you. But anything in between, I don't want to be bothered with you. So first he said, "Hi," and I just kind of gave him this mean look. And he says, "Why you want to give me such a mean look, I know you have a pretty smile; can't you just smile?" And in my head it was like, Okay Lisa, you said you weren't going to do this anymore, so I smiled. He started talking to me and I thought he was really nice. I ended up giving him my phone number and he started calling me, and I found out he lived just down the street. He was staying with a friend who lived next door to his mother or something.

It was the first time I just talked to a boy without him asking when I was going to sleep with him. We just talked and laughed and talked on the phone for hours and had a great time. I thought that was really nice. And then I did sleep with him, but for some reason it was somewhat different, even though I slept with him a *lot,* from what I can recall. Then I found myself almost obsessed with him, the ideal of him, or just the ideal of the relationship—him liking me and all this, that, and the other. And then it led to, that my whole world was him; Bobby this and Bobby that, I gotta go see Bobby, everything was Bobby. What was scary was the fact that Bobby was a really rotten kid. And I didn't find this out until . . . I don't know, maybe a month down the road. He didn't go to school, the reason that he wasn't staying at his mother's house was because she kicked him out because he was stealing from her. But by this time it didn't matter, I didn't care.

Then he did something where he was staying and he got kicked out of there. He went to his mother's house and they got into a big argument and he started throwing her stuff out the window. She called the police and he ended up at the youth authority. I told my mother that if she didn't get him out I was leaving. I talked my mother into letting him live in our home, because I "loved him so much that I could not live without him." So he came and stayed in our house. We slept together every single day, and he was there for a month. Finally my mother couldn't take it anymore, because she knew we were sleeping together, even though I said that we weren't. So she put him out and he went back and stayed at his aunt's house.

In July, I went to a birthday party for his nieces, and I got to meet everybody in his family, including his step-mother. We were having a great time, but for some reason I was so hungry. Actually it kind of started before then. I loved potatoes and sausage, and I remember I had to have them every morning and I would eat the whole plate and still want more. I couldn't figure it out, but I figured, Oh this is just a bunch of mess, because I always want that; and I always ate a lot. Also during that week I was playing basketball and I got elbowed in my breast and it hurt so bad.

So at this birthday party I ate twelve ears of corn, not including my big plate of food. And Bobby's stepmother asked me to come into the house because she wanted to talk to me. She told me she thought I might be pregnant and that I should tell my mother. She said if I wanted her to she would take me down to the free clinic to have a test, to make sure before I even told my mother. Then she brought Bobby in and explained to him what she thought was going on. And the whole time I'm just like, This is a joke, this is not happening to me. So I just sort of pretended like she was wrong, and just kind of let it all go over my head.

I went home, and at twelve midnight, which was then my birthday, my mother woke me up and told me to come into the kitchen. I could tell she was really nervous, she kind of had tears in her eyes. I wasn't sure what was going on. First thing I know my mother goes, "Lisa, you're pregnant, and you're going to have an abortion." I thought, Who told you, how did you find out? But then I just thought, Okay, solve the problem. I kind of had a relief feeling and the way she said it seemed like, okay it's just simple, no big deal.

Where the problem started was when I went back and told Bobby. He just about blew his stack: Nobody was gonna kill his child, nobody was gonna take his baby from me, I shouldn't let my mother tell me what to do, it's my child, I can have the baby if I want to, he would help support me, and blah, blah, blah. Well, during this time period I was starting to think that Bobby wasn't so great, simply because I was starting to have more arguments with my mother, more arguments with my sister. I felt like I wasn't in control anymore and I was losing it.

I would go over to his sister's house and she would argue with me, saying I should have the child and give it to them and they would take care of it. But I didn't want my child growing up on welfare; that's what they were doing. I didn't want that for myself. And I had my mother telling me, "You're gonna do it." My mother was the one who personally took me down to the Ob/Gyn for an examination right on Monday after she first told me. The soonest I could have the abortion was in August, and that two-week span was when all this confrontation went on.

On the date I was supposed to have the abortion, my mother took me in, but she couldn't pick me up because she had to work, so I asked Bobby to pick me up. I remember this like it was yesterday. I got there and it was really weird, because I thought I was going into the hospital and they were going to take good care of me. No, not even close. I went into the hospital and there was something wrong with a dressing room or something, so they made us change in this little closet, maybe three feet by three feet. And there was all this stuff in it, it was like a storage closet. There were five women, and we all had to go in one at a time and all came out with our clothes folded in a little bunch. Then she proceeded to lead us down this little hallway into, I guess, the prep room. She had us all lay down on a bed, with a little screen between us. They gave us each a shot and put in an IV, then we had to wait a really long time, and I fell asleep. Finally the nurse came and woke me up. I remember going down the hallway to the room and getting on the table and putting my legs in the stirrups. Then I remember hearing this little vacuum or suction sound and trying to open my eyes. I still can see this cloudy picture of this black doctor, a black nurse, and a white nurse. I remember his saying something about, "They just keep getting younger."

When I woke up I was so hungry I must have ate about ten packs of those little crackers they give you and drank about five of the little jugs of orange juice. After a while people started getting picked up and I went outside and looked and he wasn't there, so I took the bus home. That pretty much ended my relationship with Bobby, even though I kind of hung onto him for a while, because that was like my first real relationship. We were together . . . four months . . . six months, something like that. It was the longest I had ever been with anybody, so I patted myself on the back for that. But then on the other hand I kind of felt that was a hard way to go.

There's a story going on in my family that relates to my story. I have a cousin who's four years older than me. I remember when she was twelve or thirteen she had her first abortion, and there was all this whispering going on in the family, because my family was very close at that time. I used to be baby-sat by my aunt and I would always be over there. I always thought Denise was kind of a troubled kid, and I knew that on occasion she was living at my grandmother's house, and I thought that was kind of strange.

Then when she was fifteen she got pregnant again, and this time she had the baby. Then there was this big fight over the baby, because they felt Denise was an unfit mother. Denise wanted to give the baby for adoption, but they didn't want her to and told her, "No, you can't give this baby up." So Denise ended up running away from home after the baby was born and staying different places, finally ending up back at my grandmother's house. She stayed there for a while. Then what happened was that my aunt and uncle eventually got custody of the baby and the baby began to live with them, and Denise stayed at my grandmother's house. I don't know if she even graduated from high school. But I know after that my cousin started living this troubled life; she would bounce from here to there.

Well, things that get left in the closet, the little ghosts, do come out one way or another. What happened was . . . the little boy that Denise had, whose name was Lenny, who's about fifteen or sixteen now, was caught in school trying to have sex with this girl. Well, through all this talking we find out that Lenny's father is Denise's daddy. Now Denise's mother says it's a lie and won't talk to my grandmother, won't talk to her daughter, because she don't believe it. She says it's a lie, that her husband is not the father and all that.

Denise is really upset, she's starting to have these nightmares and these feelings. This is not her real father, it was her stepfather. There were rumors about things going on, but it was more so things with her father's friends. Then we started to piece together why she didn't want to keep that baby. She knew who the father of that baby was. So now Lenny is having a problem, because he doesn't know where he fits in all this. Nobody's talking to him, why he's doing the stuff he's doing. And now my aunt doesn't talk to my grandmother at all, not at all. She's holding onto this man that she feels like she has to have, and will give up everything. And see it's so scary because I wonder if she knew what was going on back then but just couldn't say anything, and how could you *do* that to your daughter? I did call my cousin and shared what had happened to me to let her know she was not the only one that this stuff had happened to. And to let her know, whatever you do, don't let them get to you, because she has been feeling suicidal and all these type of things, not knowing how to deal with this.

I was really scared to tell my mother I was pregnant the second time. I was twenty by then and I had been with this man for a couple of years, but I was still afraid. I think I was afraid she would tell me I should have an abortion, but this time it was like, No way, Ma, I'm not having one. But she didn't say that, she was really pleased and happy. Just to see her embrace my pregnancy and be very supportive of me made me feel different about my abortion. I wondered why my mother didn't let me have the first kid, but I think that was basically because she didn't want me to turn out to be one of those "welfare mothers." Sometimes I used to wonder what the kid would have looked like, if it was a boy or girl. I did a somewhat mourning type of thing, because I have one boy now and it would be really nice for him to have a brother or sister, especially now because he's having this problem with not having a sibling as he's getting older.

*p.103*  Sarah Maxwell, *Untitled*
(©1992, 12"x28")

*p.104*  Susan Trubow, *Untitled*
(©1984, pencil on paper, 8-1/2"x11")

*p.105*  Carol Cullar, *The Past Is Best Forgotten*
(©1988, mixed media, 42"x52-1/2")

*p.106*  Margaret Stainer, *Sacra Conversazione #32*
(©1991, charcoals on paper, 26"x36")

*p.107*  Margaret Stainer, *Sacra Conversazione #33*
(©1991, charcoals on paper and paint, 26"x36")

*p.108*  Betty Decter, *#1212*
(©1989, acrylic, mixed media, canvas, 36"x36")
*Artist's Statement:* I am often asked to explain my series of paintings
*"Women and Others"* (The Monkey Series). Some of the paintings
are metaphors of women nurturing and protecting the outcasts and
the unwanted in the world. ("This is my baby—and even if *you*
don't think it's beautiful, *I do!"*) The figures stand in for deeper
meanings and causes and cannot always be recognized immediately.
There are relationships between the women and animals that are
loving, maternal, antagonistic, political, social, and/or sexual.

In some ways the works are about choices in life: even though
others may dislike them, we have to be strong and demand our right
to make our own decisions. The recent court rulings regarding abortions, which could deny women the right to control their own
bodies *and their future lives,* are uppermost in my mind.

*p.109*  Stephanie Wilger, *Blood of the Womb*
(©1990, mixed media sculpture: wood/sisal/paint,
70"x36"x32")

---

The seven works of art listed above are individually copyrighted by the
artists, who donated the rights to reproduce them in this collection. For
further information please contact the publisher.

*Untitled*

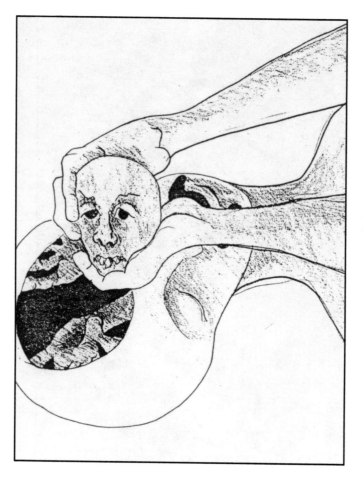

*Untitled*

*The Past Is Best Forgotten*

*Sacra Conversazione #32*

Sacra Conversazione #33

*#1212: Women and Others*

*Blood of the Womb*

# "Well . . . okay . . .
# the penis is leaving"

*At the time of our interview, Brenda was twenty-eight years old, living in an apartment with her eight-month-old son and two roommates and their two children. She was planning to start community college within the next few weeks. Her story points out the risks and struggles inherent in being a young bicultural woman in our educational and social systems, and on top of that, having to cope with her family falling apart.*

•

I came here from Nigeria when I was about eight years old. My Mom had married an American and had already come a couple of years before, then sent for me and my sister. We had spent two years in hiding because of a war that was going on there, and then all of a sudden we were uprooted and came straight to America and had to deal with the kids and everything. It was a little difficult, getting used to the name-calling and all that. I had a lot of insecurity about me just because of coming to this area and learning to adapt. The thing that really bugs me is that once I got over the peer pressure and fit in—was good scholastically and was doing my athletic events after school— then my parents broke up. I just didn't understand it.

When I was in junior high, all the kids started saying "fuck." It seemed like that was the word to say, so I said it. Then somebody, an associate of the household, he said one day, "Do you know what that word means?" I said, "No." And he said, "Well, one day I'll show you." I was about eleven or twelve and this guy was a friend of my mom's and dad's and came by frequently, so it just seemed okay. But when he proved it to me, he showed me what the word fuck meant, it kind of like . . . altered my way a little bit.

My last year in high school, when I was sixteen, I met this boy, a big football player from another high school. I didn't date really, I was mostly a tomboy, playing basketball and keeping stats for the boys' basketball team, and that's how I met him. I was dating him; it was a boyfriend/girlfriend, but platonic, thing. I was working at a clothing store at the time too, and met this girl there from out of town. I'm so nice, I said, "Oh sure my boyfriend can show you around town," right? So one night we were supposed to all go to the club, but she wants to go to the movies. I said he could drive her to the movies, but he didn't want to go dancing all of a sudden. So he went to the movies, and they did the wild thing, because I asked them both what they saw, and they didn't remember. So there was a lot of peer pressure; if I wanted to keep him, I had to do something. So I did, and when I did, it just happened that I got pregnant. Back seat of the car too, you know, so it was like kid stuff.

So we discussed it and I got the abortion. And when I'm getting the abortion, his so-called best friend had a girlfriend and my boyfriend messes around with her, and gets her pregnant. And the family is very well-off; he's got to marry this girl. So he got married to her, and I guess they had a few other kids.

My second pregnancy came a year or so later. I met this college student. We had a casual relationship—of course it had to include sex. I got pregnant by him. He was supportive, it was nothing about another girl, he was just not ready.

The way I felt about these abortions—I knew it was not the right time. But at the same time, I was one of these teenagers that believed in burning my bra and didn't believe in taking birth control pills because I didn't want nothing to harm my body. They gave me the pills, but I would take them for a few months, then go, Oh, I don't need these. Of course, I don't think I was as active as everybody thought, I was just a fertile person. Every time I cracked my legs I got pregnant.

A couple of years later I became pregnant again. I had quit school and was working. So I said, I'm going to keep this baby, but I don't think it was meant to be, and I think the Lord knew that too. The father . . . see, I don't know, that's another thing about me (at least I'm being honest), I didn't know who the father was. And anyway, I was noticing a lot of problems in a lot of people's marriages and so I just thought, I'm doing it on my own. But then I was bedridden for a couple of days and lost the baby. I was bleeding all the time, spotting, then I lost it in the toilet. And that was kind of sad, 'cause I had to take it out of the toilet and take it to the hospital, because they had to inspect you to make sure you'd gotten all the parts of the baby out. So I guess that was really a traumatic thing. So since then I said, Okay we've got to get serious about these birth control pills.

When I met my husband he had a good job and seemed like a nice guy. He tried to take me out to places, but we'd never stay. We'd buy sixty-five-dollar tickets—he'd eat the food, then it'd be time to go, because he didn't want to socialize. He could deal with computers and things, but relationships and people were kind of like another dimension. He says he was in love with me, but I think I was in love with the idea of being in love.

We bought a house. After we moved in, I was pregnant— I was pregnant while we were still dating and everything. We flew to Reno at ten at night, in a flannel shirt, curlers in your hair because you're going to work the next day, getting married. I mean, nothing romantic about it. Kicking around until about four in the morning, catching the morning flight out, get in the car, go straight to work. About four in the afternoon I said, "Hey, I got married last night." They said, "What, how come you didn't tell nobody?" I said, "It's no big deal." It wasn't, I was in my curlers and everything. What's the big deal about getting married like that? Bride of Frankenstein, that's all I could think of. I'm glad we didn't take any pictures.

He said, "Well, I don't think we're ready for a kid." But I said I wasn't ready for another abortion, because I'd had three D&Cs which is pretty much as many as anybody can take without getting into trouble. So I just went ahead and eight months later they said, "Oh, there's another head and another heartbeat." So I was pregnant with twins, and this didn't seem to make matters any better, because he and I were already arguing and there'd been a couple of punch fights. He'd leave the house, the police would come over, battered women's phone calls, stuff like that. But you know, like he said, he never really broke my ribs or gave me a black eye or a bloody nose or a tooth missing; some people walk around with crooked lips. But he scared me enough. It wasn't that bad, but it was the mental abuse, getting spit on, being pregnant and he's squishing your stomach.

But I got two beautiful kids out of the deal. Then one day he was walking around the house with a gun and stuff and the police said, "Sorry, ma'am, but we keep coming over here. You want to do something about it—just get out. If you want us to we'll stick around for a few hours." They sat there, and I just moved all the stuff I could think of. When my husband came home he started terrorizing the house, broke all the furniture, called my job, threatened my co-workers, came to the job, skidded through the parking lot. The police came and arrested him, and he called and said he was going to a psychiatric unit for a month. All the little mental bullshit, that's what it was.

So I moved with the kids, still getting harassed by him. I was getting tired, two kids, trying to work at this electronics firm where they want your life—six days a week, twelve hours a day. I got involved in crack, and uh, that was wild. At first I was trying to sell it, and that was great. I had money, you know, six thousand dollars. But gradually I found all my profits all gone and just barely scraping up to replenish, and keep whatever addiction I was having at the moment going.

This went on for about a year. Then one day he just got up and split town. So I went back to the house and all these bills started pouring in; the water got cut off, the heater stopped working. I stopped working and started collecting AFDC, because they said the twins were too young and I didn't have to work; I could stay home and take care of them. So that's what I was mainly trying to do.

But being on this drug, it makes you lose your self-esteem, your respect for yourself. All you want to do is stay in the same clothes and just find the hit, people coming by your house at three in the morning, wanting four or five dollars' worth, not even a twenty dollar hit. I don't know what it is, but the drive for you to get up at three in the morning, just to go out there. . . . Sometimes you get a good deal, sometimes you get a bad deal, sometimes you get nothing but soap or wax or whatever, because they're trying to scrounge up the money for themselves —whatever they want the money for, be it booze or whatever.

So that didn't really help issues at all, it messed up a lot of my relationships. My husband didn't know about it—Freddy Kruger was not too sure about what was going on. When we were selling the house in February of 1989, and he came down to finish closing the deal, he started asking me and the kids to move back with him, and just would not understand that I was not going to. We had another big fight out in the street. I called the police. I had been planning to rent the house back from the guy I sold to, but I didn't want my husband to know that. When the police came, they told me to go and find a place to live. They told my husband to keep the kids while I got a place. So he had my house, he had all the house keys, and he had the kids.

So I got on the bus and went down to the next county, looking for an apartment or something. I don't know what I did. All I know is that when I came back to the house, my husband and the kids were gone. I thought, well, two weeks with the kids is all he'll need, he'll ship them back. So I got a part-time job at a pizza parlor, bar-hopping, hurting a little bit because the kids were gone. I knew that was a bad trip; I didn't know what was going on, but it was not the way it was supposed to happen. Then I don't know . . . I had a few other people I was seeing at the time, and the next thing, I became pregnant. I said, Oh boy. I was staying down here with my mom, and it didn't really look like too cool of an idea. I went in and got a definite pregnancy exam and everything.

My mom and I got into a fight. The people where I took the pregnancy test help single moms with drug problems or whatever. So they shipped me to another city and I was staying with some nuns—"the devil meets the nuns!" It was all right, the cleaning up and all that, and I still had my little shape and I was cute, I had my little suits, no stomach protruding yet, I looked healthy.

But they said, "You have to be in at five o'clock." I said, You must be crazy; I'm not going to be in by five o'clock. So I had to find another way out of this avenue, I was getting bigger and everything. I went to this church that does work in the community and met some people. They showed me how to live, how to get those one-week homeless hotel vouchers and this and that. That really wasn't working because every week you've got to take your big old green bag and move to another hotel. I did this for a few months and it was just tiresome.

When I was living with the nuns I was thinking of getting an abortion because I didn't think it was fair . . . my mind was saying it was not fair for me to have twins, give them up to this crazy person, and here I am bringing another child into the world. It's just not fair, I have to clean my slate with my kids. But, you know, I'd get up in the morning, run around, get my vouchers and everything, and make an appointment to go to the abortion clinic. And something would detour me . . . you know, I'd find me a nice bus driver and we'd get into a good talk and I'd go out to the end of the route with him and come back around and we're still talking. The next thing I know I've missed my appointment.

Anyway, I just finally came to grips with myself. No more drugs—at least crack, I don't use crack anymore. This church kind of helped me with the steps to take, first to build confidence within myself, put goals out for myself, find things to do. So I was staying clean and the baby grew inside me and finally it was too late for me even if I wanted an abortion.

I was looking for work but I was pregnant and the kind of work I do, warehousing, logistics, and driving trucks, no one wants to hire a pregnant woman, knowing she's going to leave. I know how to do data entry, but it's all in the material handling area, so I would have to do some sort of lifting. I had this great friend, he was the first Caucasian man I had been with, and he really sort of took care of me. He just kept my courage up and backed me up, whatever I wanted to do. After I had the baby, he was the first person I called, I told him, "We got a baby boy." Still, I go up there, they have a big picture of the baby. We kick back, drink some beers, order some Chinese food, and smoke weed. I still smoke some weed, I don't think I'll ever kick the habit; I've been smoking weed since I was in sixth grade.

I finally went down to see the kids. The thing about going down there . . . I was afraid of that man, that man has such . . . I say he's like Freddy Kruger, he has this horror effect on me, I'm scared of him. But I went on Easter and I saw the kids. He's been wanting me and the baby to move back in with him. He says he's really tired of the kids, he needs a break, he doesn't have a job, it's depressing. I'm telling him there is a system you can utilize temporarily, until you get back on your feet. Either that, or bring them back.

With the Lord's help I've been able to keep with my goals. That's part of what I did with my crack program—I broke the habit, I had a healthy child with no problems. And I decided that I'm going back to school to better myself for my children— not just this baby, but all my children. Because if we ever do decide to finally file for divorce, I want to make sure that I'm ready . . . to be able to do what I have to do for my children, and not be afraid.

I guess I'm just above water in everything I do. I mean I'm able to break the habits and do whatever I have to do to get me to another point in life. So now I'm registered for school, and I feel like even if Michael would let me have the kids, my college has a very good day-care program there, where they teach them while I'm at school. I have a great baby-sitter for my baby, this woman I've known since I was a teenager. It's somebody I know, so I know nothing will go wrong. I mean here I'm talking about me and drugs, but I'm worried about my child growing up in a drug atmosphere, so now I have to be cautious about what I do.

My ex-roommate is eighteen now, and she has a two-year-old baby that has cerebral palsy, so she has got the double whammy. She's just now being able to get into some of the local clubs and party, and now she has this handicapped child. And I think it's bad. Just because you were in love with this guy and you got your first dick . . . excuse me . . . your first penis when you were twelve or thirteen and then you got pregnant doesn't mean you have to keep the child. Because God's not going to punish you for saying I'm too young for that. A lot of people do it because they think if they do it, this penis will stay with them for life. Well . . . okay . . . the penis is leaving. In fact, he's probably got six or seven other holes he's digging into, you know. I don't think anyone's pressuring them to keep it. Some of their moms don't even know until they come home with their stomachs poking out.

And then it's expensive too. If their parents are middle-class families or parents with work, it's hard for the children to get social services, MediCal, to be able to get the abortion. I know that the two people that got me pregnant, their parents were well-off. A lot of these people don't have the money to get the abortion, or they're too young to know that they can go to social services and get a sticker to get this abortion, that some sort of grant is there for them. They feel like they have to endure this burden, when they don't have to. So that's what the children need to stop doing is having babies—babies having babies is not healthy. God blessed me with three beautiful children, though in a way he punished me by giving me twins. But he forgave me; he knew I was ready. Where if I had had my child when I was seventeen, there would have been a lot of repercussions.

Maybe two was too much at the beginning, and this was the second chance I was given to show that I could be a good mother. I know I could have been a good mother to my twins, but there was just too much going on. The baby's father, I don't really know who he is, and maybe that's the only sad part about it. And when it comes to that I'll tell him the truth. But . . . I decided to keep him. Hey . . . I don't know who he is, but I decided to keep him.

# "You have to choose one side or the other"

*Elizares is a twenty-eight-year-old Chicana woman from a large family in the Southwest. She currently lives on the West Coast and works as a bookkeeper. She describes herself as a political activist and her primary focus is on immigrant rights and solidarity issues, particularly within Central America. She still considers herself a communist, although she says that with all the change going on, she's not quite sure what that means now.*

*One of the things her story brings out is the political polarization in American politics around the abortion issue, and its effect on many women's ability to fully express all of their feelings, especially those which seem to contradict their political beliefs.*

•

Until I was twelve, I lived with my grandmother. I'm not exactly sure why, except my mother got pregnant again right after I was born and she gave birth to twins the next year. There was also a lot of violence in my family, and that may have played a part. My mother doesn't really talk to me about my family. She doesn't want to and neither does my father.

My grandmother gave me a lot of free rein to do what I wanted to until I got my period. Then she became a lot more strict. I think my grandmother was trying to protect me, but she just didn't know how, so she did it in a really controlling way. I started my period very young, when I was nine years old. I became very rebellious then. I wasn't really rebellious in my actions, but very much so in my thoughts. I told my mother I wanted to lose my virginity because girls weren't supposed to do that and it was all right for boys.

My grandmother told me not to let anybody touch me until I got married or I would get pregnant. She did not elaborate beyond that. When I got my period, she told me about it. I got a lot more of my sense of what it is to be a woman from my grandmother than from my mother. In some ways my mom kind of feels more like my sister than my mom.

When I was twelve, I went to live with my parents. I really didn't like it. I remember the first couple of years I would just stay in my room all the time. I was exposed to my father's alcoholism, his violence, and beatings. In some ways though, my life still remained quite separate from my sisters' because I still had my grandmother, and she would buy me things when I needed them and stuff like that. My situation was a little better than my sisters' because of my grandmother.

Where I grew up, the population is about fifty percent Mexican-American, so I didn't feel so isolated around being Latina. I did feel isolated around being a woman and feeling oppressed and not having anyone to talk to about that. A few times my mother did leave my father, but she would always go back to him.

When I moved to the West Coast I went through cultureshock. The community is very different here. (The food's better.) I went to a white middle-class college. For a while it was okay, actually kind of healing, then I had to start dealing with the racism issues. At a certain point I wanted to drop out, but I did finish.

I was twenty-six before I became really sexually active. Yeah, I was old. I was raised Catholic. There was a lot of heavy guilt stuff in my religion about sex, but I don't think that's why I waited so long. I think it was really more because of my family history. I saw sex as a power thing and I really didn't want to get caught up in it. I was afraid. I didn't have romantic relationships—no dating or anything like that. I did the classic thing. The guy I liked was unavailable, and when he was available, I didn't want him.

I don't necessarily think it was a conscious thing, not dating. I had a gay Latino friend who once told me I really turned men off. He implied I gave off this negative signal. Also, I have always been heavy. All the women in my mom's family were slender, at least when they were younger. So I thought, Why date? I'm ugly anyway. In ways, I did feel isolated, not dating or having a relationship; but looking back, I really wasn't ready.

The story about my first sexual experience is really embarrassing. I know that women do this kind of thing all the time, but then when you tell them, they act so shocked. So . . . I met this guy in the laundromat. He called me a few times. At this point, I was living alone. He asked if he could come over.

He came over, and, you know, one thing led to another and that's what happened. I guess I felt curious. I felt old. I was twenty-three and I had never done anything. He was kind of cute, my type. I remember when he was touching me, thinking, Ooohhhhh, is that all there is? That's it? You know. It was kind of funny. I did feel kind of rushed, and kind of angry, too. I remember he asked if he could spend the night. I said, "Okay, but I'm going to sleep." It was funny, he was trying to be romantic or whatever, and I was thinking, Oh, get lost guy. [Laughs]

I saw him a few times after that, then it was over. I had a lot of mixed feelings about that relationship. I felt myself dragging my feet. He would call and ask me if I wanted to go out and I would tell him to go away because I had to study. I put out a lot of mixed messages.

I was worried about getting pregnant. I used something, but I still got pregnant. I was using only foam. It was weird because I knew about birth control. I had read about it, but I wasn't sexually active, so I really didn't expect to need stuff. I did have this foam put away in case something happened, but that was all.

Now that I am sexually active, I feel there is a big discrepancy between what you are taught and what your actual needs are when you are sexually active. Specifically, women aren't taught to be assertive. I've been with various lovers and they all don't want to bother with diaphragms and gels and stuff. It's real interesting that they all assume you're taking the Pill. It's like when you don't take the Pill and you use other things, you're acting to inconvenience them. People may tell you about the technical aspects of birth control, but they leave out a really important message about a woman having a right to protect herself. For instance, with condoms there is this strong message that guys don't like to use them. Well, if they don't like it, they can have sex with someone else. We have a right to protect ourselves, a right *not* to get pregnant, but none of that is reinforced.

Anyway, after I had that first sexual experience, I felt myself getting tired a lot and my period was late, so I got a pregnancy test. I found out I was pregnant. It was interesting, because I had always thought if I got pregnant I would have the kid, but when the receptionist told me, I didn't even think twice. I told her I wanted an abortion. It wasn't an issue for me.

I feel so angry around abortion rights issues. The "pro-life" people trot out all these women who say that having an abortion was the worst thing that ever happened to them and it was a terrible mistake and everything. Maybe for them, but for many women it is a really clear decision. I didn't need a guilt trip. I felt more guilty because I was so clear about what I wanted than I did about my actual choice, because I didn't even consider having the baby. I just knew.

I had to wait about two or three weeks because I was working. I had to pay for it myself. I was upset that I was pregnant and I had to make the choice, but I didn't really feel bad about my choice. I am a woman of color, and my experience in life reflects that, but, in spite of my culture and tradition which is really against it, I decided to have an abortion. When it really comes down to it, it's your individual situation that you consider when making a decision like this.

Two things happened which bothered me at the abortion clinic. The woman who told me I was pregnant said, "Unfortunately, you're pregnant. These things happen, it happened to me and I had to have an abortion. Regrettably, we can't always live up to our responsibilities." I thought that was kind of strange. It upset me. Then, when I wanted to move the abortion up a week, they said, No, we need to stick to the original time. They did not give me a reason for this.

I had the abortion in a private doctor's office. He was a man, a white man. Afterwards, he came in and said, "Now, don't get pregnant again." I thought that was weird, so weird for him to tell me that. I felt the doctor was racist. I really felt that coming from him.

The actual abortion was not painful. I remember a nurse came in and held my hand during the procedure. That was nice. A friend took me. I didn't really feel that tired. I didn't have too much bleeding, just that day, and my next period was pretty normal.

I only talked to a few friends about my abortion. This is another strange thing about this issue. So many women have had abortions. But, even your really close friends sometimes don't tell you. I found that out when I told two friends about my abortion. They had had abortions too but had never told me until I told them about my own experience. It is so common.

I was really scared just about being pregnant and the thought of delivery. I was afraid of how much it would hurt. I was working as a long-term temp, so I did not have benefits, so the financial end of it scared me also. I thought if I kept the baby, I would have to move home, pregnant and not married. I would be a disgrace to my family. I did not want to go back home. I didn't want to tell any of my family members except one sister, and she had had an abortion herself.

I'm not exactly sure how being Latina comes to bear on this experience. I have mixed feelings about that. Most of my friends who are Latina, or other women of color, are pretty independent and politically active. They are also mostly educated and have the financial resources to obtain an abortion. Even with that, there is still the family pressure. If you don't live close to home, and you're not doing anything obvious sexually, such as living with someone or getting pregnant, you can still pretty much do what you want and your family will look the other way.

Once you get pregnant, I feel there is a lot more pressure for women of color to keep their babies. Your family definitely wants you to have and keep your child. I'm not sure if this is the same experience other women of color have, but that's my experience. There is also a real pressure to get married in my culture. A very strong pressure towards that. There is a sense that if you're pregnant your future is basically made for you. That's very prevalent.

There are definite preferences within families about having a child out of wedlock versus having an abortion. It varies within the Latin community. I think it depends somewhat on how far removed your family is from Latin America. It seems that if your parents were born and raised in another country, these values seem to hold a lot stronger.

I've seen some weird things happen in Latin families. I had this friend whose cousin got pregnant when my friend was still living at home. The cousin's father kicked her out of the house because she was pregnant and wasn't going to get married. My friend's father let the cousin live with them. Then, when my friend was about twenty-six, she got pregnant and decided to keep the baby, but she had broken up with the baby's father. When she told her father—by then she lived in another state—he told her she couldn't come home.

On the other hand, my other cousin got pregnant when she was sixteen (our family is second or third generation in this country) and her parents wanted her to have an abortion so she could go to college and continue on with her life. She really wanted to marry the father of the baby and have it. So, see, it's pretty weird. I think a lot of it, bottomline, is lack of respect around women.

Often men in my culture don't want you to have an abortion. They want you to keep the kid, but they're not going to support you and they also don't want to take precautions while you're having sex. I feel it's really complicated by generation, degree of assimilation, and how religious you are. There are a lot of Latinos now who are born again to evangelism. In a lot of ways, this religion is more restrictive than the Catholic Church. I have my Catholic background, but I know a lot of Catholic women who have abortions and use birth control.

In my community, economics is also a really big factor. Even if a young man wanted to get married and support his family, more and more young Latino men cannot find jobs. Drugs are a big issue, too. More and more drugs are disrupting family life in my culture. I used to think that rural settings were safer from certain things. Now when I go home, I see how that's not true anymore. And the economy there, whew! The economy is so bad now that the sorts of things people used to do to help themselves just don't work anymore.

I just had a second abortion a week ago. I am twenty-eight now. Oh, God, I don't want to talk about this . . . . I had been seeing this guy for about a year. Oh, God, it's hard to talk about . . . . The relationship was primarily a sexual one. It was pretty rocky. He has lived in the United States for about a year. It was interesting. We were very different. He's more traditional, a construction worker. We had a lot of break-ups around how I wanted things to be versus how he wanted things to be. We would always be fighting about it.

I finally got tired of the shit. I'm referring to the struggle in our relationship. We had a date and he called to cancel because he was going out with friends. I told him to go ahead and go out with his friends, but not to come back. All this happened when my grandmother and my mother had come to visit me.

While she was here, my grandmother invited my boyfriend over to dinner several times. She liked him a lot. My grandmother was born in the United States, but my grandfather was born in Mexico like my boyfriend.

My boyfriend and I were using condoms for birth control. I have irregular periods, so I didn't know immediately I was pregnant. That month, I knew my period was late. I had a pregnancy test and it was negative. I talked to the doctor because I wanted to know what was the matter with me. My back hurt and I was nauseous. He told me to make an appointment with an Ob/Gyn.

I went to the Ob/Gyn and she said she thought I was pregnant. I panicked. Luckily, my family had left already. It would have been worse if they were still around. She did an ultrasound and it was inconclusive. I had to go the next week for another ultrasound and it turned out I was eight weeks pregnant.

I was really scared. The political situation with abortion is so volatile now in this country that you never know from one week to the next if you can get a safe and legal abortion. I wasn't certain of my decision but I was scared I might not have a choice.

The week before I found out I was pregnant, I had had one of those big fights with my boyfriend. We had this pattern of having big fights, not seeing each other for a week or two, then getting back together. Of course, then we'd have another fight! It was a somewhat abusive relationship.

I went to see my sister. She had had an abortion before. She told me just to have an abortion and not to think about it. I didn't know whether or not to tell my boyfriend because I was worried he would leave me if I did have an abortion. I considered marriage. Carlos had told me I was getting old and we should have a baby, so it seemed like a possibility. I had told him I wasn't ready to have a baby yet when we had talked about it before.

I remember one morning when we were laying in bed he started talking about getting married and having children again. I told him that he was too irresponsible and he would have to be more responsible before I would consider marrying him or having his child. Our relationship was not stable either. I didn't feel I could depend on him. He got mad and got out of bed and went to work. On the way out he told me that if I became pregnant and had an abortion, he'd leave me. He said I'd lose them both. I said that I would rather lose them than lose myself.

When I realized I was pregnant, Carlos and I weren't seeing each other and he never called me after that. In many ways, it did feel ironic because our relationship had made some strides the few months before that. We had talked about him coming home with me for Christmas to meet my family. He did not have papers, so we talked about getting married so he could have dual-citizenship. After that, we planned on going to Costa Rica where his family is and living there for a while. I even told him I would consider having children once we got back from Costa Rica. So, here I was pregnant with his child, and we weren't even speaking to one another.

I did not have much time to think about it, because I was already ten weeks pregnant. Kaiser would not do my abortion at their clinic if I was more than ten-and-a-half weeks pregnant. But, they couldn't give me an appointment for more than two weeks. So, I had this waiting time, which was awful. I had pretty much made up my mind except I didn't know what I would do if Carlos called me in the meantime. It would not have been out of character for him to call me after about two weeks of separation. I didn't know if I would tell him or not. I was still wavering a lot.

I kept thinking about what it would be like if I did have the baby. I did feel like Carlos would be supportive of me and the child emotionally, and devoted to our family. I didn't know how well he would support us financially, though. Also, all my friends that knew Carlos did not like him at all. They would always tell me to break up with him.

Part of me did not want to tell anybody about this abortion. I was so ambivalent about it. I thought I was more upset about breaking up with Carlos than being pregnant, but when I worked on this in therapy I discovered I was really more upset about being pregnant. I felt a lot of turmoil. I *did* want to have the baby, truthfully. But I felt like I couldn't. I didn't have a job. I would have to go home. I didn't consider my family's feelings of shame so much this time. I thought, Aw, fuck 'em. But I didn't want to *live* there.

My life had been really changing. I felt like the work I had been doing in therapy was really starting to pay off. I felt good about myself. I started doing jujitsu. I was working in my workbooks. Things were really starting to turn for me, and I didn't know what would happen to all of that if I had the baby. I would feel trapped if Carlos came back. If I told him I was pregnant, I didn't think I could get rid of him.

I started thinking what my everyday life would be like once I had the baby. I want to go back to school. I want to continue with my jujitsu and therapy. I would still have to work full-time. How could I keep doing all of this with a baby? If I hired a baby-sitter, would my baby know me? I finally decided not to do it. I didn't want my child to go through the kinds of struggles I've had to go through. Right up to the end, I was unsure.

My body really changed this time because I had the abortion so late. I really felt the changes going on. I was tired. My appetite changed. My body configuration changed. I talked to the baby this time. I wondered more if my baby had a soul, and what happened to it if I had an abortion. Different people told me the baby does have a soul. One woman told me that the baby's soul goes to heaven if you have an abortion. Someone else told me she thought it was the same child until you have it. I really wanted my baby to know that even though I wasn't going to have it, it wasn't because I didn't want it, it was just because of circumstances.

I felt strange about people's reactions. Many of them said how terrible it was that I was pregnant. That's not the way I felt. I wasn't unhappy about being pregnant. I was very upset that I didn't have the support or the resources to bear and raise the child. I didn't feel like I had anyone I could talk to about my mixed feelings. The way the abortion issue is so charged, you have to choose one side or the other. You can't have turmoil.

I told a close friend of mine. I thought she would be understanding because she is a lesbian woman, single, who wants to adopt a child. She didn't approve of Carlos. I was too embarrassed to admit I was considering off and on marrying Carlos and having the baby. After that I didn't want to talk with her about it.

I asked another friend to take me to the clinic. She did not like Carlos either. I felt embarrassed. I got caught. I got caught with this guy nobody likes. I still considered being with him. I felt so politically incorrect.

My born-again sister kept calling me. She drives me crazy. She just got married, and she claims she and her boyfriend didn't have sex for two years. I told her I was pregnant. She said, "Oh no. That's terrible!" I told her I was going to have an abortion. She told me she couldn't support my decision and she wanted to come see me right away.

This abortion was a real turning point for me. At first I felt that if I had been more together with my therapy and my recovery, I could have had the baby. Now I don't feel that way. I accept who I am.

I am sorry I didn't have the support around having the abortion this time. Most of my friends just *assumed* that I shouldn't have the kid. My sister assumed that I *should.* It really made me mad. I don't feel guilty now that it's over. It was harder, and it is going to take me longer to grieve it. During the time, people were not sensitive to how I felt. They said stuff like, "How can you even consider having this kid? You don't have any money. The father is a loser." I felt like telling people to just fuck off. People didn't allow me any room to have contradictory feelings or thoughts.

One of my friends told me she felt like I deserved what I got for being with this jerk in the first place. He had no right to tell me that. This was unplanned. I didn't *deserve* this. Then my sister called and asked if she could send me an after-abortion counseling book. I told her "No" and she sent it anyway. It was one of those horrible "right-to-life" booklets that show the baby week-by-week. I'm really glad I didn't get it before the abortion. I sent it back with a note saying I didn't appreciate her disrespecting my wishes.

I bought a book and it had these exercises and meditations for grieving abortion. I bought two candles, one for me and one for the baby. I lit them both and did some ritual. I felt better. I guess I'm still a good Catholic girl!

# "I was a stranger to myself"

*Hannah lives in the western United States and is in training as an acupuncturist/midwife. At the time of the interview she was not in a sexual relationship, and was still searching for a partner with whom to have a child.*

*Her story is unique. At a time when "open adoption" was almost unheard of (see Introduction, p.21), she arranged an adoption for her son that was at least partially open when she was only seventeen years old. Her story tells of her fight to demand rights for her and her baby. Then several years subsequent to that she had an abortion, which has been the source of a great deal more pain for her than relinquishing her child for adoption.*

•

Well, it was 1976, I was sixteen years old. The summer I turned sixteen, everything in my family just sort of fell apart: my parents separated, my dad lost his job, we lost our house. So I ended up moving up to Boston, and I got pregnant, just acting out—doing my sixteen-year-old thing from a distressful family. I was a vegetarian because I didn't believe in killing animals—morally, that kind of stance—so I couldn't bear the thought of abortion.

I think it was the first or second time I had ever had sex with the person. It was someone I didn't know well, but I was very drawn to him. I knew the second I got pregnant, both times I got pregnant, I just knew. He lived up in Connecticut; I think he was maybe nineteen. He was really kind of magical about it when I first told him. We went out to dinner and celebrated. We weren't sure what we were going to do, but just the whole magic about it was really kind of nice. That was probably the best time of the whole thing—it went downhill from there. But we had one dinner out that was really great.

It was a very hard period altogether. My parents had always been very focused on us kids (they were terrible with each other), and suddenly my mom was starting to date just when I was going through this really big thing. I came from a physically abusive background; my dad would beat me, and my mother and I were always very close. I had my predictions of how people were going to react when I told them. I thought my mother was going to just say, Well, okay, we'll deal with it. I thought my dad was going to beat the shit out of me. I thought my sister would laugh. My sister was the only one I was right about. My mother really hit the roof. She didn't hit me, but she just had utter rage. I felt like she just thought I was so out of control, particularly sexually.

With my father, there was this whole huge drama where I was terrified to tell him. I was in hysterics for days, but I still had to go tell him, so I went to his apartment. This was after they had separated, so he was suddenly this different person I had never experienced or known before—he had all this space or relief. So I told him I was pregnant and he just said, "So, okay, what are we going to do?" They switched roles on me. My family was actually very supportive through the whole thing. My grandmother just said, "Well you made a mistake and you have to live with your mistakes." It was very out in the open. My brother was in the army at that point, stationed in Germany, and he wrote to me a lot. We became very close at that time—never again since then, but then.

So I lived up in Connecticut in this huge house. I had been going to an alternative school and I didn't want to go back to public school, so I had dropped out. I guess there were five or ten of us crowding into this apartment, and they were all doing drugs and stuff, and I was being pregnant and being good. I quit smoking and started doing all this stuff to take care of myself, probably for the first time in my life. Ted, the dad, would come down and see me every once in a while or I'd go up. The people in my house were really there at first, then everybody kind of lost interest and went on their way.

It was a very strange time; I don't remember a lot of it, it was like a dream. Part of it was that there was shame, because I was so young. I was pregnant and going to work and people didn't know, my body was changing, and I'd never . . . I didn't know what was going to happen. I always had to deal with things before I should have in my life. I didn't have guidance, and I was very poor, so I didn't have good health care. My parents couldn't help. In fact, for a certain amount of time that summer after I left home I was the only one working, because everybody was out of work and we'd lost the house. The house that my parents had saved all their life to get we only got to live in for four or five years.

So then we got robbed at knifepoint in our apartment up there. The guy almost me hit over the head but my friend stopped them, saying, "She's pregnant." I don't know why that stopped them, thank goodness it did. My father came up and got the five of us that were living in the apartment and took us down to New Jersey—my dad's really good at rescuing, he comes through for those crises. We had an apartment in the same building that he was living in that we did work on in exchange for rent. He took the little money they had from selling the house and was renting out the dining hall to try to start a restaurant, because he just couldn't get work. So I spent from February 'til August down there with my friends trying to make this business for my father.

I remember it not showing to people. The baby was due in July and I remember in June having my shirt come off my breasts and just graze against my belly because I was just holding myself so tightly. I still wore my same pants, just open with safety pins. I wasn't letting myself really bust out of there—though I did in that last month. But there was just this whole kind of containment and embarrassment, even though my father was really great in being unashamed of me, very supportive of me. And whenever anybody found out they were good about it. It was just my stuff.

In May or so, one of the women I had lived with called me. She was in college in New York, and in one of her classes they were doing some sort of women's health thing and they were talking about adoption. She had mentioned me, that I was a teenager and interested in giving my baby up for adoption. Her teacher came up to her after the class and said, "I know a couple that really wants to adopt a baby. Can I give their lawyer your friend's number?" So she called me up to ask me. Before that time, I had checked into social service things, and I was really in quite a panic. What was available was that they would take the baby, select three sets of parents, put it in a foster home for a number of weeks, then decide which parents it looked like the most. In New Jersey this is what they were doing. It sounds weird to me when I say it, but this is what I remember that they were going to do. I couldn't have any access, I couldn't learn anything, it was all secrecy, all based around secrecy. It was freaking me out.

It felt like that would be totally irresponsible for me, since I was trying so consciously to have this child and give it a life—then to give it over to just anybody, seemed like I might as well keep it with me, you know? So when she called me and asked me, I said, "sure." So the lawyer got in touch with me, one of the most famous adoption lawyers in the country. He's a really fine person and has helped me since then. So he got in touch with me and he sent me an outline of who these people were, how much money they made, what their religion was, all this stuff. I ended up not going with them, but staying with him. We developed quite a relationship. We wrote to each other regularly, talked to each other regularly. He would always sign his letters or memos to me, legal things, with personal notes. I felt genuinely cared for by him. He didn't treat me like a little kid, and he just let me be where I was—ask for what I wanted, go for what I wanted. He told me within the limits of the law what he could offer me at the time, and was very supportive of me and very respectful.

I wanted to meet the parents, and that was almost unheard of in 1976—you didn't meet the parents. You didn't see the child and you didn't meet the people. At one point there was a couple that wanted to meet me, and I was packing to go to meet them in Los Angeles and the lawyer called and said that they couldn't deal with it and had canceled out at the last minute. We had had all these negotiations and talking, but it scared them too much for me to come and meet them. They were scared that I'd come back—you know, the fears that are there. This was in June and I was due in July, so I was starting to freak out, because it was coming soon, and I didn't know what was going to happen. Looking back on it I really feel like I was graced in a lot of ways, because I got the chance to take a lot of power and to really act in my own behalf and to act in the child's behalf as I felt I needed to. I always felt like I did what I needed to do as a mother. I say I'm the biological mother, but it always felt like the true—not like true martyrdom, but the true place of the mother. When it's something that you really care about and you want to offer it the best, sometimes you give up being with it. I just really had that experience of being able to feel like I did the best that I could.

A week or two later, these other people got in touch that I liked. We started talking and talked with each other a lot. I ended up going out to Los Angeles and spending the weekend with them. It was very short, but we spent a lot of time together, they showed me the house. They were in the motion picture industry. They had a lot of money, but they had made it on their own. They had had nothing, but had just followed their passions and created something for themselves. They had things that were important to me back then, which are different than what are important to me now. I was into alternative education, and one of their children was going to an alternative school. I was brought up an atheist and it was very important to me that they not have one religion that they brought it up in, but to also feel more relaxed than my family did about exposing the child to different religious beliefs. I wanted the child to know that they had been adopted in a way that it was okay, that it wasn't something that was a secret or an embarrassment. And that they could really communicate that it was an act of love. That was really important to me.

They had two other children, a fourteen-year-old boy who was biologically theirs, and an adopted daughter who was seven at the time. I liked that too, in terms of the fact that she knew she had been adopted. We had a great time, and I ended up sending her my teddy bear and stuff. So I ended up telling them that I wanted them to adopt the baby. They were very caring towards me, and they paid for everything. I got my phone bills and doctor bills paid, so finally I could go to the doctor, I could talk to Ted on the phone, I could get maternity clothes. They wanted to pay for my education and I wouldn't do that. I just wanted my expenses covered; I wasn't selling the baby. I was very principled back then, much more than I am today I think. That's probably what carried me through, that attitude that this is what I have to do and I'm going to do it.

Back in New Jersey, it was hot, summer. I remember just lying on the bed with all limbs stretched out, trying to keep my breasts up so nothing would touch, pouring with sweat. I was working twelve to sixteen hours a day, on my feet waiting tables for my dad till the day I went into labor. Ted had showed up in the beginning of July finally, and it was very bad, so I was consumed in that. I just remember crying a lot. My dad of course had turned back into the monster he was because he was under all this pressure from the business, so he was not available. My mother had this boyfriend, so I was pretty much alone. So it was a really . . . challenging time and I pretty much felt like shit. But I remember these moments when someone would connect with my belly and there would be this soft moment of the miracle . . . I would get aware of the miracle. I felt like there was so much going on all the time that I didn't really have a lot of space for the joy of my miracle. And my body was getting so big—I gained a lot of weight. I had smoked since I was eight years old and I had stopped smoking and we had this restaurant, so I was eating. My dad and I would just sit around and eat ice cream all the time; that was our way to pacify ourselves with each other.

My friend Susan had been going to my Lamaze with me. Ted had started doing it with me, but it was not working out and I got Susan as a back-up partner. I just had this feeling . . . he had a date he wanted me to have the baby by, because he wanted to leave. Susan is the one who ended up coaching me through. What was funny about that was that when we met in fifth grade, my nickname for her was Coach. And that was kind of the finale of our friendship; after that we separated.

I was in southern New Jersey, which was very backward. The doctor that I had gone to for my prenatal care told me I couldn't have the baby put on my belly after birth like I wanted, because it was too slippery and the baby would roll off. This is what he really told me. I was swelling up totally and he told me nothing about diuretics or what to do. He was the most patronizing asshole of my whole experience; he treated me like a piece of dirt. So I tried not to go to see him very much because he was really a jerk.

The baby was three weeks late. The night before I went into labor, my mom was sleeping with me and I couldn't sleep. We lived half a block from the beach, so I went walking and I walked all night long. I was just stirred, and I loved the ocean and the water. And I remember the sunrise. When I went back, I was aware of light contractions. Around eleven in the morning I remember lying with my head on the lap of my friend Susan, and her just stroking my head, as the early labor contractions were happening.

So Susan went with me to the hospital that afternoon, and we played cards, hung out. Then they took me into the labor room. My mom came for a little while, but it was too much for her to hear me screaming. My dad was in the hallway, clowning around. He had found this wheelchair, and when I would scream he would roll away, then he would come back and talk to people. Ted had gone, he went about a week before the baby was born, off on his travels. That was a very hard moment, and I was in all this turmoil about it. I threw the *I Ching* coins, which I believe in very strongly. When I looked at the interpretation, it was about this tree and bending with the wind and going on. I shut the book and I just went on. I felt like a weight had lifted, just really a tremendous kind of feeling, almost that he had to leave before I was going to have that baby. You know how women do that, they kind of tidy up things; that was what I had to tidy up.

While I was in full-on labor, they were trying to get me to sign a paper that said that I wouldn't see my baby. Susan was my advocate. She would say, "I know this woman and if she says 'No,' it's *no*." I could say "no" once, and then she would reinforce it. And they were relentless: "You don't want to see it, that's going to be so hard for you." They had all their projections, their feelings about it. I might have been the first person to do that with them, I wanted to see the baby. They were also trying to get me to take drugs. Sarah finally just screamed at them, "Just leave her alone; if we want anything we'll ask for it." The one thing that kept me together was this woman they put in next to me who was totally losing it. I'd turn to her and say, "Breathe, do like this." And as long as I could take care of her I would do fine. They had me on my back, they wouldn't let me out of bed; things have really changed, it was very backwards.

Finally, I was fully dilated, and they couldn't find the doctor anywhere. They were wheeling me into the delivery room and he ran in at the last minute. They strapped me down, my hands and my legs, on my back. They did have a mirror, but it was tilted so that all I could see was my thigh. They were telling me not to push, but I was thinking, I'm going to push anyway, I'm going to push this thing out of here, and I pushed the baby out. They didn't let me hold the baby at first. They took me back to my room, and I was bleeding a lot. They didn't have enough blankets and they had the air conditioner on, and I got a cold. So I had to have a mask on the whole time when I held the baby, I couldn't kiss the baby, which was really sad to me.

When the baby was born the adoptive parents sent me a telegram, saying, "We love you." So I had four days in the hospital with the baby, a little boy, eight pounds, six ounces, twenty-two inches. I named him Ian, which means God's gracious gift, and H., which is my brother's middle initial, because my brother had been so wonderful to me, and I really wanted to honor him.

I got him circumcised, and some stuff which I regret at this point that I did. I couldn't imagine for myself having this being in my body for all this time, and then not seeing him. I know women who haven't, but even if the child died, I just can't imagine not making the child real. I didn't tell any of the women in my room what was going on. They were all talking about their babies . . . . My dad came to see the baby, when he was in the nursery. He couldn't hold the baby, he just couldn't hold it. He took pictures—my dad's always hidden behind a camera. He took about twenty pictures of the baby being held up by the nurse, and it's just the same picture, over and over again, of the baby just lying there. But that's as close as he could get.

The day came when I was going to leave the hospital. They had to have me take the baby out of the hospital and hand it over to the adoptive parents so the hospital wasn't liable. So I remember that day I got dressed and took the baby. My dad and my mom came for me and the adoptive parents came and met me. We were outside, the New Jersey lawyer was there . . . we were out there and they met me, and I gave the baby to them. [Crying] I don't remember what I felt at that moment, because I think it was just so surreal . . . I don't know what I felt.

And then I got in the car, my mom and dad were in front (and they were separated). I'd never seen my dad cry in my life and my mother was always kind of . . . she was present, but she was always trying to protect me from feelings. I was sitting in back and I just put my hand on the back of the front seat, and my dad put his hand on top of it, and my mom put her hand on top of that, and we just all cried. It was such an incredible experience in terms of . . . I'd never seen my father cry . . . I mean I don't know if it was the first time, but it was one of the times that I just got how much my decision had affected other people, what I had done. I think it was very hard for them, I know it was very hard for my mother that I gave up my baby. That's why for them, in a way, it was better if I'd gotten an abortion—they could have dealt with it better. And so we cried, we just cried. That was really good too, because my father had always been . . . he'd hit me when I'd cry. It was not okay to have those kinds of feelings, so to have this space with him was very incredible. And then I said, "You know what, I want a hamburger and a shake," and we went and had a hamburger.

I don't remember what it was like when I came home. I remember, days after, just putting on clothes that I hadn't put on in a long time, just trying to get on with my life. Within a month I left New Jersey, heading for Colorado. I never made it, I made it to Michigan. I just really needed to leave. I think I was just really numb at the time. I just think it was something big beyond my comprehension. I was sixteen or seventeen at that point. I just wanted to find where my friends were and get back there. I didn't have any tools to deal with it.

Six months later I heard from the lawyer that some paper that . . . I didn't realize this until they told me, but you have a six-month period where you can change your mind. I didn't know this—or I might have been told but I didn't get it until the time it came up. So it was this big surprise in December, like, Well do you want the baby? My mom was really good with me then, because I wavered a little. But she was really clear, saying, "You can't do this, you can't bring that baby back."

[Crying] And I know she was right, and I signed it. But I remember that being hard, just having this temptation.

And I wish I had made different agreements, I wish I had made it more of an open adoption, that I could see him and watch him grow and be sent pictures. It was open until a point, and at that point the doors were closed. Once I gave the baby up, the doors were closed. My lawyer was very big into, "Let this family have its chance and don't interfere, don't ask for pictures, don't . . . . "And that was one of my hardest points back then and it still is. We all got into a situation that was complex by choice, all of us. And I feel like it's not . . . I think we could have done it all right and have kept the door open. I wrote a letter saying, for the next eighteen years (because come age eighteen he gets access to his records, in California), if I ever see you it will be from his choice. I felt like it had to come from him because something had been done to him beyond his choice, and he needed to have the decision to get out of it. Which, I also at this point have different feelings about.

A few years ago I tried to get in touch with them. He was ten or eleven at the time. One of my friends had a son who was born two weeks before him. I've watched him grow and I've talked a lot to him and asked him how he would feel. He's given me a lot of feedback, and he gave me actually a lot of encouragement that it would be okay, that kids could handle more than we think. I really felt like I wanted to know if he was alive or dead, I wanted *something*. I ended up writing them at the address I had. It was this whole big deal, my family went into a panic. It was about the time that they found that little girl that had gotten beaten to death, the Steinberg kid? It was something like that that had happened, and it sent them into a panic, particularly my dad, who really runs with fear, most of the time. He was saying, "What are you doing, they're going to be scared." All this stuff. There was this real conflict, and I didn't want to buy into it.

I felt like I had always been really honorable about it, and yes, I was changing an agreement. But I was trying to do it by sending them a letter and saying, "This is what I would like to do. How do you feel about this?" instead of just showing up on the doorstep. The letter was returned. I had sent it certified so they had to sign for it, because I wanted to know that they got it. They hadn't signed for it, it said they had moved with no forwarding address. It wigged me out. So I called up the lawyer and asked if he had a forwarding address for them. They looked in their files, they were very helpful, and they said they had moved a few months after the adoption was final and left no forwarding address.

So they've disappeared. I did see a television show about six years ago and happened to catch the credits and saw their name there. So I do have information so that I could find them. And they wrote a book, which I have. If I really wanted to investigate, I think I could find them. But I think it was so hard, just doing the letter, that I stopped. I'll get that back together at some point. Particularly as he gets older, I really want to know. And I think that he's old enough that he can tell me to fuck off if he wants me to. But if he's anything like me, he's going to want to know me. I just have that feeling.

I get pulled to him sometimes. Every year on the day that he was born, I either get my period or . . . one year they had a special day where they did all these songs from 1976 on that day. Just weird things have happened. Ted has since moved out to California, and I bumped into him on Mother's Day. I was sitting in this cafe reading Dorothy Bryant's book, *The Garden of Eros*, where she's having the baby at the end. He comes in and the only place to sit is right next to me, and it's the birth scene. My mom and gramp came to visit me and we went to the flea market and opened the door of the car and the door of the car next to us opens and it's him. Taking care of a friend's child I ran into him once, just these things I don't understand at all. But I know where to find him. He doesn't have the same interest that I do, but I don't really know how he feels about it. I'm actually interested in talking to him at some point about it because I heard through common friends that he's doing recovery work with his family finally, so I feel more open to talking with him. And I'm not angry the way I was. I was furious. I just trashed him to bits. I felt very betrayed.

So that's how it's been. I got a profound interest in midwifery, actually right after the birth. I ended up becoming a birthing assistant, and I've been at a lot of births. The part that I always have trouble with, which my teacher pointed out, is the postpartum care. She said, "This is the place that you can't get it together, I think because of your history, and you've got to work this out." I'm still in the process of doing that.

I also had an abortion about two years ago. Talking about that is harder in a way, that's really harder. Since I gave the baby up, I started learning a lot about myself. Part of why I didn't want to keep the baby was because I was afraid I was going to abuse it, because I had been abused myself. I didn't know enough about the cycles of abuse, but I knew enough about my own rage that it just scared me. I knew what my dad had done to me. So I had done a lot of work over the years with a lot of the focus being wanting to prepare myself to be able to have a child.

A few years ago I was looking for a sperm donor, because I wanted to have a child. I didn't have a partner to have one with, and I wanted to do it. To make a long story short, I met this person who wanted to become a sperm donor, and we got involved with each other and held off doing the sperm donor thing because we'd fallen in love. He didn't really want to be a parent—or if anything, a part-time parent—that's why he was willing to be a sperm donor. So it got too complicated. We had thought that maybe down the road, maybe in more years. . . . So kind of for the first time in my life, or in a lot of years, I let go of my vision of getting pregnant, even though I had terrible hungers all the time for it. One time I was out visiting my family and I was with my nieces and my nephew and I got baby fever really, really bad. We were using natural birth control, charting my cycles, and I came home, and I ovulated nine days early, almost at the end of my period. I always ovulated late if anything varied. And I got pregnant. I had just moved in with him here, moved from another town to be with him.

Basically what happened was that it destroyed our relationship, it destroyed me. I got in a situation where I felt like it would be so painful to have his child and not be involved with him—because he couldn't be involved with me if I was going to have the child, because of what he wanted to do in his life. And I was so much of a relationship junkie at the time that I talked myself into thinking that . . . he made promises . . . I'd give up the child now and later we would have . . . . It's part of my sickness around that kind of stuff—just a lot of working out of stuff with my father. That was the hardest decision I ever made. I mean, the adoption decision was clear, I got to it quickly, it was just very there. The abortion decision was a lot more complicated, I did a lot more consulting my oracles—the *I Ching,* the Tarot, I did some trance work to talk with myself and the being or whatever there, to get some insight.

Paul, the father of this child, went through a lot of stuff too. He got very opened, and at one point decided okay, we'll have it. We just went through all the possible ups and downs about it. We had to make a decision very fast in a way, because we had to decide in time, and it was ticking away every day. So finally I decided to have an abortion. Actually, I set one up, then canceled, that's how clear I was. I told Paul that he needed to be ready, that I was going to lie down on that table and I was going to jump up, that's how open I needed him to be. Because I was doing something that I never thought I would be capable of doing in my life. I always thought of it as something that someone else does. I had no space in my self . . . I mean I would never, I thought, have done something like that. I had to almost find another person in me that I didn't know and get acquainted with her in order to do it. I was a stranger to myself.

So I set up another abortion, Paul went with me, and it was horrible. It was painful, and I almost felt like it was rightfully so, like it was my due. It was like the struggle, the struggle in my womb. And it is a struggle, you know, you're pulling on something that doesn't want to go. [Crying] It's the one I haven't healed from as much. I think the adoption I've always been able to live with better. But the abortion, I just don't know. I know that death is a part of the cycle of life and it happens, and every month we have our periods and it's just part of what happens, but it's not my way. I've always had a real hard time with killing things as a way to deal with the problem, and I did it. And I have to live with that. Sometimes it will come up and just be very, very painful.

Also Paul had come from this family that never had any problems and nothing ever happened, so it was this whole new world for him, and he was totally overwhelmed. He was saying he was fine, but he wasn't fine; he was acting out and doing all this stuff. So he was not there for me, he needed all this caretaking, and I couldn't do it for him. Our relationship just went up and down, up and down, really bad—it was just so bad, bad, bad. I got in a situation where I was losing . . . I lost the baby, I was losing my relationship . . . . I had agreed when I moved in here that if we broke up I would move out, because he had lived here for a long time, so I was going to lose my home. I was just losing everything . . . I felt totally . . . I felt terrible. I also felt like anybody who knows me knows how important . . . what I've gone through about the adoption. And I came to him wanting a sperm donor. That says a lot in itself.

I think at this point what it's done is make it very clear to me that I can't get involved with anyone seriously unless they're willing to have a child—that's really what the bottom line is now. Because I can't do that again, God I can't do that again. I have to live with what I did and not beat myself over the head about it, but that's the hard . . . . I always get so pissed, the "pro-lifers"—I hate that term—the pro-lifers make it like women just have these abortions and it's no big deal, and they use it for birth control and on and on. You see these women and you know, I mean sometimes it's easier for people, but the options are just not great, not at all great.

That was two years ago. They say it takes the whole year—that you continue your cycle, and I really found it true. Around my due date I really lost it one day, and it occurred to me that was probably the day I would have had the baby. I went into terrible self-pity and all that. I called up my mother and I ended up talking to her for two hours, crying on the phone to her. She didn't hide me from the reality, which I thought was really good; she didn't try to take care of me in that way. She just let me mourn. And that's really been hardest. At least with my other child I have the possibility of seeing him if he's still alive, or I'll get to see pictures of him if he's dead or something. But there's a whole promise that went down the tubes, literally.

And I'm thirty now, and it's becoming an issue, a big issue. I don't know what to do, because I want to have a kid. I just want to find somebody, I don't care if it's a man or a woman, a lover, or a friend; I just want someone who wants to have a child. In a way I've thought it would be easier to find somebody who wants to partner with me and raise a child together—I mean friends last longer than lovers. We don't even have to be lovers. I've seen all different kinds of arrangements at this point, so I'm not attached, I'm just attached to having a child, and not single parenting. Because I feel like I'm out of the danger zone now in terms of abuse, but I don't want to ever pretend like I'm so far away from it that I could be a super-parent. Even the most patient of parents is tested.

Do you want to see a picture of my baby? [We look at pictures] They changed his name, but the hospital sent *me* the birth certificate, which I was supposed to turn in to them. But I never did, I still have it. I'm going to tell him that he's got another name someday, so he knows.

# *Unveiling*

## by Ann Perkins

One month after the abortion
My doctor says
"Ann you've done well"
She says this
Because
My uterus has shrunk back
        to its obligatory size
And I sit bolt upright on her interrogation table
silk blouse on
reading the *Wall Street Journal*
with a block of sanitary paper
across my abdomen

She doesn't recognize the child
Whistling a tune in the dark
For the child
That is dead
And there is no nice word for it
Finally the truth lies naked
Sucked out of me
Untidy
Without anaesthesia

# *Our Town*

## by Ann Perkins

To you my hazy child
I ascribe the title of burden
a hundred voices cry
there is no time   no time   no time
for you

no time for me
to indulge in the fat luxury
of motherhood

because all that time
that precious, wooing, loving, magic
time
makes no money
makes no success
makes hardly a passing nod from strangers

because, here
mothers don't get to have faces
without finessing and exhausting and cajoling
and I suppose, yes, defeating their purpose

so, I do the sensible thing.

# Conspiracy

## by Lisa Woods

Dear child,
you never happened.
That's what they'd
have me believe—
They drugged me
during your entry
into life
to dull my memory;
snatched your
newborn flesh
from these unwed arms,
falsifying records
for the sake of Propriety
(and some barren
woman's pride);
denied your existence
to me—
the one
who gave you life—
and turned me out, tainted,
after harvesting
the fruit of my womb
(and called it Charity).

And now—
fifteen years later,
my Soul is bloody
from pounding against
iron Bureaucracies,
trying in vain
to clutch a morsel of proof
that I once had a son . . .
that these
scars on my belly/
wounds in my heart
are not
my imagination.

# Conversations

## by Lisa Woods


Test said, Positive . . .
Boyfriend said, How do I know it's mine?
Sister said, How could you be so dumb?
Mother shrieked and ran from the room,
throwing her apron over her head.
Father said nothing (though I hear he cried,
grieving for what *he'd* lost)—

Banker said, You're fired.
Boyfriend's Priest said, Get an abortion.
Boyfriend said, It's your problem.
Doctor said, A fine kettle of fish!

Lutherans said, Go to the Catholics—
Nuns said, Bad girl.
Hospital said, You can go now.
Social Worker said, Sign here.
Accountant said, You owe us more
(the Baby wasn't enough)—

Psychologist said, There, there;
bored with his barren wife
and newly adopted daughter,
he jumped at the chance

to delve into
the recently vacated womb—

Bureau of Vital Statistics said,
We find no record of such a birth;
could it be under another name?
Legal System said, You have no rights;
you signed them all away—
Caseworker supposed to reunite us
said, Today's my last day.

(So far) My Son has said nothing—
(guess he's a lot like Dad . . . )

# *Lament*

## by Justine Tot Tatarsky

From this tree of love
to a winter earth
fall your ungiven names.
I send you back
up the dark river
whose currents you have swum
bringing me this truth:
Not yet my own guardian
I cannot be yours.

Against all intuition
with every reason
flicker of life, I have snuffed you out
though your breath was mine.
Fragment of renegade hope
cry of rebellion
against the world you wished to enter
only when you were substance
could I render you shadow.

To the dance of loving I will wear
this veil of grief.

# "I got pregnant on Good Friday"

*Erica, now thirty, is a nurse-midwife living and working in north-ern California. She lived on the East Coast at the time she became a birth mother at age fifteen. She remains childless at the present time.*

•

I was fourteen, going on fifteen. At first I denied I was pregnant. It was only the second time I had even attempted to have sex; I had never actually had sex. I got pregnant on Good Friday, a good Catholic girl getting pregnant on Good Friday. My parents were in the middle of a custody battle, and were just due to go to court, so I wanted to try to hide it, thinking my father would lose custody, which would be devastating for me and my sister and brother.

But once I found out for sure, reality hit and I said, I've got to do something and I need help—I need my father's help. So I told him about it, and he was immensely supportive and very loving. My mother completely lost it, told me I was going to have a deformed child, that all sorts of horrible things were going to happen. But my father, being very level-headed, said, "Well, first you need to see a doctor, and then you need to think of the options." We went to one doctor, who we knew. I was over three months pregnant, so it would have been a second trimester abortion. But I was so young, and also in the first month of the pregnancy I had possibly been exposed to German measles, so the obstetrician really felt that I should have an abortion, and scheduled me for one. But my father decided to think about it and have a second opinion. So we talked to a Catholic doctor who said, "Don't have an abortion. Come to me, I will take care of you for free. I realize your family is having financial problems. I will take care of you and deliver your baby for free."

My father also investigated a home for unwed mothers at that point. The home was run by Catholic charities and staffed by the nuns. We looked into me going there and continuing my schooling, getting the basics for high school. I was still in junior high school. My father said that one thing we could do is look at adoption as an option. So I thought about it and said that that would be fine. I was very scared and really let my family help make that decision. I remember realizing that it wasn't just all going to disappear like I had hoped it would.

So I went to live at a Catholic home for unwed mothers. I had gotten pregnant in April and went to live there in September. I started high school there; I was the youngest of all the young women. Everyone else was much more experienced in sex and just in life than I was, and I felt very naive.

My mother was very conditioned to think that it was bad, partially because they had gotten pregnant with me before they were married. And being more the good Catholic children than I was, they disappeared and came back, pretending to have gotten married and had a child already. She had enormous guilt about that, but proceeded to have two other children before they actually got married in the Catholic church. So she really felt like it needed to be kept hush-hush.

I don't remember actually lying, but I remember being really uncomfortable. I just disappeared and reappeared. And then finally somebody a few months down the line confronted me in the hallway at school, a very cocky young man, and he said, "So—rumor has it that you had a baby." I just thought

about it and I turned to him and said, "You're right, I did."
And I felt very free. I thought okay, the secret's out; I'm glad.
I didn't want it to be a secret. He was floored.

The father was the same age as I was, so he was fourteen.
I thought he knew I was pregnant. I was good friends with a
young woman who knew him, and she said he did. I thought
he didn't want to be involved, because he hadn't called or anything. So I just got very stoic and said, Well, the hell with
him, I'll do this by myself, I don't need him. I put up an angry
front, my defense mechanism. But when I was eight months
pregnant I found out that he had to sign the adoption papers.
So I called him up one night and said, "I'm pregnant, I'm going
to be having *your* child, and I want you to sign the adoption
papers." And so he said, "Uh, okay." And that was the end of
that conversation.

After the child was born I took a picture of her over to
his house with the adoption papers and had him sign them. He
took the picture and it was all . . . it was fine. I mean it was
tense; we were so young and so immature. We didn't know what
to quite make of it. I found out years later that he used to show
that photograph to people and tell them that this was his child.
He was very proud of that photograph. That felt good to me.

I blossomed in the pregnancy, I enjoyed being pregnant.
I was healthy and I felt good. I remember at the time the coun-
selor saying that I was sitting on an emotional time bomb, that
I was not dealing with my feelings, I was just coping. I remem-
ber having my "tough" walls up, thinking, These are the cards
I was dealt, and I have to deal with it.

One thing I wish I wouldn't have had to do is go through
the birth alone. My father was able to stay with me for a little
of it, then I was left by myself in a labor room. I was very
medicated, and I was also given a drug, an amnesiac called
scopolamine, which was to make me forget. I asked for and
received a lot of pain medication. So there are large gaps in my
memory. I had asked to have an epidural, which was new at the
time, and I was denied that request. They thought I wasn't

going to be able to push the baby out because I was so young. They thought I was going to have to have a C-section, and then I didn't, so they gave me more pitosin to make my labor come stronger. Eventually they take you to the delivery room and they put you on the table and they wait until you're actually having a contraction, then they give you a general anesthetic and they put you out. You get the baby almost down to being born, then they gas you and they cut you, and they forcep the baby out.

So my birth experience is lying on the table, starting to have a contraction, breathing heavily, then having the anesthesiologist come and slap a mask on my face. My last memory is fighting him, hitting him, and him screaming, "Nurse, strap her down." And then waking up a few hours later, after the experience was over.

Right after I woke up from the anesthesia, my mother and father were there. It was in the wee hours of the morning. I said, "Did I have a boy?" They said, "No, you had a little girl, and she's fine." After I sobered up a little from the anesthesia, they wheeled me over to the window, and my father was there, and I was able to see her. She was asleep, and she had a scar on her cheek from the forceps, and both her hands were covered. I remember looking down at my own hands and seeing all the blisters on the palms from pulling on the bars for pushing.

It wasn't until that next morning that I actually got to spend time with her. I wanted to be able to feed her and take care of her and spend time with her because I thought, I'm only going to have this one week. So she came in for regular feedings while I stayed in the hospital for three days—bottle feedings. Also I had requested that I be able to get pictures of her; you know how hospitals give photographs. But the nurses had taken it upon themselves to decide that it was inappropriate that I receive photographs. They said, "This is our policy; if you're relinquishing your baby, then you get no pictures of your baby." I just thought, Forget you guys, and my father came and brought a camera and we took pictures.

On one side, I was bad because I was pregnant; I was an unwed mother, I was a teenager, and I was giving my baby up, so there was guilt and shame. The other side was that I had kept my child, I had not opted for an abortion. I had given a child life, and I was giving an infertile couple a chance to raise a family, and was glorified for that. So you had this shame and you had the glory, both. And I had actually identified with the glory more. I thought the shame was just . . . well, I internalized it a little bit more than I thought, I realized years later. But I thought it was just all hogwash. I thought, I'm doing a really good thing, I'm nurturing this baby, I stopped smoking cigarettes, and somebody will be really happy. I'm giving them the best gift of their life. And I felt that was very powerful, so I related to that side more; I tried to. I was so young that it was very easy to make that decision and feel comfortable with it.

There were some women in the home for unwed mothers who refused to see their babies. There were also very racial distinctions between who was keeping their babies and who wasn't. Mostly the young white women were giving their babies up and the young black women were keeping their babies. There were two who actually relinquished their child, then came back and said, "No, I've changed my mind." Those were all the black women. There were not very many white women who kept their babies; none in fact. They all were giving their children up.

Sometimes I think about trying to find her. She's fourteen now, the age I was when she was born. I work as a nurse-midwife, so I work with women delivering babies. I just took care of a young woman the other day who was fourteen years old, born the same year as my daughter, whose mother was fourteen when she had her. It was a black family; she kept her daughter. She had been born in the hospital and was now coming back to the hospital to have her baby. So her mother is now twenty-eight and has a few other children, and now she's going to be a grandmother. I think about that; I'm almost thirty, I could be a grandmother. My daughter will be turning fifteen real soon.

Anyway, I brought my daughter back with me to the home for unwed mothers, and she stayed there in the nursery part. We were there together for a week, and I had her christened. My family came, we had photographs, she was baptized, and then that's when I relinquished her; I signed the papers and left. And my sister remembers this time very clearly. She says that she remembers me turning and looking back and looking very sad. I don't remember that. I remember crying a little bit, but still just feeling, I'm going to make it, it's all right.

About six weeks later, I went back to the home to see some friends who delivered after I did, and to see their babies. I went into the nursery and found that my daughter was still there. And I said, "I would like to feed my daughter." And they let me. I had specifically not wanted her to live the first six weeks of her life in a baby farm, I wanted her to be with a family. She had these wide eyes and she was just really eating and I felt like she was needing attention and love. I felt very sad and I called up the social worker and said, "I feel really angry that you didn't listen to my request. I wanted this child adopted." And she said, "There was some red tape. The adoption is becoming final this week." So they placated me at that point, basically.

But they were right, the emotional time bomb was there. I went into a major postpartum depression within the year, and it took me many years to recover. I wasn't grieving the loss of my child so much—it wasn't a conscious grief for her, because I felt like I made a good decision for her. I grieved the loss of my childhood, I grieved the loss of things the way they *were*. I grieved that life had changed so radically, that I no longer fit in. I went back to high school, and I was years beyond everyone else in maturity. Everyone was into trivial things, and I felt depressed and removed, and started spiraling into drugs and alcohol. I spiraled down *deeply* for a number of years, and then just started abusing my body in other ways, being very loose, promiscuous.

During my pregnancy I had received an enormous amount of wonderful attention, especially from my father. It was the first time in my childhood that I was nurtured. And I grieved the loss of that, because life got back to normal, and I was still really burdened emotionally. I remember being very depressed. And who knows what it was; was it being an adolescent, was it being postpartum, was it the grief that I was coming at in other ways? I don't know. But whatever it was, it was very destructive for a period of time. I became a ward of the court at sixteen and was placed under county custody and was in a girl's home. So I essentially didn't live with my family much beyond the age of fourteen. After it was all over, I never entered back into my life and my family fully. And that was how I suffered more than actually giving up the baby.

In my work, I don't automatically take the teenagers when they come in. I don't automatically nurture them a little, maybe because it touches too close to home. Instead of being able to do that, I see how naive I was, I see how naive they are, and I think, Oh, little girl, you just don't know what you're in for, you just don't. So I don't know if I have as much compassion in that area as I do in other areas of birth.

One of the other midwives I work with seemed to feel that I wasn't as good in the postpartum care. I've been very slow to learn the tricks of breast-feeding, the tricks of helping families bond, and things like that. Her perception of it was that I never did that for myself; I never got that reward of actually having the baby. My postpartum experience was essentially very negative and very sad. She's right. When it comes to taking care of the baby, then I don't know, don't truly understand. I keep looking forward to the time when I will complete that process.

I actually conceived again as a teenager, when I was nineteen. I had a miscarriage, and I *grieved* about that, I was sad. Then a year after that I got an IUD, and two years later I had a massive pelvic infection and have not been able to conceive since then, because I have a lot of adhesions and scar tissue. I've actually never actively tried to conceive, I was scared. There are only a few things in life that you think are about the worst thing that could happen to you in the world. And the worst thing that could happen to me was not to be able to have any more children. I had made a bargain. I had said to myself, "If you have this baby now, you will always be able to have more children, you'll be able to take care of them." And I just felt like, I'm being cheated out of something, this is really wrong. This is not part of the bargain.

I guess a year or so ago, I decided to look into whether I was fertile, even though I didn't want to get pregnant yet. I found out that, yes, my tubes are very scarred, yes, I have a lot of adhesions and would need to have surgery to have them removed. And that felt better to me. I knew all of a sudden, and I could deal with it.

I still hold in my mind that I will have a child. And I wonder why I procrastinate with the decision for the surgery. Like, when is a good time? But when *is* a good time, who knows when a good time is? A few years ago I saw a play by a woman, a one-woman show based on her experience of having given up her child and trying to find her years later. And one thing she said was that women often will go on and have many babies, to replace their lost child. Or they will have no children, to preserve their only . . . to preserve *the* child that they had. I'm hoping that that isn't what actually happens to me.

I thought when I was younger that I would wait until I was in my early thirties to have a child. And it's looking like that's what's going to happen, if the process does happen. I joke around and say, "Yes, I'm going to be a high-risk mother all the way; too young and too old."

# "If you would just go away, I could be free"

*Carol is a thirty-two-year-old woman from an Italian Catholic family in the Midwest. Currently, she is a social worker living in California. Carol has three children that she has raised primarily as a single parent. Her story poignantly illustrates some of the troubles many women have when raising children without important resources. She also has interesting things to say about her religion and its effect on her sexuality and her choices when faced with unplanned pregnancies.*

•

I was a high school dropout. I went on and took my GED and passed it. After that, I went on to college. I eventually graduated with a major in sociology and a minor in English as a second language. I went to two colleges before I finally finished my degree, and it was a real struggle.

I grew up knowing that children were highly valued. I should say, I grew up knowing I did not have a choice about reproducing—that was just something that women did. My grandma had thirteen children. [Laughs] Sexuality was not discussed in our home, except for growing up with the idea that you were not supposed to be sexually active unless you were married. During your marriage, you should be sexually active only when you want to reproduce, so sex wasn't pleasureful.

I can remember thinking, when I first heard about sex, that I would become a nun instead of ever having somebody touch me. I didn't understand my own sexuality. I do have memories of being very young and feeling stimulated. I began to feel guilty when I felt stimulated, it came in somewhere from the environment. It wasn't specifically from my parents, but maybe just not discussing sex at all had something to do with it.

So, I was never really prepared while I was growing up. I was sexually active first when I was fifteen years old. I felt guilty for being sexually active. I knew that I could never let my parents know, or they would kill me, I thought they would kill me. Even so, my first sexual experience was good, in fact, my first boyfriend and I are friends to this day. That's really nice. The only bad thing was that I felt displeased with my body and I had no cause now that I look back at it, except that I was raised in this culture. Women just grow up always feeling displeased with themselves, and that started for me when I was a teenager. There is always something wrong, you can never look at yourself and say "Oh, I'm just wonderful." We're always looking at the aesthetic, and not at how our bodies work. As I look back at it, I realize that my body worked really well for me, in all areas; I was an athlete.

When I first got pregnant, it was after I had lost my father. We buried him on Christmas Eve of my fifteenth year. A year after my father died, I was raped. It really caused me to isolate myself. My mom had no knowledge of the effects of rape, so she couldn't help me, couldn't see the symptoms. I really pulled away and was feeling really insecure.

I cared for a friend of mine's child during the summers of both my junior and senior year. He was five months old when I started tending to him. I really enjoyed it, and it also gave me a chance to be by myself. I didn't have to be social anymore. I was always very social, and suddenly I wasn't very social. That's when I got the notion in my head that I would want a baby of my own to care for, and that the baby wouldn't just go away very quickly, like my father did. I was really angry at him for dying, not that it was his fault, but still, those feelings were really alive then.

I was dating somebody who I didn't feel very close to at this time. Prior to that, I had had closer relationships with boyfriends, but since the rape, I had a hard time being intimate. Still, here was this person, I wanted a baby, and so I got pregnant. I had no idea what it meant to have a baby, to be responsible for somebody else, financially or in any other way—that wasn't a part of my thinking. Nobody had discussed it with me. I just remember being afraid to tell my mother. That was the only fear I had. I was seventeen years old.

My boyfriend and I were both from a really working-class Catholic neighborhood. When I told him about it and he suggested an abortion, it was totally out of the question for me, that wasn't a part of my vocabulary. I wasn't anti-abortion. I had friends who had had abortions, I had gone with them to have abortions, but for me, it wasn't a choice.

We decided to get married, but we didn't get married until I was almost six months pregnant, because . . . I really didn't want to marry him. I wanted a baby. But then, I was also feeling guilty, and guilt was such a strong component of my family life. When I think of my family life, it is so intertwined with Catholicism, and Catholicism is completely intertwined with guilt. I felt like if I didn't marry this person, I would have to stay at home. I had two younger siblings. The youngest was in fifth grade. My mom was working full time and going to school, and I could see how stressed out she was, and I had already added to that. I didn't think I could stay at home.

The biggest shame for me was that I had sex with somebody I didn't love. If I could have said I was crazy in love with this guy and couldn't help myself, that would have been one thing, but to do it with somebody you didn't *love*, that was the worst. I couldn't face the situation that way, so I married him.

I cried on my wedding day, cried when I went down the aisle. I wanted to run out of the church. All this, only to find out later that my mother wanted me to stay at home. She never wanted me to marry him. She looked at him and thought, this young man will never be a responsible caretaker and all of the burden is going to fall on Carol. She wanted me to just kiss the relationship good-bye and come on home. She never said it.

I was still in high school after I got married. I wasn't able to finish school and get my degree with the rest of my classmates because my baby was born before graduation. Here I was, married to this person who loved to party, he didn't come home at night and the bills weren't getting paid. It was horrible.

We got married in the winter, I had my daughter in the spring, by the next fall, I didn't want to do it anymore. He got busted when he was with somebody who was trying to rob a garage so that they could get money to buy drugs. I took my daughter, got everything out of my apartment, put it in my mother's garage, and I left to stay with my sister who was in college in another state.

I lived with my sister and her roommates for a while, which was fine. I didn't know anything about welfare. I was doing crafts and selling them. I thought this would support us. Once in a while my husband would send money down. He was trying to hang on to the marriage because he needed a "mom." That was me.

At this same time, my sister was involved in a church that is worse than the Catholic Church. It's a born-again church. They were talking to me about being born-again and Jesus and heaping *more* guilt on me. The biggest one was, "You can't divorce this person, you're married to this person for the rest of your life. If you divorce, there's no way you're going to heaven."

I felt very frustrated. I read the whole Bible from cover to cover. Of course that didn't help the situation any. I didn't understand a lot of the things I was reading. I didn't know what to do. So, when he wanted to see me and work things out, everyone in the church, the pastors, everybody, told me I had to let him because if I divorced him, I was going to hell. I could never marry again anyway. That was the way it was. There was no way I could leave him without being up shit creek with God.

He came down and it made me sad again when he was there. I was using a diaphragm for birth control and got pregnant with my son Joseph. Up to this point, I never felt like my decision to have my daughter was a wrong one. I knew it was insane financially, but I really loved her, and emotionally I was handling it well. I was reading a lot of books to be sure I was parenting right. I loved parenting. The thing that frustrated me was just the tie I had to this man.

I remember the day specifically when I got pregnant. After I found out for sure, I knew I couldn't stay with my sister. I had to go home to my mom. My husband knew I was pregnant. He came back home and got a job on the railroad. Actually, I never saw him make a sincere attempt to get a job. A friend of his basically handed him this job which was a very good job, especially for someone who didn't have a high school education.

He kept saying it was going to get better because he was working and that whole thing. I was still staying with my mom until I applied for welfare and got it. I found a little apartment for myself and my daughter and the baby I was going to have. I painted it, I fixed it up, and I moved in by myself. When he started working, he moved in. Then we moved into a bigger apartment. I was never really happy, and I never really trusted him. It wasn't safe for me to be with him because I never felt I could trust him. He had given me so many reasons not to.

Part of the problem was that, in the neighborhood we grew up in, there were a lot of drugs. I contributed, I did a lot of drugs from eighth grade to my junior year. I was high every day. Actually it was the rape experience that ended it. When I got cut off socially, I just had no desire to get high anymore. There were other things I wanted to do after that point. A lot of it had to do with reading and education and just focusing on me . . . and separating. I didn't understand addiction. He's an addict, he can't say "no" to drugs.

I realized the addiction really strongly when we moved back in together. He kept getting high, specifically on heroin. He's older than me, he's from the "Woodstock Generation," in fact, he was at Woodstock. There was a lot of heroin in the neighborhood. When I started getting out of the whole thing, it was more PCP and cocaine. He still is an addict.

When Joseph was eighteen months old, I was formulating in my head all these ways I was going to get out of my marriage. I needed to get out. He could really sense that. I was distant and we were not sexually active. Again, I was doing crafts in the house. Sewing and making jewelry and selling it. He would be very verbally abusive, always putting me down, and so I just distanced myself. We weren't really talking very much.

He wanted me to be sexually active with him and I said, No, I don't want you to do that. The badgering went on for several days. He was saying, "You're supposed to do this, you're my wife, I go to work every day." Of course he was blowing all his money on drugs. He was going to work for that, not to support us. Actually, he started saying things which scared me. He would say, "Well, if you're not being sexually active with me, maybe you're being sexually active with someone else. If that's true, I'll kill you."

I was very afraid of him. I was using the diaphragm again. That was all I had. I don't know why I didn't try the Pill; I guess because all the women in my family had gotten sick from it. Besides, sex made me sick, the thought of having sex made me sick at that point in my life. It was one of those, "Okay, if it'll make you shut up, I'll get on my back and you can fuck me." That's what happened. And voilà, fertile Myrtle, I was pregnant.

I remember waiting for the period: the period doesn't come. I was so angry. I cried a lot. I actually remember pounding on my belly, like, If you would just go away, I could be free. It wasn't going to be that much longer. I got the pregnancy test. It was positive. I was crying when I came home. He was sitting on the couch. He said, "Why don't you just get a fuckin' abortion?" I could not do that. At that point, though, I was thinking about doing it, or giving the baby up for adoption. Something! How was I going to support another baby?

I knew that I was going to leave this man. Somehow, I was going to leave him, I was not going to spend the rest of my life with him. I just hated this baby so much. I would tell it every day, "I hate you, I hate you, I want you to go away." Until one day, it was Christmas Eve, I was three months pregnant, and I started to hemorrhage.

My mom packed me up and took me to the hospital. The bleeding started to slow down a little bit, so they told me, "Just go home and keep your feet up and we'll see what happens." That was in the morning. By the evening I was hemorrhaging so much, losing so much blood, that my mom brought me back to the hospital. I remember how frustrated the ER doctor was. He said, "The baby is obviously dead, there is no way for you to bleed like this and have the fetus remain alive. Your body is obviously rejecting the fetus. I want to do an abortion on you."

If he would have said, "I want to do a D&C on you," I probably would have said, "Okay, go ahead and do what you need to do." But, he used the word abortion, so I said, "You can't do that, you can't do that to me." He kept trying to convince me but I was adamant against it. He finally said, "Would it make you feel better if we do an ultrasound on you so that you can see that the fetus is dead?" I said, "Yes, and if the fetus is dead and I know it for sure, then you can do it."

They did the ultrasound and the fetus wasn't dead. You know, it's a very sketchy picture, but you could see his little heart beating, and all his little limbs moving. I was three months along. At that point, they don't have a chest plate, so you can just see the heart moving. I could see the fingers, it was all really little, but I could see it. I said, "See, you can't do an abortion. I have to try to keep the baby." It was probably at that point that I said, "As much as I hate that this is going to slow me down, I'm going to keep the baby."

I stayed in bed to keep the baby. Up to that point, I had never been just on my own. As bad as this jerk was, he was still there, and there was enough money coming in so that we could maintain. It was extreme poverty, mind you, because he was blowing so much money on drugs. Still, I had never tried to go out to work and support the kids. I'd never tried to deal with day-care and all those things.

So I had my third child. It was a boy. Sometimes I wonder what decision I would make today if I got pregnant. I would have an abortion, although I can hardly say the word. I couldn't support another baby. Not at this point in my life. I have raised three kids basically on my own since my oldest was eighteen months old. My mom helped me as much as she could, but she is living on minimal. When we lived in the Midwest she helped me with day-care, but now that I've moved to California, I don't even have that.

Now that I really know what goes into raising children, this is what I'm teaching my children, that abortion is an option. When communities took an active and vital role in helping to raise children, I don't think abortion was so important; now I think the option to have an abortion is crucial. Because most often, a mother doesn't get community support. It's her: If he walks out, she's going to be the primary caretaker. It's crazy to think that two people can raise a child and meet all of it's needs; emotional, spiritual, financial. Or, just teaching it cultural values. It's crazy to think that two people, a father and a mother, can do that. But to expect one person to do that?

I'm raising my daughter to think about things like that. The chances of him helping you out with that child if your relationship doesn't work out are minimal. He might help for a while, but statistically, the help really dwindles. He has got to be a really special guy to want to continue in the care. I tell her, if you have a job to support yourself and a child and if you have the support a caretaker needs in the nurturing process (which our culture doesn't provide), then you can think about having children realistically. Otherwise, abortion has to be an option.

It's still really hard for me. I still cry about once a month because I'm never making it. I have a salary now—I make too

much for the government to help me, but I don't make enough
to cover the bills that are coming in. So, you cry once a month
when you're doing your bills, and you think this is never going
to end. I need to buy food, so I can't pay this bill, because food
and rent are the most important bills, and then transportation.
I'm always prioritizing, and I have at least one person every
month who sends me a letter saying you're behind on your
payment. That's the economic part, the black and white part,
because it's so obvious, you can see it. Maybe George Bush
could at least understand the financial part of this bind because
it's so concrete. Maybe, if he was willing to look, he could see
it and feel compassion. Maybe . . . I don't think George Bush
has that in him, but . . . .

I had to toss the guilt of being a single-parent family out the
door. I've seen a lot of my single-parent friends who feel guilty
all the time and so they don't create boundaries, there are not
appropriate rules in the family. The kids are the ones who pretty
much dictate what goes on in the home, then they become fourteen years old and they're doing crazy things outside the home.
That doesn't happen in my house, at least it hasn't happened,
but our rules are real clear, and the kids are afraid of me. I don't
feel guilty because I am doing the best that I can do.

My education in Women's Studies has helped me a lot
with being a single parent. Being angry at the fact that sex wasn't
discussed in my family has helped me a lot. I feel like, "Wait a
minute, sex is so much a part of being human, and it's such a
big responsibility, how could they not discuss it?" My mom
would say, "Well, it was never discussed in my home growing
up." Mom didn't have a boob tube in her home growing up,
she didn't have billboards, she didn't have fashion magazines.
It needed to be discussed and she did not do it. I know that she
didn't really know how, so, in a way I can't be angry about that.

I feel very frustrated because I'm always having to work
beyond my limit in order for the family to function. To have
the kids grow up and be healthy. I work forty hours a week and
raise three kids by myself. I "have" to work full-time to mate-

rially support my kids, but it leaves so little time to actually
have relationships with them. There is no time to just work on
relationships and conflict resolution.

The legal system has been a joke as far as getting any
money out of the kids' father. The year that I left him, in 1982,
he was making twenty-five thousand dollars, in the Midwest
where the cost of living is a lot less than here. So he was making
very good money and we weren't even paying the rent. He paid
me while I was living with my mom. Then when I got my own
place, suddenly the support stopped, when I really needed it. I
was working almost full-time and I had the kids in day-care. It
was just insane. Then when I made the decision to go back to
school full time, he never paid support again. That was September of 1984.

I went to court so many times to try to get the money I
so desperately needed to support my kids. The first time I went
*pro se* and the judge did no more than give me a patronizing
pat on the back. The next time I went to court I had an attorney,
and I actually won a judgment. I never got the money, in spite
of the fact that my husband signed papers repeatedly promising
to pay. We went to court every other week for three or more
months. My ex-husband perjured himself constantly, and the
judge did nothing.

There were two times when it looked like the judge was
actually going to take action and I would finally get something.
Both times my husband found a way to get around it. The first
time, a couple of weeks before the final court date, my husband
started going to work late deliberately. He got laid off work, so
we could not attach his wages. He was a union worker, and he
knew they would get him back on. They did, but it was too
late for me.

The second time, my husband checked himself into a
drug and alcohol treatment facility one week before the court
date. Again, they could not attach his wages because he did not
have income. The judge gave him a big pat on the back for
trying to change his life. The only time my husband's wages

were successfully garnished was when the state went after him. They got the AFDC they had paid me.

The last that I know of, he owes me about thirty thousand dollars in back support, which I'll never get. I pray that he dies. Great Spirit, if he would just die, I would get Social Security money, which would make such a difference for me. But he'll die when my youngest turns eighteen. His spitefulness is very deliberate.

If I had to do it all again, would I change it? You bet I would. I would have been really solid in my use of birth control. I would not have given in to having sex when I didn't want to. With my generation, and all the Catholicism around me, it was really hard to develop a good way to take care of yourself around sex. If you feel really guilty about having sex in the first place, then you aren't going to get birth control, because that is an admission that you are deliberately, pre-meditatively, having sex. So you don't get birth control. You won't even let yourself think, "I'm going out with Joe Schmo this weekend, and we are going to do it up, so I better bring birth control. He had better use a condom and I should use a diaphragm, so that we're doubly protected against getting pregnant."

That would be the thoughtful and responsible thing to do, but if you're not supposed to be having sex in the first place, you don't even think about birth control. Birth control was something you heard about, but I never got it. No one ever came into the school and educated us on birth control, which I think is necessary.

I get very angry about my lack of financial and emotional support from my community and culture. I love being a mother, but it has been so incredibly hard for me, and I don't think it needs to be that way. Most of the women I know who have had abortions have done so because their parents thought it was a good idea or the person they were with didn't want to have the child, not because they didn't want the child.

I think we live in an extremely immature culture. We get old but we don't mature to the point where we are making real good, clear choices about our lives, especially women. I have studied abortion cross-culturally, and in more indigenous cultures, women go through a complex decision-making process before deciding whether or not to have a child. What is the yield, what kind of sicknesses are there in my community? If I bring a child in, are we going to be able to nurture it properly? The decision is made on a mature assessment of resources. If an abortion is decided upon, it is because having a child would be a drain on the community at that time, rather than giving to it. It's not out of guilt, or not wanting anybody else to find out, or things like that. I think it's possible to feel really good about a decision like that, even though it is painful. It would be painful for me to have one, even though I would approach it in that way. There isn't enough of me to raise another child.

# "Everytime I had sex I got pregnant"

*Celia is now in her mid-thirties, married for the second time, with a professional career. At the time of the interview she is five months pregnant with her second child. She has a ten-year-old son.*

•

The first time I had an abortion was when I was about fifteen and a half. My periods weren't regular, and I didn't really have information about pregnancy and birth control. I may have been given the information, but it didn't sink in. We had that little talk at about fifth grade, but neither my mom or no one else spoke to me formally. So when I missed my period I didn't really think much about it. I had a regular boyfriend, and his mom and dad worked in the afternoon and evening and we would hang out at his house a lot. I was having sex, and I had no conception of . . . of conceiving. By the time I really thought about what was happening and went to a local clinic I was so far along that it was a matter of days before it would be too late. They were saying, "You have to go tell your parents right now and you have to decide what to do; otherwise you're going to have this baby."

At the time I don't think I was really in touch with any feelings, I was just like a robot. I felt like I was a little girl and the big people were in charge of me and they were telling me what I needed to do. When I told my folks, they said, "Yeah, you have to have this abortion." And I said, Okay, I'll have this abortion. When my mom and dad were talking to this person about the procedure, about the saline, I was just kind of sitting there. There was really no permission for me to have any feelings, so I just sat there and took in the information. When the woman said, "Let's talk about birth control," my dad said, "She's not going to do it anymore," and I said, "Yeah, I'm not going to do it anymore." And so right there I got the message ingrained that it's not okay to have sex; you're not supposed to do it.

My folks were very distant from me. They didn't give me any permission to feel and didn't create any space, at least with me, to express what they were feeling. About a year ago when I was doing some deep body work, I kind of relived that whole experience. I didn't realize until then that they basically dumped me off at the hospital; I was by myself. I don't think they could handle it. See, I had to have a saline, which means that they extract a certain amount of the amniotic fluid and replace it with saline, which put me into contractions, which put me into labor. Sure, I knew the words contraction and labor, I knew the baby was going to come out, but I had no idea what that meant.

When the contractions started coming, it was so painful and I was so scared, I just remember biting onto that thing they give you. I was in a big room and there were other people in there, I imagine in different stages of having the same thing happen—I didn't exactly talk to anybody, they had a curtain around me. They'd come in and check on me, and I was just scared and trying to be quiet and keep it all inside. And then I remember them rolling me off and I'm sure they doped me up. I can't really think of what was going on. I remember that when the baby did come out, some nurses were making faces, of disgust or whatever. I remember looking at *them*—I was too terrified to look myself.

When I did the deep body work, the first thing that came up was the intense feelings of abandonment at just being dumped off at the hospital. Then I was reliving the pain—the needle going in and pulling out the fluid—with someone there comforting me and giving me permission to feel how scary it was, and I found myself saying, "I want my baby, don't take my baby."

My dad said that my boyfriend couldn't come over anymore. He didn't say I couldn't see him anymore, but he definitely didn't want him at the house. And nobody talked about the abortion; we never talked about it again.

About a year later I got pregnant again. This time I didn't have any intercourse. I had no idea that just during foreplay you could get pregnant. My dad had said I wasn't going to have sex, so I tried not to have sex, and to me that meant intercourse, because I thought that was how you got pregnant. I knew I was pregnant that time really fast. But by this time it was like, Okay, you get pregnant, you get abortions. That's how you deal with it. Of course the guy I was with was totally freaked out and saying there was no way he could have gotten me pregnant, because he didn't understand the concept either.

This time I got the car and told my mom I was going shopping with a friend, and with the friend I went to this clinic. I had gone into this room and put the gown on and was sitting there waiting, but then it was time to get the car back. I had to take the gown off, take the car back, and somehow talk my way into being able to go somewhere else with my friend. Then my friend got her car and drove me back. I barely even remember; all I knew was that this was how I was supposed to do it. But I look back and it seems so bizarre—you know, I'm going shopping, I'm just going to go get an abortion.

After the abortion, my friend drove me home and I just said "hi" and went back into my room and sat there by myself. But see, I was molested when I was a kid, too, and I think I had learned early on that whole numbing response, tuning things out and detaching. It was just like . . . okay, well, whatever you guys have to do to me. This was just part of what my life was all about. I had no concept of having a choice, or of saying "no," or "I have a right," or "I have these needs," or "I have these feelings," or any of that. It's taken me a long time to have a sense of being in tune with my body and being able to ask for what I want. With being molested, before I even had a chance to know what my body was like and what it needed and how to be in tune with it, somebody else came in there and was directing my body and my energy, and so I was robbed of that ability. So I just knew that you kind of numb out, that's what I knew.

Actually I did get pregnant two more times. I mean, I always tried not to have sex. Since I'd been molested, I did have a sexual urge or drive, and of course I've always masturbated. One time I was teaching my sister and my dad came in and just flipped out and was so mad. I got in a lot of trouble. Anyway, it was almost like I had this relationship to masturbation and I would have orgasms, but I had no idea what was really happening. I didn't really make a connection to sex with guys.

After I got pregnant the second time I totally avoided relationships. Then in college I had a boyfriend that I was totally in love with and my dad thought he was the greatest. He wasn't pushy about sex at all, and I just told him that I didn't want to have sex with him. We must have been together for a whole year and just never had sex. Then I realized I wasn't in love with him, so I broke up with him. That was in junior college, so that was two years; then I didn't go out with anybody at all during my third and fourth years.

Then I met the man who became my son's father, and it was almost like I felt, Oh well, here's someone, I should just take someone. I should just be glad to have anybody. He wasn't that exciting or that interesting, but he was there and I hadn't had anybody for a long time. We started living together and I remember working with this older black woman, who was really angry—I'm sure she had her reasons. But she didn't trust men at all, and she started saying to me that I shouldn't just live with this man. If I was going to live with him I should make him marry me, and then of course there were my parents;

we were pretending we weren't living together. Again, I was still this little girl that didn't know what I wanted. It was like my energy had stopped and I had no control of my life really. So I felt like I should get married.

By that time I had gotten a diaphragm but I still got pregnant before we were going to get married and of course it was like: you're not supposed to get pregnant before you're going to get married—you have to get rid of this child, and then you go through your wedding and have your marriage. By that time I was an expert on getting abortions. My husband was addicted to marijuana, and he wasn't really that involved. I just remember going through the motions, and doing it one more time. And I think I was using the diaphragm correctly, to the best of my knowledge at the time. At that point I was consciously trying to use birth control. But it's almost been like this theme, that I've avoided having sex, and every time I had sex I got pregnant. It was like I had no control over my body.

I kind of went through this crisis then. I had gotten my bachelor's degree in psychology, and what can you do with that? I started a master's program, and got discouraged with that. I thought I was going to do a teaching credential program, and did about a semester, and didn't want to do that. So what else do you do?—You have a baby. At that time I was a nanny to an eight-month-old and a two-year-old, so I was kind of living that lifestyle anyway, so I thought, well, I may as well have a kid. It wasn't exactly the best circumstances to have a kid, but it was almost like I had decided on my own, really, basically without my husband, that I was going to have a kid. I've always joked that it was like immaculate conception—the second I said I was going to have a kid I was pregnant, boom. But it was just a wonderful pregnancy and an incredible birth, and my son and I have been bonded ever since.

Then one more time, after his father finally left, I was with this really young man. He moved in and was real attentive and loving, but then he just kind of got blown away. He was only nineteen, and suddenly realized, wait a minute, I can't be doing all this. We were using the diaphragm too, and I got pregnant. This time I had more awareness and I went to this person who did some body work, and I went to a psychic counselor. I had my friend come in with me during the abortion and help me breathe and talk about it and say how I was feeling when it was happening. It was almost like a healing thing—a conscious abortion. It felt really complete and really different.

# "I was officially and formally declared immoral"

*Donna was in her late thirties at the time of our interview. Like many birth mothers, she has remained unmarried and childless, and has lived with a great deal of pain and grief. Unlike many, though, her pain has been related less to relinquishing her child and more to the shame with which she felt branded for being sexual and becoming pregnant. She currently works as an educator and counselor for women in crisis.*

•

I grew up in Nevada, in a town which was very small at that time. My parents ripped us away from Los Angeles and moved us when my brother and sister and I were all adolescents. I had two alcoholic parents, so I come from a pretty wobbly family, especially with this whole disruption of being moved to the middle of nowhere. It was a real chaotic time, and none of us ever did too well.

When I was sixteen, I managed to get pregnant. I was a junior in high school and my boyfriend had already graduated. He had no plans and no options and was either drafted or joined the army, as many small-town boys do. This was 1969 and the Vietnam War was in full force. At his going-away escapade, I got pregnant. I was trained by the experts in denial, so I didn't know I was pregnant for at least two months. The thought must have been seeping around the back of me some-where because I can remember, I guess as most women do, waiting for my period. Every time you go to the bathroom pulling down your panties, hoping, hoping, hoping there's blood—for weeks on end. And it didn't happen.

I was devastated. It was just horrible for me. I didn't know what to do. I had no one I could discuss it with—certainly no one in my family. My sister was out of the house by then; my parents were completely inaccessible. As far as I knew, I was the only girl in my high school who even had sex. So I was stuck and I didn't know what to do.

My boyfriend came back to town at the end of basic training and I told him. He was so dear and so sweet, I love him to this day. He wanted to get married, but I said no. I was only sixteen, after all, and he was in the army. I must have been further along than two months. He was slightly more resource-ful than I and abortion didn't even come up as an option; like, could we somehow get enough money and get someone? I can't even imagine how grown-up people with money got abortions in in our city. I don't know if they were possible then, but they sure weren't for teenagers with no money. An option he offered was to have his parents raise the child. But I didn't want to do that either.

He was only home for about a week before he got shipped off to Fort Ord, in preparation to go to Vietnam. We didn't resolve anything before he left and there I was—still pregnant, still in high school, with nobody to talk to. I just sort of shut down again and didn't do anything—didn't do *anything*. I did try to abort myself. I remember doing tremendous jumping, leaping, throwing about of my body. I'd heard of coat hangers, and I thought, What the hell do you *do* with a coat hanger? I didn't know physiology; I didn't know exactly what a uterus looked like. I remember one day taking the coat hanger out of the closet and dismantling it and thinking, Okay, I'm going to shove this thing inside me, but then thinking, I can't, this is horrible. I didn't know what it would do anyway.

After a few weeks of leaping and jumping and hot baths, it was clear that nothing was going to budge, so I just sort of let it go. I would freak out and try to do things, and then my denial would kick back in and I'd pretend nothing was wrong. All the while going to high school and trying to be normal and feeling *so* different. I know there was terror in my heart—I'll be found out, everyone will hate me—tremendous shame.

So the months went by and finally one day my PE teacher said to me after class: "Donna, are you pregnant?" I said, "Well . . . sputter, sputter . . . yeah, I am." She said, "Well, you know, you look it. So I think you must be fairly far along." I said, "Yeah, probably." She said, "You know I have to report you to the administration and you'll probably get kicked out of school." This was May, maybe. I said, "One more month, come on." But I was maybe five months pregnant. She said, "I can't do it. I would if I could, but it's too obvious." She said, "What about at home, do your parents know?" I told her no. She said, "Well, you're going to have to talk to your parents. You're going to get kicked out of school; you're pregnant." And that was the end of her helping me.

So that night my father was out of town on a business trip and I knew I had to tell my mother *that* night—as if she didn't know. So before dinner, we were sitting there together reading the paper; my heart was pounding and I was thinking, I have to, I have to, I have to, but I didn't. Somehow after we had finished cleaning up, I squeaked out, "We have to talk." It was the hardest thing I've ever done. I'm not completely sure why, except our family motto is, "If you can't say anything nice, don't say anything at all." And this was not nice.

I think I said, "Well, you probably know that I'm pregnant." She said she had suspected it or something. I said, "So what's happening is that I'm being kicked out of school." That was basically what I felt I had to tell her, that I was kicked out of school—not that I was pregnant, but that I was kicked out of school because I was pregnant. She said, "Oh, well, what shall we do? How shall we tell Dad?" I said, "I don't know."

And she said she would tell him and I said "Fine." So we made these tentative plans. We probably spent no more than fifteen minutes talking about the whole thing. She talked to our local family doctor about who I should see. Here I am five or six months pregnant, no prenatal care obviously, this teenager starving herself trying not to look pregnant, wearing girdles and stuff. It was determined that I should seek medical attention in the the city thirty miles away, so as to avoid as much local contact and *shame* as possible. In such a small town it's not likely that *anybody* who knew us didn't know within twenty-four hours.

So somehow Mom and I sort of negotiated what we would do, which was basically nothing. She did say, "How come you didn't get an abortion?" I said, "How could I?" She said, "Your friend, Mrs. Anderson, doesn't she know about these things?" I said, "I don't know, I didn't ask her." So Mom's basic thing was that I should have taken care of it myself and now she'd do what she could, but I should have taken care of it—a high school child in a small town.

I did get kicked out of school, but the home teacher came every two or three days to finish out the term. And I went to the prom. I think it was an oversight—they must have forgotten to expressly forbid me to. My boyfriend was back on leave, so he wore his military uniform and I wore a straight-fitted dress with my tummy just sticking out. It was pretty wonderful. That was the saving grace—I had a little fun. Our friends were happy to double-date with us, and it was fun, we looked wonderful.

In the course of going for my prenatal care, we also started going to the welfare department to talk about adoption. Unlike a lot of teenage birth mothers, I never felt like I was forced or coerced into anything—it was my choice. When it finally became real to me that I was pregnant and that I would in fact have a baby, I didn't have any doubt that I would have to place it for adoption. Because I had to get out of this little town and I had to get out of my family, and I knew that. The only way to save my life was to get out of there. I couldn't as a teenage mother with a baby, and that was why I did it—I had to get away. I could have gotten married. I could have had my in-laws raise the baby. I had options, and I chose what I thought was the best one for my child and me. I didn't think the in-laws would be good parents. They were old, like my parents, and they were alcoholic, too. My child has four alcoholic grandparents. I'm so scared for him.

We'd go to the welfare place and they were really . . . oh, God, I hated them. This was the situation where my mother expressed the most shame and embarrassment. They had all their social services in one place; I think even entering welfare freaked my mother out. Before I agreed to anything or signed anything they were really nice to me. But that was only for the first couple of visits and after that they were really condescending and rude. Basically all they wanted to know was, What color is this baby going to be? What race is this baby, and are you in good health? That's pretty much all they cared about. I thought, Well, lucky you, you're getting a one hundred percent Caucasian baby, yippee skippee, you know? And I was . . . I was a little bitter. Even then I knew what was going on, that they were just using me, that they wanted my baby; they certainly didn't want me. And they never *pretended,* they never even suggested that they were offering me any kind of counseling or support or information. You got a baby you want to get rid of, we'll take it, period, end of discussion. So every time we'd go over for my medical, we'd check in with my "worker" and say, Yes, everything is fine, and yes, I still want to give up the baby. A creepy routine.

Summer was kind of fun. It was the closest I ever was to my father. He's very distant—pretty typical of a man of his generation; no emotions. But he was really nice to me that summer that I was pregnant. Unlike my mother, who was a total bitch, as she always has been and always will be. We made homemade ice cream together almost every week and he strung up the hammock for me in the back. My mother continued to be ashamed. She would always ask me if I didn't want to wear a wedding ring when we went over to the city. My brother was livid at me, saying that he couldn't bring anyone home because they would see me and he was so embarrassed.

I did focus in on the baby and spoke internally to it, telling it what was going to happen and that it was the best thing. I really connected—I think I tried not to, but I couldn't help it, I couldn't help it at all. I remember kind of playing with him. When they kick and move, you can kind of push back in, which was kind of fun, because he would react. I could interact with him, in and out, so that was okay. But I realize now that I did withhold some of what I could have done, and it was the pain of knowing that it would have to end.

I kind of remember how labor went. I had to drive the thirty miles—with Mom. Here I was, I'm now seventeen, and I was home and my water burst. It was pretty freaky because nobody, not even the doctors, had told me about labor—how to predict when it was beginning, what it was like, nothing. So I called my mom at work and told her I thought I was starting labor and what should I do? She didn't say she'd come home; she just stayed at work and told me to call the doctor.

As my mom and I were driving down the highway toward the hospital, she said, "Well, I suppose you know they'll shave you." I kind of looked blank. "Shave me?" "Yeah, they shave you 'down there,' and they'll give you an enema." It was almost taunting and malicious, not like, "Well, dear, prepare yourself for the worst." Those were her only hints on what happens in labor.

In the labor room, my mom was there some, but she was mostly not there. It hurt like hell, and I felt like I was ignored. I was the only person in this labor room; the nurses would come in every ten or fifteen minutes. I was all alone and it was kind of grey and it was cold. I felt like it was appropriate punishment—I deserved all the punishment I was getting and this was more of the same. Finally, the baby arrived. In the delivery room, they were pretty neat to me. I watched the birth in the mirror, and I liked that. They did some of the tests and stuff there and I kind of watched, but they didn't offer him to me. They didn't let me touch him. Then they took him away and that was it; I never saw him again, never touched him, never got to see him when I was not drugged.

They stitched me up and wheeled me off to a room by myself, where I fainted and threw up. It was just really sad and grim. That's all I remember really is emotional pain—this incredible sorrow, and that I deserved all this pain. I was so empty and lost. Then I came home and those guys were walking on the moon. I always kind of equate them in my mind, because it was just a couple of days later. I couldn't walk stairs, so I had the guest room downstairs. Everyone else was in the next room watching TV twenty-four hours a day and I was in there all alone with a tight bra on; my breasts were all full of milk. My breasts hurt, my crotch hurt, my heart hurt, my brain was empty.

The hardest part was when, five or six days after the birth, two women in navy blue suits came to the house with the final adoption papers. My mom was at work and I called her—or anyway she appeared. I was in my nightgown and bathrobe and there were two ladies in navy blue suits and my mother. I think my mother was sitting next to me, but not touching me, just adjacent to me. I was sobbing. I was sobbing, and this was just so symbolic of the tremendous pain of it all. I will never forget that feeling—so vulnerable and so small. Our house had really high ceilings and when I picture it I see this tiny little person in her nightgown, not dressed, with these fully clothed, powerful people sitting around me. And I was sobbing so hard I could hardly hold the pen to sign the papers. And I'm glad. I hope they all got the message that this was no small thing. I don't know—I hope it made them uncomfortable at the very least. When I look at my relinquishment paper now, I see my little childish teenager signature, all round. And that was that, that was the absolute end, over, it was done. It was never discussed in my family ever again, ever, not once, until I brought it up in recent times.

My mom went back to work, I went back to bed, and the women in the blue suits went back to the welfare office, and that was the absolute end as far as they were concerned. Of course, it wasn't the end of it for me by any means; it was the beginning. But I didn't know it at the time. What I do know now is that within about six weeks I started taking drugs, and I didn't stop for ten years. He was born in July, and before school even started I was taking LSD, smoking dope—taking drugs all the time. I stayed stoned for the next ten years. I had so much pain, and even with all my mother's good training, I couldn't summon up enough denial to make it all go away. So the drugs helped it to go away. It's been a long process to get out of it—it still hurts. I think the hardest part about it then— and they do adoptions differently now—was: You'll forget, everyone will forget, we will forget this, this didn't happen. So I thought that was right. I thought that was true. I had no idea that you can't just make things go away by willpower. I think that's the element that made it last so long.

My mother said to me about three or four years ago, "What makes you think I care about your child?" I was harping on how important the search for him and the work of uncovering the pain and working with it were. I said, "This is a person, this is a person that matters, even though I don't know him." What makes you think I care about your child?! She doesn't *know* that we're talking about her grandchild—it doesn't sink in, she doesn't even know what's going on somehow. This is her *first* grandchild.

I never felt guilty or that I'd done the wrong thing with the adoption. I was made to feel guilty for having had sex and having gotten pregnant. That was absolutely the sin, and I've carried that guilt all along. But I never felt guilty about relinquishing him. And all along I told him that this was absolutely the best thing for him—if he knew the options, he'd agree. The people who could be in your world are horrid; whatever you get will be better than the families that have this legitimate claim. So I always felt like he must somehow know that I was making the best decision, that that's what this was about.

I didn't know that I could have seen him or held him. If I had known that I had some rights, that I wasn't a total scarlet woman, I could have held my baby, I could have gone to the nursery, I could even have nursed him. I mean, I could have interacted with my baby—I had every right to. But I didn't know that. Now I send him conscious thoughts of love, real formally, as often as it comes to mind. So I'm still communicating with him in that same way, because it's all I can do. I can't seem to find him, so I just send it out there and hope he'll receive it.

I went back to high school for my senior year. In home economics class we all had to take this test called, "The Betty Crocker Homemaker of Tomorrow" Search. It actually was a search for a scholarship. So my home ec teacher was really pleased to inform me that I'd gotten the highest grade in school in this Betty Crocker test, and about a week later she came back and was just beside herself. She told me, "You have gotten the highest score in the entire state of Nevada and you won the scholarship. You *are* the Betty Crocker Homemaker of Tomorrow." It was a two-thousand dollar scholarship and a piece of jewelry.

Well, I was pretty pleased. But then a few days after her telling me, I was called into the guidance counselor's office, and this school counselor said to me, "Did you have a baby this summer?" I said, "Yeah, I did." She said, "Thank you very much. You can go back to class now." A few days after that, my home ec teacher said to me, "Well, this is very disappointing, but I have to tell you that you are being denied the scholarship. We are requested by Betty Crocker to sign an affidavit of morality for the prize winners, and we find that we cannot verify you as being a moral person, so I'm very sorry, you won't get the scholarship. But you do get the necklace."

So I was officially and formally declared immoral and that . . . God . . . that just really confirmed it for me, that what my mother was telling me was right—I was an absolute fallen woman, and I was pretty much good for nothing because I was so bad morally. And not because I relinquished a child for adoption, but because I was pregnant, because I had had sex. It seems like most of the pain of the women I have worked with was about the relinquishment. Most of mine was about how I got there in the first place. And I think that's part of my not getting married and not having a more conventional life. I'm immoral, I'm a bad woman, I'm lucky to get anything. I never felt like I deserved a nice husband and house and children. If they had not taken that scholarship away from me, it might have allowed me to go on with my life, like they said I could and would. If they had said, Just put this behind you and go on with your life—but there was no way they were going to let me. They wanted to punish me.

Also, I got the weirdest messages about sexuality in my family. Like, to be a good woman you should be very sexual. We had *Playboy* magazine on the coffee table—I had grown up looking at *Playboy*. How women should be is sexy and available, on the one hand. And then this real uptight, fussy, critical, condemning attitude about being nice and polite and doing the right thing. It was very confusing. But I think what won out was that the best I could do was be sexual—it was my best shot at being a woman. So I said, "Okay, I'll be sexual." And I got a good payback. I got this wonderful boyfriend who hugged me and kissed me and just adored me. I got . . . love. It was worth it, in a way.

After my son was born, I went on the Pill and took it incredibly diligently for ten or eleven years. I never made a mistake, never flubbed up—I took it absolutely the right way. Then, of course, I began reading about how it might be adversely affecting my health, but I was so paranoid about getting pregnant, so absolutely terrified. Most of this time that I was on the Pill I was in a steady relationship with someone, so I examined and started using other methods of contraception, but I was really fearful and cautious. I began to use the rhythm method more and more, where I would just refuse to have sex when I felt like I was fertile, even when I was using other methods. I felt like that was safer, and I had this tremendous fear of pregnancy, bordering on phobia.

I used to see pregnant women and think, How can they go out in public like that, aren't they ashamed, don't people throw rocks at them? I couldn't comprehend how anyone could get pregnant. It didn't make any sense to me. This was just pure emotion—it's bad, it's fearful, you'll be hurt. I couldn't even imagine how women could proudly walk around being pregnant, when to me it was the most shameful, mortifying, dangerous thing you could do. And I've managed to keep this attitude. I'm thirty-eight now and almost past questioning it. I won't have any kids. I've got the one who's out there in the universe somewhere, and that's it.

I can sort of hear some part of me saying to him—because I think most of us fantasize about knowing this person again—some deep, dark part wants to say, "You meant so much to me that I couldn't have any others." Somehow that takes away some of my guilt. I think it's something about knowing we will reconnect or want to reconnect and being able to say, "If I couldn't keep you, I couldn't keep anybody." There's such tremendous guilt around that. How do you say to someone, "Please don't feel abandoned or rejected; it didn't have anything to do with you"?

*p.192*   Anne Ardillo,
         *Who Came First #1* (©1990, graphite, 33" x 26");
         *Who Came First #2* (©1990, graphite, 26" x 19");
         *Who Came First #3* (©1990, graphite, 26" x 19");
         *Who Came First #5* (©1990, graphite, 48" x 36")

*p.193*   Lois Llewellyn, *Scarlet Letter of the 1990s*
         (©1990, film collage Kodalith, 8"x9")

*p.194*   Barbara Milman, *No Choice*
         (©1990, oil/acrylic on canvas, 37"x48")

*p.195*   Barbara Milman, *Children Having Children*
         (©1990, oil/acrylic on canvas, 37"x48")

*p.196*   Bernice Kussoy, RWC, *If the Shoe Was on the Other Foot*
         (©1990, welded steel)

*p.197*   Roberta June White, *Not Gravid*
         (©1989, 24"x29")

*p.198*   Sheila Pitt, *Broodmare*
         (©1990, woodcut/monoprint)
*Artist's Statement:* In the print *Broodmare*, a woman is depicted as
an animal, giving birth. I often use the horse metaphor to illustrate
my views about attitudes toward women, who are thought of as
breeding animals. This view treats woman as though she is still a
child herself, and only others can decide what is right.

---

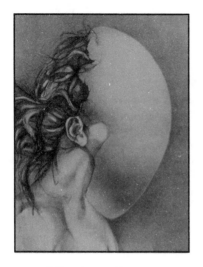

*Who Came First #1*

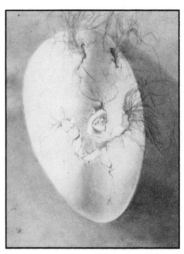

*Who Came First #2*

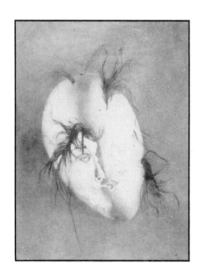

*Who Came First #3*

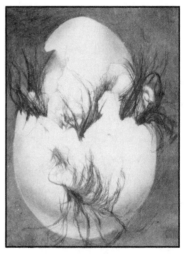

*Who Came First #5*

*Scarlet Letter of the 1990s*

*No Choice*

*Children Having Children*

195

*If the Shoe Was on the Other Foot*

*Not Gravid*

*Broodmare*

# "I should have danced all night"

*Jenna is about forty years old at the time of the interview, and has been in recovery from alcoholism for two years. She is working on a license as a Marriage, Family, and Child Counselor. She gave a daughter up for adoption twenty-one years ago, when she was a college student. In her thirties, while her alcoholism was still rampant, she had two abortions.*

•

It was the summer of love. I was nineteen, in college in the Midwest. I was working on some idea of a rhythm method, so I thought that I wouldn't get pregnant, but I did. I tried to get an abortion, but this was twenty-one years ago, so it was really hard to find out where you could get one.

I managed to find one abortionist in Cleveland and went by myself; it was really scary. He put me on a table; I had never been examined before. Then he left the room, leaving me lying there for a long time; it was really weird. When he came back he said he couldn't do it because I had some kind of infection. I felt like he was discriminating because of my youth and insecurity, and because I was by myself.

So then I went home, and it was Thanksgiving. I told my parents and they had the boy's parents (I was going steady with this boy) come down and they all talked about it. I had already decided that I wanted an abortion or to give the child up. It was decided that my father and I would fly to Puerto Rico. My father and I didn't talk, we had a very hard relationship. I hated him—he was an alcoholic. So my father and I did our first father and daughter thing, which was to get on a plane and fly to Puerto Rico for an abortion. But in this hospital the doctor said, "She's too far along, we'd have to do a caesarean cut, she'd have to stay here for a couple of months." The place looked really creepy and dirty, so we just left.

I went back to college, and my father went home. When I talked to my mother, she said I had to get married. I said, "No, I'll give the baby up for adoption." I didn't want to get married, I didn't want to *have* to get married. I wanted to finish school, and it just didn't seem right. I left school at the end of the quarter, making up some lie to everyone about my family running out of money or something. Then we went around to find a place for me to stay, like a home for unwed mothers. My boyfriend's parents had a lot of connections in New York City. The first place we went was terrible; it was one of those Florence Crittenden homes, I guess. The woman was just all weepy, saying, "Oh you poor dear." In the dining room they were making baskets or some kind of garbage, and all the girls there were still in bed. It was really depressing, horrible.

We didn't know what to do, whether I should get an apartment by myself, or where we were going to squirrel me away. Then we went to this other home which was just wonderful. It was a New York brownstone, and the woman who ran it was really nice, down to earth and matter-of-fact. Over the fireplace there was a statue of this pregnant girl, which said, "I should have danced all night." I liked that, and it was all college girls like myself, and they had healthy food. So I went there. There were counseling groups, but we never really worked through anything that I can remember. Maybe I was just so totally shut down. I think we were probably all pretty shut down.

The adoption was handled through a private agency in New York. The social worker, I remember, kept saying, "It's your choice." I felt like, Bullshit, this isn't my choice. I don't want to get married, and I can't have a child by myself . . . what would I do? And the shame involved, and my parents . . . . The only time my father ever cried was when he found out I was pregnant; he was so upset. It wasn't about, Oh my daughter will be going through pain. It was more about what people would say. And then he stopped crying and said, "Oh well, it happens in the best of families."

The birth . . . oh . . . yuck . . . it's funny—I didn't expect to cry like this. Well, at three or four in the morning I started having the pains, and some sort of plug came out. So I went down and told Mrs. Marlowe and she had this other woman go with me and we walked down Lexington Avenue, a couple of big city blocks, to the hospital. I was in a lot of pain, and I remember just being a total wimp. [Crying] But I was by myself and it was really scary. They acted like I was a real irritation. I kept begging for drugs or something for this pain you know. They finally gave me something, and I remember crawling up the sides of the crib they had me in . . . this bed was like a crib.

When I had the baby I was out of it and I don't really remember. I remember them saying "push" and I was trying. I don't have much memory at all of the actual birth. It was like I wasn't there. I don't think it was a real long labor.

My plan was that I wasn't going to get attached to her. I would just have the baby and give her up and that was my decision and I wouldn't have anything to do with her. But after it happened I started thinking, she's in there all alone, she really needs some . . . she needs . . . she needs her mom. [Crying] So I fed her all the time I was there. And I'm glad I did, because I don't think she should have been left alone, you know? I just . . . it didn't seem right. So that was about a week I was in this ward. The nurses were such bitches, oh they were so rude. I guess it was that we were unwed mothers, or because I was in the ward with all the poor people. I remember I had infected stitches, and I was in a lot of pain. The nurse was nasty and shrill with me until she finally looked at me and could see it was all infected.

When it was time to go home, I went to my boyfriend's parents. I was so angry with him, because he got to stay at school, he got to totally *not* experience this. I got letters from him while I was in the home. He was in his fraternity and life went on. It was this big secret, and I was squirreled away with the shame, having the shameful results. He came to visit me at the home and he wouldn't walk out on the street with me because he was embarrassed, or he was afraid someone might see us. His parents took over for him completely. They took me out to lunch, his mom made me clothes. They were there for me one hundred percent.

I was in so much pain, and he didn't even want to hear about it. And then after the birth he wanted to suck my breasts, because there was milk in them. I was so mad I broke off with him. I still loved him, and I was hurt for a long time after that. I just always thought that we would get married someday, that kept me going through the whole thing.

I knew after the baby was born I wanted to keep her and I knew I couldn't. I loved her, it wasn't that I didn't love her. I loved her and I wanted her to have a life. I found out about the parents and they sounded very nice. They had already adopted a daughter. I thought that sounded good, because they'd already been through the process, they knew what they wanted and had experience. That made me feel good. They just sounded like a nice couple with culture and all the best things, you know, all the nice things.

I had to go back to the hospital and sign the papers. And since she had had thrush, I wanted to see her. They put us in a room, and she looked so cute [tears], just really bright-eyed. She looked just like me, like my side of the family. I just spent some time with her, and it was really hard. I remember standing by the window overlooking New York City, and I thought about jumping. It was just the drama, the histrionics of it, just thinking of the sadness, the pain. I mean I didn't seriously entertain it, it was just in my mind, like, what do you do here, you know? Well, you just go on and sign the papers and go through with it. But part of me just wanted to jump, in my mind.

I don't know what I did in that room with her. Now I would do the good-byes, I *know* stuff now. But at nineteen what did I know? Did I talk to her, was I just there with her? I have no idea, I don't know what happened. I just knew that she was okay. I remember the little pajama suit she had on, thinking it was used, it was faded and washed. You could tell she was in transition, she was going to go from me to her parents. Now, in retrospect, I think of all that time she was in the hospital—it was a couple of weeks—and I think, God, I hope she's not borderline, I hope she had that connection, I hope it was soon enough, I hope things are okay for her.

She was born in June, so I had the summer before school started again. I was depressed, and on every TV show, every commercial, there were babies everywhere; baby food, diapers, mothers with children. Mothers with children were just dropping out of the sky in my face. It was really painful for me. Who knows, though, I didn't feel anything in those days. I drank a lot, I was an alcoholic. But thank God I didn't drink while I was pregnant, that my baby didn't drink with me. At least I wasn't out of control with the drinking then.

I did entertain those fantasies of keeping her. Then I'd say, No, let's be reasonable, let's do the right thing. But I never let go of her, and I thought when she was eighteen she'd probably want to get in touch, and I went through all the paper work with the hospital in New York. Then I found out it was twenty-one, so I waited 'til this year, twenty-one, and I registered with the New York state adoption agency and I got in touch with the father. After all these years I received a very nice letter from him, saying that he had been wondering about it too, he'd just recently gotten married. His young wife's sister is the age of the daughter, right? And he was wondering what his daughter would be like. It showed he had at least thought about it some, and that took away some of the anger I'd held at him, I kind of lightened up toward him.

I talked to this social worker in New York, and she was very short with me, she said: "Well, they don't usually get in touch, a lot of them don't." I was surprised because I thought she'd have a natural curiosity and when she turned twenty-one she'd just go. It's on file, it's all ready to go. If she puts forth, it's there, if her parents agree. So I was excited, and now I'm kind of sad again. I have to just let that go and realize that maybe she'll never want to get in touch with me or maybe it's just not the time. Maybe she's not even alive and I'll never know. And who knows what she's gone through, God knows, maybe she was put with alcoholic parents. Nobody knew at that time. Who knows what kind of shit she grew up with, or *abuse* . . . ahh . . . just don't know.

There's part of me that would be afraid to meet her. What if I didn't like her or she didn't like me? I am grateful to be in recovery, with all my training and knowledge that I've gotten. So I feel I'm in a good space, I can handle anything: bring her on, I can deal with her. I've seen so many TV programs, too, that showed children reuniting with their parents that had given them up for adoption. And there was anger there, you could see it. It's been many years since I saw this, but I remember watching it and thinking, Those kids are pissed off, they're mad. It was nice the first couple of minutes, but then you could just see it, boom, the anger came out: You gave me up.

I could try to find out where she is, but I don't know if that would be the right thing. I think I want to make things up to her, I want to explain, say, Don't take it personally. If you've got abandonment issues, it was a loving thing. What's really difficult for me now is to see women having children without being married. At that time I just didn't have what it took to have a baby out of wedlock. Now I think, I could have just said, "Who cares what the world thinks." But then I see how I've been for the last 21 years, and I think she may have had a good break being with someone else. I never grew up, I was an alcoholic, I came from a really dysfunctional family. She might have gotten the break of her life. To trust, just to trust.

He was an engineer, who knows what was going on there; maybe they broke up quickly, maybe she never had a dad anyway.

My mom had had an abortion before I was born, which I hadn't known about. I had two older brothers, ten and eight years older than me, and then my mother had an abortion somewhere in there before I was born. It was back-room, she started hemorrhaging and had to go to the hospital. So I know that when I was born I wasn't wanted, but they made the best of it. I wonder if I somehow internalized something about not being wanted, acted out in giving up a baby, I don't know. I'm just wondering about my own birth process, what went on with my parents with my daughter's birth process, and the fact that I've never had any children since then and haven't wanted to.

I'm sure I have a lot of anger that I'm still working out, a lot of grief. A couple of years ago my therapist suggested that I might do some grieving around this. And it just struck me— grieving!? This was a loss, I had a loss? Whoa, I didn't even know it. [Crying] I couldn't talk about for so many years, *never, ever* did I talk about it. And then I'm sure later on I'd get maudlin and drunk and cry about it or something.

I couldn't remember her birthday—I didn't want to, I didn't want to know that date. Then after about fifteen years I wrote to the adoption agency because I wanted information again about the parents. Actually they wrote me with some little different details from the first time. And I wanted to know the date then. But I hadn't wanted to go through life with, Oh my God, it's June 12. I didn't want to go through the pain. I didn't name her either. I didn't think that was my place, that I had the right to give her a name, although now I sort of wish I had. Maybe I just didn't want to give a name to the pain.

I guess I feel some terrible guilt that I have impacted or affected a life in a totally irresponsible way, although I was as responsible as I could be with what little I had. I smoked, but I didn't know about that.

I was pregnant twice after that and had abortions. When I was twenty-four, I had gone to Europe for a year and was living with a guy. He went away for the summer and I went off the Pill, then he came back suddenly. We were using rubbers, but I got pregnant, just when we were coming to California. I was really grateful for the abortion. But it did bring up the feelings of the adoption, the shame and the secrecy involved, the feeling I was stupid and bad again, I was doing something wrong.

Then when I was thirty-eight . . . I don't know what that was. Probably I was just drunk and I wasn't careful. I used a diaphragm, but I got pregnant. Shortly thereafter I had a hysterectomy due to a large fibroid. So, now I can't have children. It's funny when I think about it: I would have had three children, I got pregnant three times. At the time of this abortion I was completely shut down, as far as my own body, what the process was, having any feelings of loss. I was probably at the very height of my rampant alcoholism at that time, because it was very shortly thereafter that I got sober.

I woke up today and I wasn't even thinking about our meeting. But I thought—abortions—is there something in there, does this qualify as a loss, is there something that I should be concerned about here? I've never dealt with it. I remember the one abortion was really horrible, it was just kind of obscene. I think I was aware that they were joking, they had the vacuum and were saying something like, "Well here comes another one . . . ." Just crass, unfeeling. I just felt really angry about the way it was, like some kind of conveyor belt. And the doctors were very disrespectful, ugh, just an awful feeling. I don't believe in abortion. I mean I do, but it's not a pleasant thing; it's a horrible, ugly thing.

I don't know what it's about that I didn't want to have another child. I can imagine how much I would love a child. If I had one, to think, Oh what you gave away . . . ahh. I couldn't love this child more, and I have another one out there.

Sometimes I wonder why I didn't get married. I had this whole fantasy of how it was supposed to be, though, that we would go through college and then we would get married.

There's a part of me too that feels like he didn't want to marry
. . . well, he *didn't* want to marry me. I don't know how I felt,
I was reacting from him. I felt that I wouldn't want him to
marry me if he *had* to, and I think there's a lot of pain around
that. So I wonder what's going on when we choose abortions
or having babies and giving them up, feeling, Oh I don't want
to put this guy to too much trouble, if he has to marry *me*. I've
had dreams that I'm getting married and the guy does not want
to get married. He's not even there; it's like I'm getting married
to nothing and nobody, who doesn't want to be there. It's these
feelings like, Who am I, I'm nobody to be married to.

# "What would I be doing now if I had a child in a wheelchair?"

*Jillian is in her early forties at the time of the interview, married, with one adolescent son and a professional career. She tells the story of an abortion she had a few years earlier when an amniocentesis revealed that the fetus had spina bifida.*

•

Gary and I had really planned on having only one child, when we decided it was time to have kids. I would say that he was very influential in that. I had been married previously, and I had actually been pregnant and had a stillbirth. At seven months the baby died, and I had to go through the birth. At that time . . . that was about 1966 or 1967 . . . none of the prenatal stuff or Lamaze was around. So that birth was something I had never really worked through until I went through this abortion. It was interesting to me to realize that there was so much left over.

At the time that I had the stillbirth, I was really dumb and naive. And I was super-woman. I had taught for a couple of years before I got pregnant, and I don't think I missed one day of work, that kind of thing. And I certainly wouldn't miss any fun. So here I was seven months pregnant, and I went out on a boat ride, on a speed boat—hitting the waves, bam, bam, bam. That was on a weekend, and then on the following Monday, I didn't feel anything. I went to the physician and they told me they couldn't hear a heartbeat, but we'd just give it some time. But you know, there never was a doctor that would acknowledge, "Oh no, that wouldn't do it"; there never was a doctor that would acknowledge that. And when the baby was born, the diagnosis was that at the time the respiratory system was forming, something went wrong, and basically the respiratory system just stopped forming. Well to me, it made a whole lot of sense. And I think I held onto that as being . . . that one of my stupid activities caused this baby to die.

But when that baby was born, was delivered, that was the end of it. We had moved, and no one in the new neighborhood knew that the baby was dead. So all that anyone in that neighborhood knew was that I had a baby, but it didn't live. If I'd stayed in the place where I was when that was diagnosed, I would have had that pity, you know, which I just didn't want at all. So I hadn't really dealt with it—the grieving process. And that's what I did in this one. The grieving process that we went through was very allowed and supported. I think that I did that for both of them then. Because at the time of the first baby it wasn't very acceptable, it was a sign that you weren't very strong. There was no debriefing afterwards, you just got over it. I don't think they even acknowledged the postpartum blues at that point, or anything, especially if you didn't have the baby.

When I got pregnant with Darren, our son, it was really very wellplanned. We had been married five years, I could quit work. I could experience the pregnancy without having to go to work every day, I could get the house ready and stuff. And after he was born, we acknowledged that it was a big job, and probably, ideally, every child should have two adults. So we were very content at that point with having only one child. When he got to be six, I guess we felt we'd been pretty successful, and we were still at an age where we could change that decision. I had used birth control pills during my early years, then had used an IUD. I had gone back to using a diaphragm and was getting tired of that and thinking I should do something permanent.

So all that transpired into thinking that we were still young enough to have another child, and that financially we could do it. But I was at an age, at thirty-eight, where there was a question mark. So we went into it feeling like we were very confident that we would have the amniocentesis—and we were thinking of the Down syndrome more than anything—and that we were willing to terminate the pregnancy, based on what the findings were.

I actually had several miscarriages and it took almost two years until we had a viable pregnancy. I felt good and was working. I got fairly good-sized before we did the amnio, and that was something that surprised me. Because I hadn't anticipated having to acknowledge the fact that I was pregnant before doing that. Later on I realized that was a really hard part of it, because people already knew, and then you had to give an explanation for what you did. I think a lot of the guilt came out there. I found myself wondering what other people thought, and that had not entered my consciousness before then, that that would be a consideration.

Some friends were pregnant at the same time, and that was exciting to find out. They hadn't planned it, and they were thinking about aborting. Then when we got together, they had decided to go through with it, so I was thinking, great, this must be just right. So we were all in the same time line for the amnio and all that. Then I got that call from the doctor saying, "We have a problem—it's not Down's syndrome, but you have a spina bifida baby." It was just like . . . oh, pain . . . I could hardly believe it. Then it really set in, this was a reality. I don't believe that I ever felt like I couldn't give the baby up, I can't remember feeling that. Because I really had gone into it so conditioned. But it was sad, it was very, very sad, and that part was hard. There were a lot of tears, and a lot of emotional working-through. We went to Stanford and had them explain everything. We took Darren. He was six, so he was old enough to know what was going on, that we were going to have another baby and all that. We didn't take him into the counseling session, but he knew what was going on.

I didn't share it with my family until the night before I went in to abort. I grew up in a very religious family and I was afraid that my mother would not be able to accept it. But somehow, I knew that if my daughter was in that situation I would at least want to know. So it was hard to make that call, and then I was just totally supported, and that was a wonderful feeling. There was total support from Gary's family also, at least if there wasn't, they did not give any indication. They were very concerned about my health, and gave us the strokes that we had a wonderful family and they recognized what we needed to do. That was the biggest issue—Could we take on a situation like this? And we had made the decision that we couldn't, prior to getting pregnant. We were both early in our careers. Gary hadn't been out of school that long even and we were still paying for that, thinking of buying a house, and we had put our son into private school because he just really was a very bright kid and we had that choice.

Part of the process was getting another ultrasound, which by that time gave a really clear picture. In spina bifida, the spine is separated. The spine just basically did not connect the lower part of the body. So what that meant in this case was that probably the paralysis would be very extensive—the child would never be able to control bowels, never be able to walk. There was also fluid on the brain. They were talking about draining that, but at that time I don't even think they were doing that *in utero*, where now they can do some of those corrections while the baby is growing. There were really no alternatives at that point, at least at Stanford there was nothing offered. They weren't saying, Oh we could do this, we could repair that.

I found myself lying there on the table while they were doing the ultrasound and seeing this live being right there—you could see the spine, you could see it move, you could see the head, everything—and just not being in reality. I'm sure it would be much harder for a person who had gone into this not having made the decision or maybe the pregnancy was not planned or, I don't know; I'm sure it could have been a lot harder for me than it was. The hardest part was to know that there was a fetus that was going to be, basically, terminated.

Then the clinical aspect of it—we had to make the decision of what *way* we were going to do it. Are you going to abort the baby by a natural process where you would actually go into labor and actually deliver? They like to have that done, because then they can do an autopsy and it can be, basically, the university's project. And the other way is that they go in and they crush, and then they just get the tissue; it's like a major D&C type operation, suction and all. I just could not . . . I don't know which one would be worse, but I could not even consider delivering the baby. I'm sure it was more to take care of me, psychologically. In the earlier pregnancy, as a twenty-two-year-old when I had the stillborn, they just let you wait until you went into labor, that's what I had to do. And you know, I never actually got to see that baby or anything, but I could just envision . . . of course, I probably *could* have seen it, but I just thought, Why put myself through it?

So I think this time I really took care of myself over somebody else—or over the being that was not going to live anyway. I can still clearly visualize the difference between those two things and the . . . you know, the crudeness of crushing. I still can really visualize that, a lot. I don't think of it—unless I talk about it. The process was actually then very methodical after that. Gary really stuck with me the whole time, which was certainly important. I can imagine how hard it would be if you were making that decision all by yourself because your partner didn't want the baby or you were too young to have the child and be responsible or you didn't want your parents to know, or whatever.

The process was to go in the day before and have my cervix stimulated with . . . it's like a little cigarette kind of, and it stimulated the cervix opening. I remember going in there and having the doctor say, "Now once we do this, it's not reversible, so this is the time you sign this life away." And then you kept this in all night and came back the next day and went into the procedure. By that time the cervix was opening and they could go in and do what they needed to do. I basically was just unconscious of what was going on, so I guess it was a general anesthetic—yeah, sure it was.

In dealing with it afterwards, I think the hardest thing was dealing with people, because I just felt really guilty about doing it. I didn't even know anyone that I was concerned wouldn't appreciate and respect my decision. But still, there was just an awful lot of guilt there. Part of it had to come from my very rigid Christian upbringing, that you don't have the right to take a life. The other part is just the mother in me. And I don't know if I was feeling more guilty about having a defective body that made this baby that couldn't live or whether I felt more guilty about making that decision.

But I didn't find myself dwelling on it. I'm really a very active person. I think the other hardest part was that I found myself making another decision and feeling most of the time that I wanted to stick with it. And that was that I didn't want to have another one, admitting that this was going to be my last try, because I wasn't willing to go through that again. And yet, you know when I was a kid, I probably would have had ten babies. If I'd been in a situation where I'd gotten myself married early—and I did, I got married at nineteen—but married to somebody who really wanted to have kids, I probably would have had ten. And so it's taken me a long time to get over the fact that there's not going to be another baby. Finally, I think I'm very content now.

I was really sure afterwards that I'd made the right decision and I think Gary was too. I fantasize, What would I be doing now if I had a child in a wheelchair? And there happens to be a very, very wonderful child that's just the same age ours would have been, and I watched her grow up. I don't even know her name, but I keep up with her through people in the school system. She's in the regular system right now and she has her own equipment, her own aide and stuff. And I think, Boy these parents have really been her advocate. But everything revolves around that child. I could not be doing what I'm doing, my family couldn't be doing what they're doing, all of that would have been different. So I don't feel at all like we made the wrong decision and I don't dwell on it or anything, but I guess the hardest part was knowing that I didn't want to go through it again and as a result that meant you just didn't get pregnant again—period. That's all there is to it.

# "I was simply incapable of making the decision"

*This is a self-written story. Sena, the author, is now in her mid-forties. She has been in recovery from her eating disorder for the past several years. She works as a educator and advocate for women while pursuing her own creative work.*

•

I was twenty-five or twenty-six years old, living alone in a studio apartment. I was a compulsive eater, and though I'd been going to a diet club and lost a few pounds, I still weighed probably 250 or more. I was in graduate school.

I had met a guy who was living with his dad and mom in an apartment across the driveway. Dan was a roofer, a beer drinker, a country music kind of guy. He loved Charlie Pride. He was sweet, with curly reddish hair, a mustache, a slight build. He was shy and kind. He probably treated me better than any man had until then, and perhaps than any man has since.

I liked him, but I didn't take him seriously. I didn't take any man seriously who was interested in me, cared about me. After all, what kind of man would be interested in me? Certainly not one that I could consider someone to take seriously. I was inhibited with sex, silent, passive. With the kind gentleness of this man I grew some. It still did not seem safe to let him know I liked it, really. My first response was always "no," and I had to be coaxed. But I was willing to be coaxed, though my attitude was often that I was doing him a great favor, that he was my small, needy boy that I had to take care of.

Dan had a five-year-old from a previous marriage who his ex-wife would not allow him to see. It was very painful to him. I think he was trying to earn enough money to take her to court.

I guess we'd been lovers for a couple of months when I missed my period. I don't even remember what kind of birth control we were using, if any. Becoming pregnant was not a reality to me in any sense, though I know a part of me wanted to become pregnant, to prove that in spite of my weight, I really was a woman. I kept thinking my period was coming, because I would cramp and spot. Finally I went for a pregnancy test, and when it came back positive, I was dumbfounded. Suddenly I, who loved babies, could not get a grasp on what it meant to be pregnant, on what babies were. I could not make it real. I thought I should go to the hospital nursery and look at the babies, to remember what they were. But I never did.

I don't know what I wanted or expected when I told Dan. I remember standing outside his apartment house in the evening and talking. I remember how closed off I was, angry and resentful and blaming. But it seems like I was that way even before he told me how he felt or what he wanted. He said that he already had one marriage all screwed up and one child he couldn't see. He didn't feel ready to take that on again. I know I didn't expect love, perhaps not even kindness. And he was kind, and gentle, and apologetic. And he probably would have helped me, however he could. He probably would have married me, if I had pushed it. But I cut him out. I didn't really see him much, if at all, during the time I was deciding what to do.

I remember thinking and writing that I didn't see how I could have a child and care for a child when I wasn't a woman yet myself. I meant that I hadn't had the chance to come to terms with myself as a woman, or even believe I was a real woman. I felt, somehow, that because I was obese, I gave up my rights as a woman. And the idea of my having a child seemed like a sham almost.

I felt so lost, so alone. I don't remember talking to friends, though perhaps I did some. I didn't have as many friends then, or use them in the same way that I do now. I talked to my male therapist. I called my sister. She was shocked when I told her I was considering an abortion and begged me not to do it, saying she would take the baby if I didn't want it. But I knew beyond the slightest shadow of a doubt that it was not in me to carry and give birth to a child and give it up. It was not really a matter of not wanting the child, not wanting a baby. My sister called back the next day and apologized. She had talked to her husband and realized that perhaps abortion would be the best decision for me.

I went to the doctor expecting to hear that I was too fat to have a baby, that we both would be endangered, and that I would have to have an abortion. But he said that, although it was not ideal, I seemed healthy and should be able to carry and deliver the baby without problems. But, if I wanted an abortion, he would perform one. That was a year or two before *Roe v. Wade*, and abortions were legal in California only on the advice of a psychiatrist or something like that, and were still performed in hospitals under a general anesthetic. There was some paperwork that had to be done for permission, so we decided to start that, just in case. I thought I would have at least a week or so to make my decision. But in a couple of days I got a call from doctor's office saying that the abortion had been arranged for two or three days later. I didn't tell them that I hadn't made up my mind. I just said, "Okay." I went to the hospital the night before the abortion was to take place, still not having made a decision. Someone must have driven me there, the same friend who picked me up the next day, I suppose. But no one was there with me in the evening. I didn't tell Dan I was going. There was a thirteen-year-old sharing the room, also scheduled for an abortion the next day. I was completely shocked by her, and sorry for her.

It was all dreamlike. I had not made a decision to have an abortion, yet here I was. They gave me a pill to sleep in the evening. Early in the morning they came and shaved us I think, and gave us another pill to put us half-way out, readying us for the general anesthetic. I believe I went into the operating room still not having made a decision. I just let it happen to me because I didn't know what else to do. Also, I felt the whole time that I could live with any decision I made. I simply was incapable of making the decision. I have always been grateful that they were using a general anesthetic then. If they had not, and if I had not had the sleeping pill the night before and the knockout pill in the morning, I honestly don't know if I could have gone through with it.

Dan came to visit at some point, perhaps afterward. He brought flowers. I don't know how he found out I was there; I really don't think I told him. He was puzzled and surprised that I hadn't let him know. It was comforting and surprising to me to have him there. Not something I expected or thought I deserved.

Late in the afternoon after the abortion a friend picked me up and took me to her house. I was groggy and detached. They were having a party that night. A lot of people were in the apartment. I think I tried socializing for a while, then went to bed. That night I dreamed that I found or rescued my child. She was a little miniature child, but she was alive. I experienced such relief at finding her alive and being able to save her.

She, or he, would have been about seventeen now. As the years have gone by, I have calculated periodically how old she would have been. I was very aware that first year of when she would have been born, and the next year of the first birthday.

Yet it's difficult to imagine what my life would have been like had I chosen to have this child; the road not taken. I have never had a child, and now it seems too late. I believe the only other time I was pregnant was about a year later. Dan had moved back to Portland and I saw him when I was up to visit my sister. We went out, and ended up going to a motel and making love. I believe that I was pregnant, but when I decided that nothing had changed, I had a spontaneous abortion.

What would I say to that child now? Is it you that I have longed for so often at my breast? Is it emptiness of you that leaves this space inside my chest that nothing can fill? How could I have let you go, loving children so much, having watched with envy all my life that mother who could take the infant home and have her all the time, to whom she belonged, who she called Mama, who she clung to? How could I have let you go, thrust you from my body, refused to recognize you calling me from the darkness? And now your chubby baby hands clutch at me, clap for me; your smile is dazzling.

Yet nothing in me finds a place to believe that I could have given you what you needed. That I could have nurtured you as you deserved to be nurtured, that I could have made life a kind and gentle place for you. I hurt too much, I needed too much, the doors in my heart were far too closed. I think I would have hurt you, and the pain of that could have gone on so, so much longer for both of us.

# Christopher

## by Jody Kirk

The air was putrid with the smell of you.
While I, bruised and bleeding,
Scrubbed till every pore was raw.

Too late . . . the deed was done.

Child conceived in violence . . .
Spawned with hatred from a hostile womb.

He's a man now.
I've heard he looks like me.
I wouldn't know . . .
Hell was harsh enough a place without reminders.

•

*When the rape described in this poem took place, I was twenty- one, and a nonperson . . . a no one. I had been physically, emotionally, and sexually abused (including incest) from the age of four through my late teens, and had left home as soon as I could find means to escape.*

*Although my rapist was someone I knew, at the time (1959) there was no such thing as "date rape," and there were no abortion clinics, support groups, or other places where I could go for help, hope, or guidance. Returning to my family was absolutely out of the question—I'd have preferred death to being with them again.*

*The baby was born in January 1960, healthy and beautiful. For ten months I tried to love him and be his mother, but I didn't have the slightest idea how to do either . . . loving, nurturing role models had never been part of my repertoire. At the end of ten months, I gave the baby to his paternal grandparents, who wanted him and promised to give him a good home. They were decent people who were, I suspect, trying to atone for what their son had done to me. They assured me he would have no part in the baby's upbringing, and—since they were my only viable option at the time—I had no choice but to believe them. Besides, although I felt nothing but pain and revulsion about having given birth to a baby born of rape, I did not want him to suffer.*

*I am fifty-two now, and have—after many years of torment and with much help—managed to emerge from the nightmare of my past.*

# *the lost baby poem*

## by Lucille Clifton

the time i dropped your almost body down
down to meet the waters under the city
and run one with the sewage to the sea
what did i know about waters rushing back
what did i know about drowning
or being drowned

you would have been born into winter
in the year of the disconnected gas
and no car      we would have made the thin
walk over genesee hill into the canada wind
to watch you slip like ice into strangers' hands
you would have fallen naked as snow into winter
if you were here i could tell you these
and some other things

if i am ever less than a mountain
for your definite brothers and sisters
let the rivers pour over my head
let the sea take me for a spiller
of seas      let black men call me stranger
always      for your never named sake

# to the unborn and waiting children

## by Lucille Clifton

i went into my mother as
some souls go into a church,
for the rest only.  but there,
even there, from the belly of a
poor woman who could not save herself
i was pushed without my permission
into a tangle of birthdays.
listen, eavesdroppers, there is no such thing
as a bed without affliction;
the bodies all may open wide but
you enter at your own risk.

# Upon Departure

## by Leanne Claire Civiletti

There are times when things should not be spoken.
You with your hair long and streaked with grey.
Your self-obsession.
Your doddering and my impatience.
Your arrival when I told you to stay home.

I cringe at gene pools and your stories of my existence.
The probing fingers of Chicago abortionists.
That you held tight to stop my removal.
That you read Proust while I waited in utero.
The feeling of suction, the whirlpool you entered
when they finally came to my rescue and induced my
       birth.

I'm now left with a color I can't live with.
It seeps in where it is not wanted.
It spreads and stains every image that I create.
I've soaked and scrubbed, it will not be muted.
I now know where it came from;
it's the color I saw through you,
as I waited for my exit.

# Essay On Guilt

## by Kasandra Fox

Mea culpa
the woman cried
wrapped in herself and rocking

tut tut Freud said
enough of that

and Jung agreed
and so did Adler
while nodded Fromm—and even Horney
(Horney, seeing Woman, sneered
grow up!)

a yellow bee
rested a moment in a nearby flower
fretting
you know he said
once I brought pollen
to a dead wrong place
and caused a crisis Darwin
spent a lifetime trying to explain
so I know how it is

and a fat guppy swimming by
said yum I ate my children

interesting said Freud

the woman went on crying

# "I thought it would be like taking the garbage out"

*Paula is a forty-three-year-old woman, currently a receptionist, and the mother of a fourteen-year-old son. She gave up a child for adoption in 1968. We also have an interview with Paula's mother, Trudy, which follows this one. It is an interesting companion piece: through these two interviews we get to see how two generations of women faced unwanted pregnancy.*

•

I went to high school in a small town. I met a man who was married at the time. Actually he was married the whole time I knew him. When I finished high school, I moved to San Jose with a girlfriend. When I got pregnant, it was a night I'd had a fight with a boyfriend in San Jose. Then, almost to spite him, I went back to my home town and saw the married man.

Two or three weeks later, I had the flu and lost about ten pounds. I finally went to the doctor and found out I was pregnant. Up to that point I had used no birth control, not at all. It really did not occur to me. I drank. I thought it wouldn't happen to me. We really didn't talk about that kind of stuff. You're young, you're indestructible, nothing can happen to you that you don't want to have happen. That's just the way I thought about it.

I don't know in my own mind who was the father. I think it was this married man I was seeing. I was drinking a lot in those days, and I have no way of knowing. He took total responsibility for it, even though I was honest with him about not knowing.

I did not even consider the fact that I could be pregnant. I was in shock when they came in and told me. I remember standing on the landing in the doctor's office and thinking, This would all be taken care of if I jumped. I don't know that I particularly wanted to die, I just didn't know how to deal with it. I was totally overwhelmed.

I called my parents the same night and they drove over from Modesto and got me. My jaw locked from the tension and we had to pry it open and put a spoon and washcloth in to keep me from grinding my teeth away. I had immediate, overwhelming stress.

I'm not going to say I called my parents for comfort. It was more that I couldn't think of any other options. What else could I do? I'd only been living away from home for two years and my parents had always taken care of me before then. I had no real skills. I knew you went to work and you paid your bills, that was it. I was twenty-one.

I'm trying to remember my parents' reaction, but that one's difficult because my perceptions have really changed. Back then I thought they hated me and I was a bad girl, and all this yucky stuff. But in retrospect, they were right there for me. They picked me up right away, took me back to their home, helped me figure out what we were going to do.

I insisted I needed to make my own decisions and, phew . . . there were a lot of pressures from everywhere. I remember feeling a lot of societal pressures. My parents did try to stay out of it in order to let me make my own decisions. In order to get an abortion at that time you needed the recommendation of either two or three psychiatrists.

I was definitely certifiable at that time, but my false pride would not allow me to do that. My brother-in-law was stationed in Japan and he was willing to set everything up there and pay for it, including plane fare. I was already under psychiatric care when I got pregnant and I think I could easily have had a legal abortion, but I decided it was not the thing to do.

I think part of my decision was holding out the belief that if I had the baby, the father of the baby would divorce his wife and come be with me. I think that was a whole lot of the process that caused me to opt not to have an abortion.

I went to a home for unwed mothers instead, and gave the baby up for adoption. I never really seriously considered abortion. I did not know anybody in my circle who had had an abortion. Most likely I wouldn't know about it even if they had. You didn't talk about those kind of things.

I decided to go to a home for unwed mothers because I felt a lot of pressure to not be visible in the town where my parents lived. My mom was a social worker in that town, so I really felt I had to go somewhere.

My parents took me up to a home for unwed teenage mothers. The girls were all fourteen and fifteen years old, and they were rigid and rule-oriented. I knew that wouldn't work because I was older and had been living on my own and thought I was real hot stuff and wouldn't be able to live with the rules and blah, blah, blah. Instead, we found a little home in Stockton. It was run by a couple who lived with their adult son in a main house and they would have four or five girls in a cottage in back at a time.

At this facility, I was still the oldest, but we had more freedom to come and go as we pleased during the day. The only restriction was a night curfew. My girlfriend would come visit me all the time, and my mom would come over. I went on public assistance and used an assumed name because of my mom's employment. To this day the birth records and adoption papers have the assumed name on it and not my real name, although I have written them and given them all the correct information.

At the home I was living in, it was just like three teenagers living together. We'd parade up and down the streets sticking our bellies out. It wasn't just that we were pregnant, this was our womanhood, folks, we were women now. Nobody knew us in the town anyway, so we could feel free to express that. I think the youngest little gal there was fourteen and we all had that same sense. In fact that little gal had been raped and was insisting on keeping her child. That one never made sense to me.

That's who my friends were then. We buddied together. The big event of the day was to go to the grocery store and buy yourself goodies to, you know, get through the day. It was a real sorority-type atmosphere. It was like a dorm, it was a party thing. We just kept it going. It was amazing how we all could simultaneously not face reality. We all were very good at it.

I never considered keeping the child, and it's kind of strange because I had a good-paying job and I probably could have kept the job and raised the child, but I felt like this was what I was supposed to do.

I had the baby in a Catholic hospital, which was a trip. His lungs filled up and I remember panicking. They had doped me pretty much. I'm surprised we had a live birth at all, because I don't remember participating in it. I do remember coming awake enough to see that he was in distress and that they were going to put him in an oxygen tent, and I panicked. I freaked out. They gave me more drugs to put me under.

When I came to, a nun came in and literally dumped him on my lap. She said, "You had him, you have to see him." The doctor had big orders on the records, "Baby up for adoption, mother not to see baby." I've had to work through some resentment about Catholicism and nuns in general. The doctor had told me all along that I would not see the baby. They put tags on the baby anyway and I would walk down to the nursery and see him. I would look through the window and cry, compose myself, and then go back to the window. I did that the whole time I was there and awake, so the doctor finally just said, "Take her home," because they didn't want me in the hospital anymore. I was just torturing myself.

Even though I had already made up my mind, it was still real traumatic when reality hit. I lived with my parents after I had the baby and I remember staying real busy partying and drinking to get through the first year. Back then you had a year instead of six months to change your mind and I just wanted to make it through that year.

For everything that was going on at the time, I still think it was the right choice for me, but I don't think that I would ever do that again. I don't know that I would have an abortion; I just have no idea. To have it and give it up is horrendous. I would certainly have everybody be in reality and think twice before they opted for that. I understand it, but it was just really horrendous. I thought it would just be like taking the garbage out and you're done. I had no idea what feelings were; I had always used substances to avoid feelings. I had no concept what pregnancy would be like.

With the son I have now, I was told that I was seventy-five percent sterile and I had to use fertility pills. I got pregnant to say "I'll show them" more than anything. I wanted to prove something to those people who said I was sterile. I love my son dearly, and I'm glad we've weathered all the storms, but I had him more out of my need to have somebody that I knew would love me rather than wanting a child, because I knew I had this loving and nurturing to offer. It's changed over the years, thank God.

I think the baby I gave up for adoption wouldn't have lived because I'm afraid he would have been battered. My son that I raised suffered abuse primarily because of my drunkenness and drug addiction. I would hold a pillow over his face when he cried and I would cook one-handed and hold him over pots, burning him and not realizing what was going on. I would walk through door frames and be too drunk to be balanced and ram his little head into the door jamb. My excuse would always be, not that I was drunk, but "He grows so fast I can't keep track of him."

I told the social worker that I would never drink and use during my pregnancy or after. After I gave up the baby for adoption, I went on to become an addict and full-fledged alcoholic. I remember getting drunk while I was pregnant with my first child. We used to go down the street to this woman's house and get drunk, and we'd always be back before curfew, and that was all they checked for. As long as we were in at the right time, they didn't look any further.

When I went in to see the baby for the last time, my mother went with me. I remember holding him for about two hours, trying to explain to him the situation as best I could. I wished him well and all that . . . . Just horrendous sadness and the crying . . . . Still, I would not let myself change my mind, I wouldn't let the thought surface. I kept the baby's picture for ten years. My son now and that baby are only ten days apart on birthdates. It finally hit me that as I go through all this horrendous depression and sorrow every year about the baby I gave up for adoption, I was robbing my son of his birthday. I finally threw the picture away and tried to let go of it so that I could enjoy my own child that I did keep.

# "I had to have it done, as far as I was concerned"

*Trudy is a seventy-five-year-old retired social worker, currently living on the West Coast. She had three illegal abortions, the first two of which were relatively easy to obtain. The third, after a large shift in the political climate, was very difficult to obtain. Her story illustrates what can happen when abortion goes underground, the lengths to which one has to go to find someone to perform the procedure, the great secrecy and shame surrounding it, and the increased danger.*

•

I lived in California when I met my husband, and we were married when we were in college and he joined the police force. We lived in various places around the Southwest and then moved to Costa Rica for five years. We moved back to the states after that. I worked as a social worker for twenty years and then retired. I retired at sixty-two and I've been married fifty-two years this year. I have three children, all grown now.

Let's see, the circumstances around my first abortion. I was dating the man who is now my husband. We were both in college. He was on a scholarship. We were both working, too. I worked for my board at the university and he worked for his room and board. When I got pregnant, I knew right away I didn't want kids. We just didn't have any money and we were not married, and I didn't want to have kids even if I was married, because I wanted to be independent. I was tired of having people tell me what to do. I was twenty-four when this happened.

It's funny, even when I was a little kid, I remember not wanting to have children. I had a lot of dolls, and when I played with them, I was always their teacher, never their mother.

My boyfriend apparently found out how to get the abortion from some of his students. I didn't tell anybody I was pregnant, except my boyfriend. Getting pregnant had never occurred to me. I was not a person that liked to talk about myself. I hated being around women who were talking about menstruation and their pains, childbirth and the like. I just did not like to talk about it. I guess I learned about how babies were made when I was a junior in high school at a health class we had. But then, it just never bothered me any, I just never thought about it. We drank a lot when we had free time from work and school. I was either busy working or drinking, so I really didn't have time to worry about birth control.

Anyway, my boyfriend found the place to have the first abortion. It was just a regular clinic setting. I don't know if it was really a doctor or not. You went in there and then they gave you a pill to sort of put you under and then they took you into the operating room. All I can remember, because I was almost totally under, was that when the doctor came toward me, his face was red, but other than that, I couldn't tell anything at all.

The abortion happened in Los Angeles. I never had a pregnancy test. As soon as I realized my period was late, I told my boyfriend and he arranged for the abortion. I was panicked. I knew I didn't want to get married, that never entered into the solution. I just dumped it in my boyfriend's lap, and he found out where we could go.

After the abortion, I stayed there four hours, then I went home, that was all there was to it. I remember the clinic was all white, like hospitals were back then. It was very clean, I thought. I didn't really feel like I was doing something illegal,

I felt like I was doing something I had to do. I never talked to anybody about it except my boyfriend.

I don't remember how much it cost, but I do remember borrowing the money from the Dean of Women at a junior college I was attending. She had always been very nice to me, and I told her I needed the money for books or a special project or something like that.

My feelings about being married and having children were different than many women in my generation. My father was a violent alcoholic and I just was not going to take that shit from any man. What he did to my mother . . . and she was just always trying to placate and satisfy him and there was just no satisfying him. I just wasn't going to do that, that's all. [Laughs]

When I got pregnant that first time, my boyfriend was real concerned. I had just left home to finish college, and I wasn't real sharp anyway, so, if I would have had the baby that would have meant giving up college. He still had more college left to go, and we didn't have any money; I just didn't see how we could live. I still had enough co-dependency in me to feel that his education was important and I wasn't going to be the reason that he had to quit. I was willing to quit mine, but I wasn't willing to have him quit his.

After the abortion I felt relieved, just relief. [Laughs] I don't remember any physical pain. I don't remember the nurse saying anything to me about birth control. The only thing I remember birth-control-wise at that time were condoms. I'm sure we must have used them part of the time, but, like I said, we drank a lot, and we'd rather spend our money on liquor than birth control. So, I went through the same thing again, at the same clinic and everything. Joe just took care of everything again. I don't know how he did it, we never discussed it. I don't think we have discussed it to this day.

My boyfriend went with me; we didn't have a car then, so we went on a street car. There were five women waiting in the office at the clinic. I wondered at the time if they were all there for the same reason I was. The clinic was called "Female" something. I didn't know if it was generally a clinic for female diseases or if it was just an abortion clinic. Most of the women were in their late twenties or early thirties, they were all white. I borrowed fifty dollars for the abortion. I don't know if that was the whole cost of the abortion, or if my boyfriend paid part of it.

Again, I didn't talk to anybody about the abortion except my boyfriend. It was pretty much a routine thing by then, you know, the same clinic and everything. I did not have women friends that I confided in.

My boyfriend and I got married in 1938 and, shortly after we were married, I got pregnant again. We thought we could go to the same clinic, but meanwhile there had been a crackdown and it had been closed. His mother had it all worked out that she would take care of the baby and I could keep my work. I didn't want any part of that. At that point I wasn't too gung ho about Joe even. I didn't want a kid that was raised the way he was and be the same kind of a fellow that he was. No way would I do that.

I told the woman I worked for that I thought I was pregnant, and so she arranged for me to have an examination to find out. That scared me. I told her and yet I didn't really want her to know. She was an old maid and she just looked so shocked, she was very stern. She went into this, "Oh, Trudy that hurts me terribly." She had planned for me to finish the business education classes I was taking and then I was to take the job as manager of either the women's dorm or the student union cafeteria, both of which she oversaw.

At that time, if you were pregnant and married, that meant you gave up work. When she reacted that way, I came back after the weekend and told her that I was mistaken, that my period had started. Then we went ahead with the abortion. I don't remember how we got the money for the third time. We had to get it from somewhere else. My husband never pressured me to have the baby. I think he was afraid of my temper, and rightly so. He knew that if I didn't want to have the baby, it wasn't a good idea to try and pressure me into it. He didn't try to pressure me to have the abortions either, but I just wanted them so badly and he knew it.

Anyway, I wasn't about to have a baby and have my mother-in-law raise it. My husband started asking around, and he found a dental student who had an aunt who would do it. I don't know if she was a nurse or a retired nurse or what. She gave it in her home. This was in 1938.

I remember it was a very different experience from the other abortions. She did it right in her house. She had this stinky old dog in the room. It was a sweet old thing, but really smelly. It was done on a kitchen table. She told John, I think that was the name of the fellow who arranged it, to have me take two aspirin, but what she didn't tell him was to have me take them within thirty minutes of the abortion. We lived in Los Angeles and had to take the "red car" to where she lived, which was a good half-hour trip, at least. I had taken the two aspirin before we left and that's all I had.

With that one, I had an awful aftershock. We got in the car afterwards, her car, and drove over to some ridge, a slough I guess you call it, and she dumped the baby, you know all the crap that was on the newspaper underneath me on the kitchen table. She disposed of it that way. I didn't think of it as getting rid of the baby, but something was wrong with me then. I just told Joe "I don't care what happens, but I'm not going to go through that again."

I knew nothing of this woman's credentials, only what her nephew told us. I think he said she was a retired nurse. She was an old woman. [Laughs] Not as old as I am! But, she obviously had retired, I think. She must have been sixty. I was not real curious about who was to perform the abortion. I just knew it was somebody's aunt who was supposed to be a registered nurse. I had no anesthetic whatsoever. I should think she took a shovel in there and dug it out. That's what it felt like.

It was very painful, but I couldn't tell her to stop. I had to have it done as far as I was concerned. It didn't take any more than twenty-five or thirty minutes. The reason we went out to dump it right away was that she didn't want to get caught. Something was also said about how she didn't want to have too many cars coming to the house. She didn't want any evidence left behind.

I remember telling my husband I would never go through that again. I would have the baby and give it up for adoption, but I would never have an abortion again. The first two times I was almost completely out, and really didn't feel anything. This last time was really horrible. There was something about seeing her dispose of everything on the newspaper and the awful pain. I just could not go through it again. I was afraid I would get someone like her again. When I saw her throw that stuff in the slough, it became more real to me.

We moved in 1943. It looked like my husband was going to war. I had no idea how I would support a baby, but I thought "I had better have a baby. In case my husband gets killed in the war, I'll have something to remember him by." Also my mother was telling me I was pretty old and I had better get thinking about having babies. His mother was saying the same thing. The family pressure, added to the thought that my husband was going to war and might not come back, made me want to get pregnant.

It turned out that I could not get pregnant at that time. I guess my uterus had fallen or something, so the doctor put a brace up there. I don't think this was due to the abortions . . . maybe the last one . . . I don't know.

Finally I got pregnant again. I had that one. It was a boy. Then I always thought it was terrible when people would just have one child, so I wanted another one right away. Then I couldn't get pregnant again right away. I thought I would have them nine months apart and raise them like twins. Thank God it didn't work out that way. Twenty months later I had Carmen, nineteen months later I had Paula. I had no trouble with any of the births.

When I had children, I did not just all of a sudden forget all my doubts about having kids in the first place. Tim used to cry constantly and I'd walk him up and down the canal, I'd look down at the water and wonder if he could swim, you know like puppies do. Oh, I just hated it. He just cried all the time, he'd even stop feeding to cry some. The only thing that would keep him quiet was driving in the car. Of course, with gas rationing you couldn't just drive a kid all over town and all over the countryside. Somebody gave us a buggy and either my husband or I would sit there and push that buggy back and forth like that. I thought I'd go out of my mind. I know I would have if Carmen had been the same kind of baby that he was.

Carmen, bless her heart, the only time she ever got my attention was when she would occasionally cry for a bottle. She would sit quiet and just watch Tim play. If she had been like him, I just don't know what I would have done.

Motherhood did not really take away my desire for a career or my desire to be on my own. That didn't do it for me like it seemed to for a lot of women. For one thing, I didn't feel that good at it. The kids didn't do what I wanted them to do. I couldn't boss them around and I couldn't satisfy the father.

If I couldn't have gotten those three abortions, I probably would have killed myself. I couldn't have stood it, or wouldn't have. The pressure of having those kids while my husband was working in the police department, working all different shifts, trying to keep them quiet so he could sleep, trying to keep the house half-way presentable, which I wasn't very good at and still am not.

All of that pressure just would have been too much. I was always so sensitive about what people were saying, particularly about the kids. I didn't have perfect kids, and that just threw me. I don't think I could have lasted raising six kids. If I'd had all those kids, somebody would have suffered.

# *The Visit*

## by Wendy Weiner

I remember when I first started my period. It was during the summer, right before Mr. Good's typing class. I was taking typing in summer school. FFF-space-GGG. One time I was erasing over the carriage and Mr. Good came over and ripped the paper right out of the typewriter. All the typing in the classroom stopped as heads silently turned towards the teacher standing above me. Tears stung my eyes.

That summer was right before freshman year, and somehow a bunch of us girls were taking typing in summer school. I remember us car pooling, a different mother every day sitting in the driver's seat, silent while we chatted. It was lucky everyone had a mother. I doubt you'd have been able to take typing if you didn't have a mother to share in the carpooling. Having a mother who didn't drive would have been like having no mother.

But I had a mother, a mother who drove. My mother didn't have a mother; she had died early of a burst appendix and my mother would remind me how lucky I was that she was still alive, that I had a mother, because my mother had to grow up all by herself.

So, one morning while I was waiting for Janet's mother to pick me up for typing class, I started my period. I remember hearing a neighbor lady's chattering downstairs, punctuated by my mother's laughter. Embarrassed, I hissed my mother out of the kitchen, telling her that something had happened in my pants and would she please *do* something. Now. She seemed annoyed but she did go out to the drugstore then and came back with the pads and the little belt and said, "Here, dear." So I put it on, and then I put on an ugly lime green shirt and checkered skirt and waited to be picked up for typing class. I remember being mad at everything all day. When I came home my mother was all sad. She showed me a poem she had just written. Seemed on this day, twenty or thirty years ago, her mother had died. I remember the poem talked about my mother crying because now I wore the cloak of womanhood, and her mother was dead.

Well, at least my mother drove.

•

"You shouldn't have told your mother."

"I know. But I did. It just came out."

"She's not expecting we'll get married, is she?"

"She knows better. But she said she wanted to drive up here for the appointment."

"She won't though, will she?"

"I told her to send the money for gas, save herself the trip. That got her mad. She sent a plant instead."

"Is that it there?"

"Yeah. Funny how they always wrap it in foil, like it might go stale or something. Blue foil, pink ribbon. I wonder if she told them those colors. That's something she would do. That's just like her."

"You could ask her."

"She'd never tell me, really. I'll never know."

"Come on to bed now."

"In a minute. I think the plant needs some water."

The plant was a huge philodendron with leaves as big as your face. After I watered it I went over to the piano bench and pulled out the picture of my mom and me, a portrait she had made by a professional photographer a few months ago. She had called Mick and got him to set up the session in the studio. My mother always gets everyone to do whatever she wants, one way or another. She knew I hated having my picture taken, so she went through Mick, who couldn't exactly say no to her. He wasn't family.

So there we were, both in white, matching earrings, pink lipstick, smiling for the camera. Although we don't look alike, the photographer had caught that same twinkle in our eyes.

"Eyes that shine like pools of stars in the forest of the leprechauns," I heard my father say once, when he didn't know I was around. At that, my mother's twinkle practically leapt out and grabbed him, a rosy blush coloring her cheeks, Mom has that milk-white skin you only see in magazines, while I'm battling acne, always searching for a decent cover-up. At least I got the twinkle.

I've never been the family-photos-on-the-mantel type. I don't even like Christmas. Kittens and babies bore me. After we had the picture done, Mom would say on the phone, "Is our lovely portrait out in view?" and I'd say, "Yes, Mother, I'm staring at it right now." She'd say, "I know you're lying," and I'd say, "At least you know me." We'd both laugh then. But if she was coming for a visit, I'd clean the house and drag out the picture.

I just happen to leave our picture out on the piano and at eight o'clock the next morning I get a call. "I'm about an hour outside of town." Just like that. Mick throws on his pants, grumbling.

"At least she's not *your* mother," I call from the bathroom. I don't wipe off the foggy mirror; instead, I stare through its veil of mist, deciding to be undefined today, ethereal, light as Tinkerbell. I float through the haze as the hair dryer whirrs above me, its heat stinging my scalp.

I remember coming home for lunch one day and there's this banging around upstairs, drawers slamming. It's Mom; I can hear her muttering in low tones. I've heard her muttering before, but then it's been different—softer, slower, almost like a bird cooing. It's usually been late at night when I wake up and want a glass of water. Then I hear these mumbles and creaks coming out of my parents' room muffled under the covers and I know it's not time to bug them, so I get up and get the water myself. One time when I came into their room late at night there was all this fumbling around and they were both breathing hard, all out of breath, and I asked why, since they hadn't been anywhere, they were just lying in bed. They both acted kind of mad that I'd bothered them, Mom especially.

But now it's noon and I'm home for lunch and mom is alone upstairs, muttering. "Mom, I'm home." No answer. I fix myself a peanut butter sandwich and a glass of milk. I take it upstairs to the bedroom, figuring I'll watch TV. *Jeopardy* is on.

Mom doesn't see me as I stand in her doorway; she just goes on muttering and slamming drawers. Her nightgowns are strewn all over the room, even the black lacy one she keeps in the bottom drawer, the one I secretly play dress-up in. Every once in a while her voice gets a little louder and I can catch her words. "Damn you," she says. "I won't take this." There are tears on her cheeks and she looks so sad. Then her eyes catch mine in the mirror. "Oh honey," she says. Then she grabs me and hugs me real tight like she doesn't want to ever let go.

•

The morning sickness hits me and I am suddenly hunkering down over the toilet.

"You okay?"

"Yeah. Just the usual. I'll be fine."

"We need coffee. You coming with?" I hear the jingle of keys as Mick fills his pockets.

"Give me a minute." I brush my teeth a second time. "You know, I bet she wouldn't be on her way if I hadn't left that picture out all night."

From the other side of the door I hear Mick whistling the theme from *The Twilight Zone,* which grows louder and more insistent, until he barges into the bathroom and starts tickling me under my towel, his high-pitched whistle buzzing my ear like a giant gnat. "No, stop," I squirm against his chest. But he doesn't stop, and I'm giggling and punching him and all out of breath. He's grabbing my wrists real tight and suddenly we both stop at the same exact instant and hold real still, and I feel him breathing against me, with me, against me, with me—in this moment, this day, this time, in this fogged-in bathroom with the towel at our feet.

Then he reaches down and I feel the breath of his hand as he grazes my belly. He doesn't touch the skin exactly, but just keeps his hand hovering above it, lightly, like he's reading braille or something. I grab his hand and bring it up to my face. "Hey, you're crying," he says. He picks up the towel and puts it around my shoulders, already feeling the chill.

•

The twinkle has left her eyes. "Your mother is sick," my dad says so softly we hear every word.

She keeps her bathrobe on all day. "Hey, Mom, have you seen my blue blouse?" She just turns away, arms folded tight across her stomach, staring out the window, smoking. The ash on her cigarette would grow long and fall off by itself. Sometimes when I'd come home and couldn't find her I'd follow the little piles of ashes she'd leave behind. They usually led to the bathroom. One time when I opened the door she was standing at the sink, naked, just staring down into the drain. "Mom?" She locked the door after that.

•

We drive in silence, Mick punching up the radio buttons every five seconds. Always looking for the perfect song, this guy. When I met him he was leaning against the jukebox at Swanky's, face pressed up against the glass. "See anything you like?" I had said.

"Now I do." That was a year ago last fall.

Mick and I are a lot alike. We're both slobs, for one thing. We live well together. There's an easiness we have with each other, like when I'm washing the dishes (usually three days' worth) and he comes up behind me, leans into me, starts kissing my neck. That usually stops me in my dish-washing tracks, my soapy hands encircling him, the suds dribbling down our shirts. A couple days later one of us is washing twice as many dishes, but neither seems to mind.

And he puts up with my mother. Doesn't like her much, but knows how to ignore her in a polite way. I like guys who are polite.

"How long is she staying?"

"Just 'til it's over, I suppose. She'll probably write a poem about it."

I run my hand up along Mick's thigh, his soft faded jeans so familiar against my palm. He's found a song on the radio and quits punching the buttons for a minute. It's "Cherish," and I know he thinks it's corny, but he knows I like it and he leaves it there. Mick's been extra nice ever since we found out about all this. The appointment is tomorrow and the only thing I'll miss is him being this sweet to me.

For days now I've been lying on the couch in my purple robe. Little Queenie, Mick calls me. Lying in state. I hear the clomp of his boots when he comes in, even though he's trying to walk quietly. I wipe the tears away and sit up, smiling. I don't know why I'm so weepy lately. Mick looks so cute with his new beard. When he kisses me, I feel baby chicks. "Peep, peep," he whispers, and I pull him down into the couch, into the folds of my robe. We just lie there a while, my tears wetting his cheeks.

"How about enchiladas for dinner," he says. "I'll make 'em with green sauce, just like you like 'em."

Mick even cleans up.

So now *she's* coming. To spoil it all. That's just like her.

•

I visit her in the hospital only once. I stand real still next to her bed. "Would you brush your mother's hair, dear?" She nods at the mirror and brush set on the nightstand—silver filigree, left to her by her mother, the only things of her mother's she had, along with the wedding band she wore on her little finger. "When I die, these will be yours," she often told me.

"Your grandmother was very beautiful," she says, staring into the mirror. "Did you know she once won a beauty contest?" My mother's eyes are dark hollows. I watch her thin fingers run along the patterned filigree on the back of the mirror.

She loved for me to brush her hair. It was long and red, the color of fall leaves, and when I ran the soft bristles against her scalp she'd lean back against me and close her eyes. I'd work deftly, brushing up the nape of her neck, around her ears, against her temples, up over her crown, down and around. She'd sigh and relax, and at those times I always felt she was glad to have me there.

"Would you like to brush Mama's hair, dolly?"

•

"Any second thoughts, dear?"

"Course not. What would I do with a kid?"

Mom settles down on the other end of the couch. Mick brings us both cups of coffee and then disappears into the bedroom. Mom digs out a glazed doughnut from the huge satchel she always carries and puts it on my saucer. I munch and dunk as she pats my feet next to her through the blankets. She likes doing that, I know.

"Have you read this?" she asks, pulling out a book. "I think you'll find it helpful."

She started buying these books when my brothers went bad, when they started drinking and drugging, as she puts it now. She would tell me how much better she felt, now that she could "let go and let God." She would actually say that. But by that time I had already left, so she was just a tiny voice in the telephone. I had left as soon as I could. I was the only one who left.

I barely glance at this book's cover; it's another one of those she's always sending me— *Ways to Intimacy, Roads to Heaven* —you should see the library in my closet. I wish I could return them but she has inscribed this one the way she always does, with something mushy and phony and untrue, like how beautiful I am and no matter what, I'll always be her daughter. I should write a book for her— *Women Who Think Too Much.*

Now she places the book by my side. I turn away and it falls, its pages fanning out haphazardly, dust jacket askew. She gets up so quick that her doughnut falls from her lap and rolls to the floor, leaving a sticky trail to its resting place under the piano.

Gathering up the cups, Mom takes them into the kitchen, saying she needs to be alone for a while so she can write in her journal. Good. Go away. The door swings shut but she is still here—only in the next room.

I finish my doughnut and wipe my sticky hands on my robe. She *is* writing a poem about this, I know it. In *my* kitchen.

I sit up, my ears prickling to the sound of the scratching of her pen. A sigh, perhaps a sob. Again I have caused her pain.

I push open the kitchen door and she looks up at me with wet eyes. "I'm sorry I upset you, Mom."

She brushes away a tear. "I wrote something," she says. "I should have been more honest with you when you were growing up."

"It's okay, Mom," I sigh. "You don't have to tell me."

"Remember those times when I was supposed to pick you up after school and I was late? I told you I was detained someplace, perhaps the dentist? Or the traffic was bad? You would be crying?"

She doesn't stop to see if I do remember; she is looking past me, someplace over my left ear. "Well, I wasn't detained anywhere, dolly. Sometimes I forgot. I simply forgot."

Now I do remember the little girl in the empty hallway of the school, wiping her funny nose with a scratchy woolen mitten, peering out into the grey of the late afternoon, searching for the slightest hint of a blue car veering around the corner. "Honey, is someone coming for you?" the janitor asks as his broom glides silently by. Waiting, waiting, staring out the window so hard my eyes hurt.

She's not asking me, but I do remember. What she's asking from me is forgiveness. "Forgive me daughter for I have sinned."

I feel my jaw shut tight, my tongue smothered against the roof of my mouth. Suddenly another wave of nausea rolls over me and I bolt out of the kitchen. Between all the coughing and gagging I hear myself muttering obscenities and more. I want it out of me, out of me, out of my life.

Then I feel a hand cool on my forehead, pulling back my hair. A wet cloth wipes my face. "There, there, dear—Mama's right here." Cooing sounds, lulling my eyes closed, lifting me up, guiding me back to the couch. "I'm in the kitchen if you need me."

•

Mom drives me to the clinic. Mick has to work; it's better this way anyway. She knows how to settle in for the wait. She's already reading one of those stories from *Redbook* when they call my name.

•

Oven mitts on the stirrups, doctor between my legs. Cold blue steel prying me open, white sheet separating me from my body. It's about the size of a lima bean now, I know, with a black

speck for an eye. Eight weeks. I hear soft murmurs, a whoosh-
ing noise down a dark tunnel. A pinch, some scraping, more
murmurs. Whoosh.

Eight weeks. I've seen those pictures in *Life*, so I know.
Sucking its thumb in the womb, curled up in itself, the hint of
a spine sharp against luminous skin. Breathing in my essence,
weightless, it turns in its sleep, a little fish safe within its home.
A wee babe.

So what do I do? I embark on a mission to search and
destroy.

Lost: one child, please return. No questions asked. I hear
a low moan escape from my lips, carrying with a sorrow far
beyond this body now lying on the table in this room.

"Shhh. It will be over soon." A soothing voice, a touch.
I squeeze the offered hand as icy needles shoot through me.

Boy or girl? Pink or blue? My baby will always wear
white. In a white gown of lace and feathers it nestles against
my breast. I offer it up to the priest, its tiny hands grabbing at
the rosary beads, its trusting eyes wide as the sky. The glow of
a thousand candles shrouds us in soft forgiveness. The priest
sprinkles holy water on the baby's brow. "In the name of the
Father and the Son . . . "

I wish you eternal life. Go now, my child.

•

In the front seat, I turn my face from Mom and stare at the sky,
so crystalline blue now. Muffled sounds of traffic leak through
the glass. I turn on the radio and the music blares for an instant
before Mom shuts it off, with a "Do we need this?" expression.
Now we drive in silence. I cherish the moment, because Mom
is usually a nonstop talker.

•

I may have slept. I am home now, home in my purple robe,
lying on the sofa. Mom's in the kitchen, I know. I feel all hot

and sticky, a dull ache nagging at me from between my legs, one arm pinned up against my stomach, the other hanging limp.

Knuckles knocking against the floor, I watch the swirling patterns of the wood dissolve into silky undulations. In some spots the wood grain is pale yellow, almost golden, merging into rivulets of copper. I gaze into its depths, the floor rises to meet me, and soon I am running, running through golden fields of wheat, those amber waves of grain. The sky is achingly blue, the sun hot on my neck. My hair is the color of the sun-baked wheat, and I am singing, singing up at the sky— "This old man, he played one, he played nick-nack on my thumb . . . "—clapping my hands, stomping up the dust, my dog in front of me, barking.

"This old man, he played one . . . . " The rhythm pounds at my heart, sears through me, out my closed fist, down into the wood, into the golden floor . . . . "With a nick-nack pad-dywhack, give a dog a bone, this old man comes rolling home. Rolling home . . . . "

My fist stops suddenly. Sure enough, I do hear it—a soft tapping from the kitchen, from the other side of the door: "This old man comes rolling home." "Mom?" I push off the covers and slowly make my way over to the door.

"This old man . . .
. . . he played two
He played nick-nack . . .
. . . on my shoe"

Tentatively at first, we serve the rhythm back and forth through the closed door. As we get stronger and surer, we get faster and louder. Now we are beating out the rhythm together, slapping hands on wood, stamping feet.

"This old man, he played three," Mom shouts.

"He played nick-nack on my knee," I finished from the other side, and I know what will happen next. As I burst through the door, Mom tears into me, pounding out the paddywhack on my knee, my poor knee. "Uncle," I cry, and we collapse together in a heap, our laughter filling the kitchen.

As our laughter ebbs, we still lie there on the floor, staring at the patterns of sunlight filtering through the window. Legs entwined, we listen to the rhythm of our breath as it grows deeper and more steady.

Finally, I unravel my legs from hers and sit up to examine the damage to my knee. Negligible. Then I sense the dull ache between my legs. I look over at Mom and she reads my face, quickly leading me back to the couch. She tucks the blanket around me, kisses my forehead, and I fall asleep listening to the scratching of her pen in the kitchen, the rustling of blank pages.

*p.253* Julia Couzens, *Being Exposed #28*
(©1991, Charcoal, 12"x12")

*p.254* Angela Sinicropi, *#4*
(©1990, charcoal on paper, 5'x6')

*p.255* Angela Sinicropi, *#7*
(©1990, charcoal on paper, 53"x64")

*p.249* Anne Ardillo,
*Standing Still*
(©1991, charcoal, 60"x102");
*Hidden Secrets*
(©1991, graphite, 23"x30")

*p.250* Laura Jeanne Grimes, *The Adopted Child*
(©1988, monoprint)

*p.251* Barbara Hendrickson, *The Secret*
(©1991, woodblock print, 12"x18")

*p.252* Barbara Droubay, *Birth Series I*
(©1992)

---

The eight works of art listed above are individually copyrighted by the artists, who donated the rights to reproduce them in this collection, with one exception. For further information please contact the publisher.

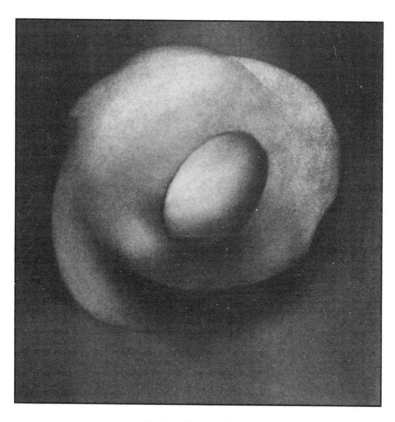

*Being Exposed #28*

#4

#7

*Standing Still*

*Hidden Secrets*

*The Adopted Child*

*The Secret*

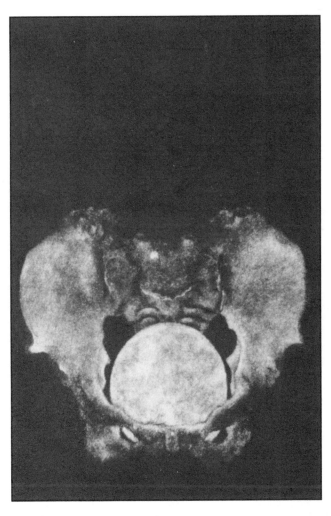

*Birth Series I*

# "And none of
# them were planned"

*Marge was fifty-four years old at the time of the interview, and had worked as a psychotherapist for fifteen years. She had recently moved with her husband to a smaller community, intending to resume her practice, but decided she'd rather garden. After so many years of taking care of other people she found she simply didn't want to do it any more.*

*Her story says much about the plight of women in the fifties and early sixties and gives a perspective on their dilemmas and how they compare to those of women in their childbearing years today.*

•

In those days, people didn't have the option of abortion, or at least it wasn't as well known or available as it is today. It wasn't a choice in those days unless you really were devastated. My mother had an abortion, but it was a terrible thing to have to go through in those days.

My children were not unwanted, in the sense that I didn't treat them like unwanted children once they were here. Although with the third one . . . . I mean, I had been socialized to want children, so I never had overtly discussed not wanting that child. It was not something that was heard of in my family, to ever discuss a child not being wanted. But that was the truth of it. And I didn't consciously even know that. I was just terribly depressed and didn't know why.

At that time, life was hard. We lived in a very cramped place with only one bedroom until after the third child was born. Then we added on two bedrooms and a bathroom. So it was a tiny little house, and it was out in this area of Southern California that no one had ever heard of. Every time I had a baby they marked the population sign with one more, because I was the only person having children. It was lonely, I was isolated, my husband was working eighteen to twenty hours a day in the business and on-call twenty-four hours a day because it was a restaurant. If I had been in a community where there were other women and other children, it would have been a different situation.

You know, in those days we all seemed to get pregnant without planning it; I don't know why. We were all using contraceptives, we were all using diaphragms. But it just wasn't part of our consciousness to really be careful. And we were conditioned to have babies, and so when it happened everybody should just be happy.

When the third son came, the one older than him was seventeen months old, and the first just over three years old. I lived in an area so rural there were fox tails blowing into your clothes, so part of doing the laundry was picking the fox tails out. That's about all I remember of that time period—mountains of laundry with fox tails. I guess I must have just repressed a lot of that . . . those bad feelings. My third son was a whiny kind of kid; he was super bright, and as an infant was just angelic. He must have known he'd better be. In fact, my mother-in-law used to say I was killing him because I was giving so much attention to number two, who was far more demanding and far more mischievous and really a difficult child. Well, he was a baby, and he was caught in the middle of two other babies. So the oldest child knew he had to be sort of the parent child. He looked out for everybody, and even to this day his brothers are fighting with him to stop being their dad. They have two and that's enough. He says he's not even aware of doing it.

After seven years of living in that isolated environment, I was so lonely and the children really needed other people to live with. So we moved in nine miles and lived on a cul-de-sac where a bunch of families had just moved in also, in a new development. And that was community for the first time in our whole lives. I had never had child-care available, and finally now the neighbors would look out for us.

I guess my father-in-law helped us get into that house. He was an extremely wealthy man, but really didn't have a philosophy of sharing. My husband was a very hard-working guy, but he couldn't work hard enough to please his father, ever. We both worked in the restaurant until I moved, then I had nothing to do with it after that. When we separated, there were lots of properties that my husband had co-ownership of for tax purposes. So I guess his father insisted that my husband contest the divorce so I couldn't claim ownership of any of those properties, or of the business. So we were thirteen years working that business and I came out with nothing. I had four children and the judge awarded me almost no financial help. In those years they didn't. He awarded fifty dollars per month per child, so two hundred dollars per month for four children. He did award me alimony payments and the house, but I had to pay all the debts, I had to pay off the house really, and sell it. And my husband never paid me alimony, and that was it.

I went to work part-time in the neighborhood so I could be close to where my kids were. Then I realized I was going to have to go to work full-time because there wasn't enough money. I had four children and nobody to care for them, and I had to go to work. And in those days there was no child-care. I think after about a year of working as a secretary, and I was a horrible secretary, I started taking college courses. And the kids just had to fend for themselves, up until the time I remarried. So for about a year and a half they were on their own. For the first time in our lives we lived in an apartment rather than a home. I thought it was wonderful, because I wasn't responsible for all the things you are with a home, but it was a very bad environment for my children. They got into a very bad situation with other kids who were left alone a lot.

I was surprised that I did remarry as soon as I did because I really loved not being married. But I did need help with the children, I had these four boys. My present husband had four children that he had to leave because of a divorce. Although he would never admit it, I think having these four children to replace his was his way of getting another chance. For the most part it was a very tough life, because you have all that step-parenting stuff to go through and money stuff. But I think we did it pretty well, considering all the problems involved in having four kids and a step-father.

I'm in therapy now with my third son, and lots of things are coming out of that. Things that I thought were being a bad parent were not the things that he brings up. He'll cry about my not making him brush his teeth. That's what stuck with him, and when he had a son he made sure that he brushed his teeth every night. But you know, he has one child and he has a lot of time and energy for that child. He took off months when his son was born, to do parenting. And I know that much of his strong feeling comes from the fact that his parents were either physically or emotionally not available to him. He's still extremely needy, which is one of the reasons I agreed to go into therapy with him. I can't make it up to him, and I always feel this sort of covert demand that makes me want to push him away, just like when he was little.

Much of my parenting was single parenting, I felt, even though I was actually only alone for about two-and-a-half years. My second husband didn't really want to be a father to my children, which was good in some ways, but as a consequence I felt like I was, again, a single parent, and I was very resentful. But he supported me to go to graduate school, and he supported all my children; their father did not.

I got very mixed messages from him. He'd say go, do, do,

do. And then he'd get really angry at me. And my children were the same way. One day I came home from school, and I said, "There are four adult people in this household capable of starting a meal, and everybody is just sitting waiting for me to come home. I quit." I had made a list of all the jobs that I thought were important jobs in the house, and I was open to taking jobs off that list, but they weren't my jobs anymore. So from that point on, although nothing ever got done again the way it got done when I was doing it all, I ceased to feel the kind of resentment I had felt for so long. And my youngest son particularly, who's the one who felt he got gypped the most (I was there when everyone else was growing up) kept saying, "I'll do it, but it's your job."

When we'd been married six years I discovered I was pregnant, though I'd been using an IUD. I don't know what happened to the IUD to this day. Since he had four children by a previous marriage, and I had four children, we decided eight children was enough, and I knew there was just no question that this time I would have an abortion. We went to a family planning clinic and had the interview and scheduled the abortion. Three of my children were born at a hospital, and you didn't get a lot of tender loving care at this hospital. And my first son was born in the army, so all my pregnancies and birthings were in institutional kinds of settings. The family planning clinic was an exceptionally good environment to have to go to; we didn't have to go to Tijuana. Nevertheless, I didn't have my own physician, I didn't have a special hospital room, it was all done in a day, and you went home. And I also went to that abortion the way I think I had done everything in life. They told you exactly what they were going to do, but I didn't understand really what it was going to be like. Here I was forty years old, I wasn't in my twenties anymore. But I just had the same attitude toward life, which was, This is what I have to do.

I was very present during the abortion. There were a lot of things about it that felt very much like delivering a baby. It was quite mechanical, they had given me the anesthetic sodium pentothal, they had you on a gurney and they had you in a hospital-type setting. One of things that I remembered in having babies was that, even though I was awake, it all seemed sort of like a dream state. It seemed that way with the abortion too. And then, after it was over, it was painful. They put you in a recovery room and you have to stay there for x amount of hours until they release you and you don't see anybody or talk to anybody during that time period. I woke up and there were women in various states of discomfort. I always compare myself to people who are the least comfortable, and think, all those people are worse off. It minimizes whatever is going on with me.

Thinking back now, I say I would have had an abortion with my third or fourth child, had it been legal. But actually, I think my consciousness would have been different all the way around. I was raised as a woman who was expected to marry and have children and not work. If it was a world like it is today where people talked openly about these issues and women had choices about everything, not just childbearing, I probably would not have married either of my two husbands and I probably would have had a very different life.

When you have your children and you raise them and you love them, it's hard to say you wish you'd had an abortion. But what I wish I had had was more of a *life* that was my own. With four children you just don't, I mean unless you're really. . . . It's interesting, I'm very angry at women who have babies and go to work. And yet I'm sure if I were a woman today I would do that. I think it's really a rotten thing to do to kids, probably because I feel guilty about the lack of bonding I had with the children I did have, even though I didn't go to work when they were tiny. I feel it's not a good way, even as a community, to bring children into the world. They're going to grow up like my third son, feeling that he'd been abandoned and that he never got his needs met, those initial bonding needs.

And that's what I think we're doing today by having babies and then leaving them. The dilemma that women are in is that if they have careers before they have children, they don't want to give them up or can't afford to. I have a daughter-in-law who has been working since she was about eighteen or twenty years old at the same company. So she now has a ten- or eleven-year career, and is at a point where she has to start having children or she's going to be in trouble. She is *very* ambivalent about giving up her career, even to go through birthing and motherhood, and is not sure she will want to leave the child, and will feel guilty about it if she does. So it's not an easy decision even when you have all these choices. If there was a kind of a caretaker that could come in and take care of that baby, the baby would get the infant bonding needs met, but it wouldn't be with the mom, and I feel really bad about that. It's just not a perfect world.

# "We never spoke of it again"

*The three children that Elena did finally have are grown, and she is a grandmother. She has a thriving practice as a psychotherapist, serving both the Anglo and Latina community. Her story brings to light the pain and danger of illegal abortion, the absolute require-ment for silence and secrecy in the Mexican Catholic community in which she lived, and the burden of keeping that silence for more than thirty years.*

•

I grew up in East Los Angeles, which at that time was kind of international, but a predominantly Mexican community. Today, forty years later or so, it's an almost one hundred percent Latino population. So it was a working class neighborhood, and predom-inantly Catholic. We lived a block away from the church, and so I was trained very thoroughly to believe the kinds of concepts that the Catholic church expounds. Of course, abortion was out of the question—in those years it was out of the question.

Fortunately I didn't go to a Catholic college, which would really have doomed me forever, or at least a bigger section of my life. I think Catholic schools are just so destructive. The doctrine of the church is bad enough, but it's the way it's given to you as a child when you're so impressionable.

I became pregnant when I was nineteen or twenty. I had been dating this man for about a year, and we had been sexually active for some time and were actually planning our marriage. But he had been married before and the church doesn't acknowledge divorces, so as far as I was concerned I couldn't get married unless he had some special dispensation. I was still involved enough in the church to want to be married there. So he was busy trying to clear his divorce, and in the meantime I got pregnant. So there was no way we could get married. That would have resolved it for me; I would have just gotten married and not have had an abortion. But not being able to get married, and living at home, my parents were just . . . . I believed it would really hurt them if they knew.

It was clear that I was going to have an abortion; I was not going to have this child if I had to die doing it. I was ready to commit suicide; in fact I was very suicidal during that period. I was highly emotional, probably from the pregnancy itself, but also from feeling that I had done such an evil, bad thing to get pregnant. If I didn't have the abortion, I would be exposed in my evil badness. It was really a twisted way of thinking, but that's how I thought in those days.

I had never talked to anyone who had had an abortion. In my family there was somebody, a distant cousin, who had a child that my aunt adopted, and there was talk in the family about the disgrace of that woman. In high school there was a girl who got pregnant. Her name rhymed with rape, so they would call her Joanne Rape, because she was very promiscuous. So it was like she was a bad girl, and she got pregnant. That was the only experience I can remember from high school. Everyone knew she was pregnant. Only bad women did that.

So we began the process of finding a way to end the pregnancy—and this man was very willing to support me in trying to find a way. He went all over talking to his friends, got me pills of all kinds; I was sick as could be. I went horseback riding trying to bounce it out, all kinds of crazy things like that. Finally he found a chiropractor who was willing to do the abortion. By then I think I had finished my first trimester, maybe even almost four months along, it was really bad, close. Then

I was burdened with, Aahh now I'm killing a human being. I felt sick, that's all I felt. When the doctor's assistant examined me for the abortion she said it was about the size of a lemon or something. That visual size, it seemed huge, rather than teeny. But nevertheless, I had already made up my mind, and I was clear I was going to do this, so I went ahead and made an appointment.

I had to plan this thing with my family, as though we were going to be gone over the weekend. We left and had it done in the office. Actually what he did was stimulate labor, and then I went home and proceeded to pass . . . so, I was in agony—well, labor. It hurt. Aahh, I just got an image of that, how it went. I was at a friend's apartment, and my future husband was with me. She and her boyfriend left so that I could be private and abort. When the time came, and I knew it was time, I got up and went into the bathroom. I closed the door, I didn't want him in there anymore, I just couldn't stand to be . . . . I closed the door, and he was asking me to let him in so he could help me or do something. I was sitting on the toilet, and I started to sit up and I could see down and whatever I had passed was dangling there. I'm screaming out what's happening through the door to him, and he's yelling back, "Take it, whatever that is, just get it and wrap it, don't let it fall in there." So I did, and I let him in and he took it and wrapped it, whatever it was—I remember it dangling there—he took it and went and buried it. Before he buried it he told me he looked at it, he examined it, and he said that it was truly a fetus; he even knew the sex. I didn't realize all that, I mean I had no idea until it happened.

But I couldn't do it any other way, it was just the only way to do it. It brings up a lot of philosophical questions about when life begins, whether it's just an appendage of your own body, your own self, you know? It was a part of me, it couldn't survive by itself, so it wasn't a person, and yet . . . getting rid of it, I feel like I was . . . I did something bad and wrong. And yet again, even at the time, as bad as it felt—and I was hysterically upset—nevertheless I knew that was the only thing to do. There was no other option that I could take at that time. And I think I would do it again, given those complete, exact circumstances. But it was very difficult. And after that, we never spoke of it again. We never spoke of it again.

I didn't realize it at the time, but I was very depressed after. I didn't reject him, I didn't want to stop our wedding. As a matter of fact, it really clamped me into being married. After what I went through with this man there was no way I would marry anybody else or be with anybody else. That was it, I was completely his—I mean literally. It was like I was an object owned by him. I was locked into that relationship.

So I think I was very depressed and very guilty. That's why I couldn't speak of it, the unspeakable thing that I did, just unspeakable. I felt worthless too, that I really didn't count. I didn't see myself as a person anymore—I was an appendage to him in this marriage. I really did feel that way. Of course part of that had to do with my training, my Catholic upbringing and my family, and the role modeling for me of my mother and the other women in my family. "Women, be subject to your husband." We were quoted that a lot.

So, we got married and never spoke of the abortion. I didn't get pregnant again for a couple of years into the marriage. It was beginning to worry me that maybe something had happened out of that abortion that I couldn't have children, but I had three. My husband was such a shit sometimes that when he would really get mad at me he would say that he wasn't the father of that pregnancy. It took me a long time to get through with that commitment to . . . subjugation. It started to happen with my going back to school. I took classes all the time, but I went back to school in earnest when my oldest child was ten or twelve, and the others were ten and eight or something.

It was such a great feeling, a world opened up to me, I couldn't believe it. Also the Vietnam War was going on, so I had an issue, I had something that I knew I felt right about, that I knew that he was wrong and I was right. I really had something here that was a terrible, vicious, horrendous thing where humans were being killed, and we had no business being there. And I had support, because I could hear people saying what I was feeling and believing, out loud. They were actually challenging authority out loud. That also gave me a lot of support to be myself, to wake up to subjugation and look for freedom. I got involved in Cub Scouts, which didn't match all that, except that somehow the women that were involved in that were moms too of kids that age, who also wanted freedom and were looking for ways of making themselves count. School seemed the outlet, taking classes that were more than just French or real estate or art, the kind of stuff we had been taking. We started taking history—history, that was great. And literature, in which I read and read—the right things, things that were stimulating to me.

I went through a metamorphosis, growth that was gigantic. I was in my thirties by then. I stayed married until 1970, and then I just finally left one day, in the middle of cleaning his camper after one of his hunting trips. I started directing a nursery school. I hadn't gotten a divorce, we were just separated. Anyway, into this school comes this young teacher, and we had such fun. She wanted to do stuff that I had always wanted to do. I was getting a taste of another way of life; she just opened up my head and my world tremendously. We'd talk on the phone for hours at night.

Then this one night on the phone I told her about my abortion. It was the first time I had mentioned it since it happened. I had never told anybody. You can imagine, after keeping a secret for twenty years, what it was like to finally tell it. It was such a powerful event for me. It still took me a while to be able to speak of it freely, but this tremendous burden had been lifted.

It's interesting how going through it and talking about it, dredging it all up again, it's still there; there's still a lot of . . . discomfort. It's not pain, like it used to be, but it's still there like an old wound, a soreness. It never goes away.

# "Because it is true
# I will not spare any details"

*This is a self-written story. The author, Lucille, is now in her mid-sixties. She is a well-known and well-respected professional and activist in her community.*

•

This is a horror story. Because it is true I will not spare any details. Only now as the Supreme Court is deliberating whether a woman has the right to a safe and legal abortion do I feel the need to share my experience.

I was thirty-nine years old in 1963, returning with my three children from Europe where we had lived for two years following a divorce from a man who used every legal tactic in the book in an attempt to deny my right to leave a destructive marriage. It seemed impossible that I could be one month pregnant. Getting the children settled back into school kept me busy while I wondered what to do. Marriage to the father was impossible. I feared going to a local doctor for help, as my ex-husband was one of them. I knew that if I had a baby out of wedlock he would use that to take custody of our children. He was still vindictive and I knew I was the better parent. I did talk in a roundabout way with a psychiatrist friend who indicated he was against abortion . . . . No help there. Illegal abortion was something that happened to "other" women, but now I was faced with finding someone who could help me.

I went to San Francisco and picked a doctor out of the phone book. (Looking back now I realize it had not even occurred to me to seek out a woman doctor.) I made up a name for myself; anonymity was important. He was cruel, telling me of all the bloody abortions he had been called in on at the point of death. He seemed to enjoy my shame and fear . . . . No help there.

I went to Los Angeles where, through a friend, I met a man who knew a technician in a hospital who would be able to "arrange something." It would cost one thousand dollars. I had to trust this man because I knew no one else and I was in my second month of pregnancy. We met at the hospital. I produced the money and was told to return home and wait for their call. The man was solicitous but insultingly insinuating. I have never felt so powerless in my life. The call came as I was in my third month of pregnancy. I was told that the technician had "cold feet," but the man had found a doctor who would perform the abortion in his office. It would cost another thousand dollars. I felt trapped and desperate and completely vulnerable. I had confided in only two friends and they were feeling uncomfortable . . . wanting, yet not wanting, to distance themselves from "the problem." We all felt like soon-to-be-exposed criminals.

On the doctor's examining table I had what I thought was a D&C. Because the doctor did not want to risk implication in case there was a reaction to anesthesia, I was fully conscious and feeling every bit of it. I can even today recall the pain. The nurse had blindfolded my eyes so I would not be able to recognize the doctor in case of his arrest. My procurer was present with more than consoling caresses. It's amazing to me now to remember how grateful I felt towards these two men who had "delivered me from evil." The doctor wanted me to return the next day for more antibiotics. I was pleased that he was so concerned.

The doctor's "clinic" was in a house in the black ghetto and I felt very white and obvious. I knew everyone knew I was having an abortion. I tightened at the sight of policemen. Again my eyes were covered. When the doctor arrived he had me on the table again, explaining that because I was so far along in my pregnancy he had not been able to abort me. I was to take some pills he gave me and come back in a week if I did not abort. Again I was back home lying to my children and friends about my frequent trips to Los Angeles, praying desperately that the pills would work and knowing that precious time was passing. The pills did not work. My return to the "doctor" of whom I knew nothing filled me with terror. His only recourse was to insert a catheter and send me home again with it in place. He was washing his hands of me. At this point I must have gone numb . . . my survival system went into automatic.

I returned home, sent the housekeeper away, did the grocery shopping, fixed dinner for the children, and while they watched television in the family room I silently aborted a formed fetus in the toilet. The bathroom was covered with blood but I carefully cleaned all the traces before I crawled into bed.

I am sixty-four years old and a grandmother to four little girls. My three grown children are contributing citizens. I am respected and have been publicly honored for my volunteer community work. In that bed, twenty-six years ago, I experienced a deep, compassionate, loving forgiveness of myself which can only be attributed to the spiritual realm of the loving Jesus or the compassionate Buddha . . . an experience of grace which allowed me to go on.

When I hear the anti-abortionists rave about killing children I force myself to see that formed fetus floating in the toilet bowl to see if I feel guilty. I see only the sneeringly righteous face of the doctor in San Francisco . . . and the power-hungry face of my manipulating procurer. If legal abortion had been available to me as it is now I would have destroyed some cell tissue in my first month of pregnancy. I would not have been forced to struggle for over three months to find an "abortionist." The delay itself forced me, in the view of these vehement anti-abortionists, to "kill a child." For there was never any question in my mind that, whatever it took, I would not risk the loss of my children and what I felt was their well-being.

# The Depths of
# the Great Depression

*This is a self-written story. The author, Anna, is a graphic artist and writer who continues to work now, at the age of seventy.*

•

These lines come to you from a woman now going on sixty-eight. This means that when I was young, abortion was neither legal nor safe. I was young during the time when women were being discovered by the tobacco industry, wooed by the cosmetics industry, and otherwise told to stay in our "place."

As with many thousands of youngsters in my generation, circumstances caused me to be left alone in the world at the age of twelve, in the depths of the Great Depression. It was fairly Dickensian; no such things as welfare, Aid for Dependent Children, or Child Protective Leagues. Life for us was very hard. The girls worked as live-in "mother's helpers," a euphemism for unpaid slaves. Otherwise it took all one's energy and wits to scrounge food, shelter, and some sort of covering for the body. Either way, there was no counseling or guidance to help us through our puberty years. It is true that the only drugs we heard about were perfectly legal, that marijuana was scarcely used except by musicians; street crime was limited to very tough "Bowery" type areas, and people did not need to lock their cars or houses. In these regards, those were relatively innocent times.

On the other hand, society had a callous disregard for the suffering individual, aside from county hospital care, so homeless children were dependent on the occasional kindness of strangers or upon themselves—and ill-equipped to deal with the realities of life.

As is unfortunately still true today, vast numbers of parents did not inform their children of the "facts of life." (What we learned from our Victorian era mothers was that sex was a nasty business, but one had to "put up with it" in order to have a marriage.) In such an atmosphere, important information was withheld altogether and the word "abortion," like "syphilis," was absent from the vocabulary. "Nice people" didn't get either, and that was all we needed to know.

There were whispered conversations, naturally, among peer groups. Somewhere along the line we found out how babies were conceived and realized that unmarried girls who got "in trouble" were a wretched disgrace, that sometimes one would "have her appendix out," which seemed to end the problem, or she was sent away for a long recovery from a strange illness. We also learned there were terrible people who removed babies from the uteruses of women "in trouble," but that this was very dangerous and often caused the women to bleed to death or get infections that killed them. Those were the days before sulpha drugs or antibiotics, and the days before licensed doctors could perform legal abortions in sanitary hospitals or clinics. We did *not* learn that pregnancy was in any way preventable.

In the midst of this educational void, however, we were (as are all girls today) constantly dinged on by the media to be sexually attractive to every man, everywhere, or else. And the companion message was there too; if we could not "hook a man," we would probably starve to death, since there was no place for females in the world of the well-paid.

Being female and alone (and far from pretty or "sexy"), I consequently eschewed all thoughts of romance or marriage (except daydreams) and concentrated on trying to make it through school. Thus, I was all of eighteen before I "lost" my virginity in the standard, bitter way of reaching out for love, and only a few months older when I found myself pregnant, by a man who didn't love me in the least. An estranged older sister whom I rarely saw became alarmed at my condition which was, after all, a reflection on the "good name" of my family—who ignored my very existence all the rest of the time. She therefore begged or borrowed the then-enormous sum of three-hundred dollars and came to me with instructions on how to reach the "person" who would "take care of the problem."

Following her orders, I hid the money in an inside pocket and used one of the two streetcar tokens she gave me to travel all the way across town to what I hoped would be a doctor clandestinely carrying on a much-needed practice. What I came to was one of the oldest houses in the oldest and dirtiest slum in the city.

The house was decrepit, paint peeling from the walls and porch, garbage strewn on the ground and on the front steps, flies everywhere, a yard untended for years, rank with old and young weeds and broken bits of machinery. The entire block looked the same. There were no trees! There were no green lawns, no shrubs, just barren misused land and ugly misused houses, most of them tumbledown apartments. And the whole street was void of visible human life. Not a child playing, not a housewife watering. Nobody. It all lay there, sweltering under an unseasonably hot sun, promising nothing. As frightened as I was already, I found the scene terrifying. What was a nice girl like me doing in a place like this? (Answer: But you're not a nice girl anymore, remember?)

I studied the house for a long time, watching to see if anyone came or went. There was no sign of life. The longer I stood there in the sun queasy with nausea, the worse were my fantasies of how the inside of the place must look. I pictured my clean and healthy body being worked on by the kind of person who would live or work in such a place, and the picture made me truly ill.

I won't ever forget those hours spent trying to make myself go up the stairs and ring the bell, knowing that if I didn't, there would be hell to pay, and that if I did, there might be death to pay. I will never forget my rage that I could not go to a decent hospital and have this problem solved in a decent fashion, with cleanliness and dignity.

In the end, I opted for cleanliness, and spent a very rough time indeed, trying to manage having and caring for an illegitimate child in an uncaring culture. It was a battle lost before it began, and I ultimately gave up a beautiful and charming eleven-month-old son for adoption because there was no way I could earn enough to support us both.

A sad postscript to this story is that, in making the effort to "do the right thing" for my child, I had to work at the only job I knew where tips were possible: waitressing in a restaurant where we carried heavy trays over our heads, eight hours a day. I had to start doing that only two weeks after giving birth, and the damage to my body resulted in my requiring a hysterectomy. So I could never have another baby, even when the time came when I could easily afford it, emotionally and financially.

Mine has not been a life of unrelieved tragedy. I later adopted three beautiful babies and now have two beautiful grandchildren. But I have never ceased to mourn the loss of my first and only born son, and I never cease to wonder whether I would have been able to adopt my three had it not been that they too were conceived when abortion was illegal and unsafe.

# Index of Choice:
## Abortion, Adoption, or Kept Child

*Keeping the Child*

*Abortion/Adoption and Keeping a Child*

*Multiple Abortions (more than two)*

*Illegal Abortion*

# Biographies of Poets and Artists

Anne Ardillo, *Who Came First (series); Standing Still; Hidden Secrets*

    I was born in 1953 in Providence, Rhode Island and have drawn since the age of twelve. I graduated from the University of Rhode Island with a B.S. in geology, headed West, and settled in San Francisco in 1976. I work primarily in black and white drawings and glass.

Lucille Clifton, *the lost baby poem; to the unborn and waiting children*

    Born in Depew, New York, and educated at the State University of New York at Fredonia and Howard University, her awards and distinctions include The University of Massachusetts Press Juniper Prize for poetry, two nominations for the Pulitzer Prize in poetry, an Emmy Award, creative writing fellowships from The National Endowment for the Arts, and being named Poet Laureate of the State of Maryland.

Julia Couzens, *Being Exposed #28*

    Born in Auburn, California, she received her M.F.A. from U.C. Davis in 1990. She has exhibited nationally in both solo and group exhibitions. She currently lives and works in Sacramento and Los Angeles.

Carol Cullar, *The Past Is Best Forgotten*

    She describes the stages of her life as "persistent (2–5), adventurous (6–9), voracious (10–12), escapist (13–18), rebellious (19–21), optimistic (22–27), romanticist (28–40), and late-blooming (41–47): 'Woke up and realized I was now old and ugly enough to do and say almost anything I damn well please—then did it.'"

Betty Decter, *#1212: Women and Others (The Monkey Series)*

    Born in Birmingham, Alabama in 1927, she is the mother of an artist and the daughter of an artist. Largely self-taught until

1965, she studied with a private teacher then enrolled in Otis Art Institute and made a radical change in the content and style of her work—from realistic portraiture to an expressionistic, contemporary mythology.

Barbara Droubay, *Birth Series I*
(No biographical information submitted.)

Cosette Dudley, *Seventeenth Spring*
Born in Sacramento in 1935, I attended Sacramento City College and University of California, Davis, where I studied with painter Wayne Thiebaud. After residing in London from 1958 to 1961, I attended Stanford University for a B.A. in English Literature. I was a social worker from 1965–1967, spent six years working in the peace movement, and was a founding member of Appletree Press, a cooperative printmaking studio, where I still work. Extensive travels in Asia have had a profound influence upon my work and philosophy. I am an Associate of the Institute for Research on Women and Gender, Stanford University.

Kasandra Fox, *Essay on Guilt*
Born in 1922, I grew up a political and social radical in the Great Depression. I learned early that the passion inside me was not attractive to many people, but its honest expression put me in touch with other very real persons, and thus I have had a full and involved life. Now I am 69 and disabled, but still earning my living in a creative and enriching way.

Laura Jeanne Grimes, *The Adopted Child*
Born in 1954 in Indianapolis, I received a B.A. in Art History at the University of Houston in 1977 and a B.F.A. in Studio Art at the University of Texas in 1986. I work primarily in monoprint and in painting, and tend to work on a series. Series I have worked on include self-portraits, children in the pool, and animals with people. My current series deals with child abuse: I have been painting doll beds, incorporating self-portrait with references from movies and television. The series explores personal survival and recovery.

Barbara Hendrickson, *The Secret*

Born in Columbus, Ohio, the first generation of child Italian immigrants, I moved to California in 1960. I retired as a professor of English and Women's Studies from Ohlone College to work full-time as an artist. I did not begin art, nor did I believe I had any artistic talent, until age forty-four. A summer class in Women's Art opened the door to my own creativity, and paintings began to emerge.

Bernice Kussoy, *If the Shoe Was on the Other Foot*

I have been a sculptor for the last thirty-eight years, exhibiting extensively during that time in museums and galleries in California and around the U.S. I work primarily figuratively, in welded metal.

Lois Llewellyn, *Scarlet Letter of the 1990s*

Lois studied painting at the Art Students League in New York City, sculpture at Sacramento State College, and photography at City College of San Francisco. She holds an M.A. in Social Work from the University of Southern California, and is currently employed at Family Service Agency in San Francisco. She has exhibited locally and nationally for more than twenty years.

Sarah Maxwell, *Untitled*

Sarah is an artist who lives and works in Palo Alto, California. She is a graduate in Art from San Jose State University.

Barbara Milman, *No Choice; Children Having Children*

Raised and educated on the East Coast, in 1979, after more than a decade practicing law, Barbara moved to Davis, California and began painting seriously. She now combines this with part-time legal employment. She writes, "My painting addresses issues that concern me deeply—military involvement by the United States in Central America, the Holocaust, abortion rights, the end of the Cold War." She has exhibited nationally in galleries, universities, and museums.

Sheila Pitt, *Broodmare*

I teach art at the University of Arizona, in Tucson. All of my art is about issues which affect contemporary women. Many of us are "transitional" women, who have been raised with traditional viewpoints. Our awareness of the harm of these traditional attitudes toward women, thought of as second-class members in our society, often develops after years of buying into the traditional point of view. Once one has this insight, there is no way to go backward.

Angela Sinicropi, *#4; #7*
    Angela studied printmaking in Italy after earning a B.F.A. in 1981 from the Kansas City Art Institute and an M.F.A. in 1983 from the University of Washington. Since moving to the Bay Area in 1988 she has been in numerous exhibitions, including *Introductions 88* and her first solo show in 1991.

Margaret Stainer, *Sacra Conversazione #32; Sacra Conversazione #33*
    Professional artist, freelance gallery curator, and published author of art research and articles, she is an adjunct professor in Fine Arts (Drawing and Art History) at Ohlone College and has served on the board of directors of nonprofit art organizations such as the Northern California Women's Caucus for Art, and WORKS/San Jose. For the past six years Stainer's studio work of predominantly charcoal drawings on paper has concentrated on the intensity and psychological aspects of two people in a dramatic moment of one-on-one communication/conversation/confrontation. Close-up views, cropping, and asymmetric emphasis in compositions and exaggerated drama heighten her mannerist/romantic sensibility.

Justine Tot Tatarsky, *Lament*
    Inside my body was a stranger—man. If i spoke my fears, would he be hurt? Angered? Confused, i intoxicated myself with passion so i wouldn't have to be rational. I abandoned responsibility, as did he. Abortion was the responsible answer to the resulting pregnancies, but a deeply painful one. Let's unearth and examine the fear and confusion between the sexes; we are burying its results.

Melissa Tinker, *Growing up with Marie*
    I was born on Guam in 1974. My father is in the US Navy so I have traveled a lot. I have lived in Pennsylvania, Florida, Sicily, Virginia, Hawaii, Japan, and California. I currently live with my family in San Francisco. A senior at the Urban School of San Francisco, I plan to attend college and concentrate on my writing.

Susan Trubow, *Untitled; Untitled*

Born in San Francisco, she received her B.A. from San Francisco State University and her B.F.A. from California College of Arts and Crafts. She has exhibited internationally and nationally, including in the U.S.–U.K. Print Connection.

Wendy Weiner, *The Visit*

Born and raised in the Midwest, Wendy moved to California fifteen years ago. She currently teaches writing at a community college in Oakland. Her work has appeared in *The Haight-Ashbury Literary Journal* and *Aurora*.

Roberta June White, *Not Gravid*

I grew up in a small West Texas town. Small-town ethics made it clear that sexual activity outside of marriage is a sin. Girls who became pregnant were labeled sinners. This attitude fostered a fear of sexuality that I have tried to eliminate by confrontation in my artwork. *Not Gravid* depicts the joy of a woman receiving her period. The menstrual blood is an indication that her "sin" has not resulted in unwanted pregnancy.

Stephanie Wilger, *Blood of the Womb*

My art comes from the part of me that seems inconsolable as an individual and as a member of society. With my love of life, the deepest hurt is the destruction of the individual. My figurative work speaks against this annihilation, embodies the inclination to change/ transform, and celebrates life.

Lisa Woods, *Conspiracy; Conversations*

A writer living in California, Lisa lost her only child to adoption in the 1960s. She established National Birth Mothers' Day (May 1st: May Day) as a day for acknowledging and mourning the loss of birth mothers and adopted children, and created a forum for birth mothers, *MayDay!—Reclaiming Our Voices*, a quarterly publication. (Details of these projects may be obtained by sending an SASE to MayDay, c/o Box 8447, Berkeley, CA 94707-8447.)